EARLY ENDORSEMENTS

"Having Dr. Hansen's special expertise and passion for change in education takes us even closer to ensuring that we can achieve the transformative movement in education we need."
— Sir Ken Robinson, TED speaker: "Do Schools Kill Creativity" and author of *Creative Schools*

"Too many young people leave their formal education believing they are not smart, not capable, and that they can't measure up to one-size-fits-all standards that define success so narrowly that most children are destined to fail. In *The Future of Smart* Dr. Hansen reminds us that the challenges of education in America have their roots in a complex system of values. Weaving together science, history and the examples of educators and young people, she challenges us to examine these foundational values and to imagine an education system grounded in a different view of the world, one that embraces the jagged and highly individual nature of human development, learning and human capability as a strength rather than a pathology. At a moment when America is seeking to reexamine its cultural narratives and transform public systems to meet rising expectations, this book is a must-read for thoughtful policymakers, advocates, leaders and citizens."
— Dr. Todd Rose, Director of Populace and author of *The End of Average* and *Dark Horse*

"I've known Dr. Hansen to be someone a step ahead, signaling where we need to be to support learners and the systems of learning that (should) support them. In this book, Dr. Hansen does it again— grounding us in what has been, making sense of what holds us back, and offering sensible and smart paths forward—if only we are intentional about remaking the learning landscape for America's youth."

> — Gregg Behr, co-author, *When You Wonder,* You're
> Learning: Enduring Lessons for Raising Creative,
> Curious, Caring Kids

"At a moment when we are being challenged to revisit the very purpose and structure of education and reconsider who we talk to and how we engage them, we need a book like this to guide us. For anyone who is really serious about seeing education through a new set of eyes, *The Future of Smart* is almost a handbook of what positions you to be a real listener. Dr. Hansen took me on a journey and I was left with a new set of tools to engage in critical conversations about education, culture and the future of this country. In this time of COVID-19 disruption, rethinking education systems and social renewal, Dr. Hansen is truly a gifted and purposeful human resource."

> — Peter McWalters, Big Picture Learning Board
> Chair and former President of the Council of Chief
> State School Officers

"For decades, our national discourse for improving the quality and outcomes of American education has been dominated by narrow and technical solutions that tinker on the edges of the factory/ industrial model without ever making true leaps towards a new vision of the system that will cultivate young people in all their infinite potential. As a consequence, we have been spinning ever faster on an ossified, paradigmatic carousel, wishing for new insights while recycling old approaches. Dr. Hansen's brilliant examination is radical in its effort to deconstruct the assumptions and values that prop up an outdated model of learning and fuel failed policy solutions that will not meet the needs of this century. This book is urgently needed as we wrestle with the ramifications of widening income-stratification and deeply rooted racial injustice, in which our educational system is complicit. If we are to meet the challenges of our age and solve seemingly intractable problems through public institutions, we must embrace new mental models and habits of being. Dr. Hansen offers an astute and historically grounded approach to begin that worthy journey."

— Jenee Henry Wood, Head of Organizational
Learning, Transcend

"Dr. Hansen provides a refreshingly new, optimistic and compelling perspective on truly revolutionizing American education. Addressing systemic challenges, she provides clarity for a future that can truly unleash the potential of all of our children."

— William Browning, Chief Strategy Officer,
United Way

"Dr. Hansen and her book are beacons. Through her writing she shines a light on the complexities of modern education. She seamlessly pulls together ideas and thoughts in an accessible way. More important, though, she illuminates the current challenges and highlights the path forward with human-centered and liberatory education. She is able to articulate and put words to the nebulous future, which gives me hope!"

— Miguel Gonzalez, Director, Embark Education

"The Future of Smart is a revolutionary and timely work. Dr. Hansen passionately takes us on a journey through the history of education to reveal how we have arrived at the pronounced inequities of our day and time that prohibit the advancement of education for certain youth. Her work brings a reality to the need for justice-oriented exploits in education and takes us beyond reinventing the wheel. Dr. Hansen's research and studies will enhance the future of education for years to come and will provide much insight for design, innovation, and equity in education."

— Alexis Gwin-Miller, Principal, Crosstown High School and Co-chair, Memphis Interfaith Coalition for Action and Hope (MICAH)

"In *The Future of Smart*, Dr. Hansen challenges us to imagine how an education system can honor and develop environments that acknowledge and build upon students' rich assets. She establishes a path to move us away from deficit-based thinking to designing asset-based models that start with students' funds of knowledge, cultural knowledge and capacity for moving between different worlds. As someone who works with families who are often systemically marginalized, I know that Dr. Hansen's push to transform education to honor different ways of being, knowing, speaking, thinking and engaging with the world would not only transform education, but students' lives and our society."

— Paola Ramírez, Director of Family and Community Partnership, Reschool Colorado

"Educators do care about the whole child. However, the systems that they teach in/counsel in/lead in are intractable and based on a very (very) old model of education. Continuing to "reform" the existing system through draconian means leaves everyone at a loss—students lose, teachers lose, leaders lose—our nation loses. It's time to look at what children truly need and create educational opportunities that are just that—opportunities. Not barriers. Not disincentives. Not deficiencies. Dr. Hansen provides us with a thorough analysis of the ways in which our current system was built, is maintained, and leaves our children in educational deficit. She then offers us ways in which to look at our current system and build towards opportunity and abundance for all children. I highly recommend this book to anyone who cares about our children and our nation."

> — Dr. Lynn Gangone, President and Chief Executive
> Officer, American Association for Colleges of
> Teacher Education

"Dr. Hansen compels readers to see development and schooling in a different way, one that is founded in more than just learning experiences but also in learning sciences. Using examples from her own life and schools around the world, she illustrates how to help create the future of smart. For any educator or community member who wants to critically reflect on our current schooling systems and work to envision a more holistic, learner-centered approach, this book is for you."

> — Dr. Emily Liebtag, Founder, Boundless

"Dr. Hansen has a wonderful way of moving between the history and systemic issues that affect formal education in the US and the implications of those issues at the learning level. Her global understanding of education is helpful for advocates, policymakers, educators, and community members alike. For so long, writing about education has been dominated by white, male voices. I'm excited and grateful to have Dr. Hansen's outstanding perspective on the future of smart added to the canon at this moment when transformation is sorely needed."

> — Anne Olson, Director of State Advocacy,
> KnowledgeWorks

"What if… Why… Could we try… Have you considered… I was that teacher, always asking questions and wondering if there was another way to meet learners' needs and impact the walled system. Dr. Hansen's research, expertise, and passion provide a path forward as we continue to ask the hard questions for our education profession, our learners, and towards an open system. Her concise, challenge ending of the book says it all… 'The choice is ours to make.' Amen."

— Linda Kerouac Barker, educator and former
Manager of Advocacy and Professional Practice,
Colorado Education Association

"At a time when the 'goal posts' in education are oversimplified notions of access and equity, those with their hands on the levers of change have given little attention to the worldviews that have created, maintained, and advanced systems that have, and continue to, marginalize and disenfranchise so many of our children. In *The Future of Smart*, Dr. Hansen bravely challenges the foundational paradigm on which our educational system (and a plethora of others) rests. Starting with the bifurcated nature of the human brain, continuing with how that inherent biological trait can create worldviews that are constraining, and concluding with a truly transformative vision, Dr. Hansen offers a divergent perspective on how we can create a system in which our children's humanity is fully nurtured—a system in which their uniqueness takes its place at the center of the enterprise, and the purpose of education becomes for them to craft their identity and discover the abilities they possess to contribute meaningfully to their individual well-being and the well-being of the communities in which they live. As an educator, a leader in the learner-centered movement, and a parent of two young children, to me these ideas are simultaneously confirming and challenging in the best way. Confirming because they align and clarify what I have been up to in my 20 years in learner-centered environments. Challenging because they uncover many of the assumptions I have around the genesis and perpetuation of the current system, while offering a glimpse into a new way forward. *The Future of Smart* is a must-read for anyone who wants to reimagine how we can best serve our children and our human community."

> — Alin Bennett, Vice President of Practice and Field Advancement, Education Reimagined, and Director of School Culture, The Learning Community Charter School

"*The Future of Smart* is a thought-provoking book about the limitations and systemic inequities of the prevailing educational paradigm in our country. It also provides an exciting vision of the structures and supports that our learners desperately need to thrive in today's world. Through her extensive research and personal story, woven together in a masterful narrative, Dr. Hansen challenged my thinking about educational design models that best facilitate learning for all children. I recommend this book to any educator who is serious about leading learner-centered transformations in the schools and communities where they serve."

> — Dr. Doug Schuch, Superintendent, Regional School District 13 (Durham, Connecticut)

"When I first met Dr. Hansen, she was giving a presentation on a learner-centered vision for education, and it was like a switch turned on in my head; it was the most complete picture I'd ever heard on the future of learning. So many of the things I had been grappling with in my head, she had an ability to put into words, and turn words into actions. Every time I've spoken with her since, I've learned something to sharpen that vision and understand the critical actions to go from *WHAT* to *HOW.*

"In reading *The Future of Smart*, I get that same feeling of learning from a true visionary. Dr. Hansen's ability to tie historical context that juxtaposes Cartesian-Newtonian and holistic-indigenous philosophies with current educational challenges is second to none. As I read, I was pulled into each passage that adds depths of understanding to the inherent inequities that pervade our educational institutions. Dr. Hansen manages to cut through complex topics to reach simple and practical conclusions that get to the roots of our educational inequities. *The Future of Smart* is the well-researched, human-centered, deeply contextualized book we need right now to create educational ecosystems that truly support the unique needs of every learner while contributing to a more equitable world."

> — Nathan Strenge, USA Country Lead, HundrED,
> and Senior Learning Designer, Fielding International

"Dr. Hansen and I met several years ago at a meeting at which we discussed the ideas she shares in this book. I was impressed by her, and since we had so many common beliefs about what needed to be done to create an equitable learning system, we have remained advocates for each other and for real change. *The Future of Smart* is a perfect guidebook to a world in which the uniqueness of each child is valued and each learning ecosystem is built around those unique needs. If you seek a transformation to models that value uniqueness and not sameness, add this volume to your reading list."

> — David Cook, Director of Innovation, Kentucky
> Department of Education

THE
FUTURE
OF
SMART

How Our Education System
Needs to Change to Help All
Young People Thrive

ULCCA JOSHI HANSEN, PhD, JD

Published by: Capucia, LLC
211 Pauline Drive #513
York, PA 17402

Paperback ISBN: 978-1-954920-13-2
eBook ISBN: 978-1-954920-14-9
Library of Congress Control Number: 2021915954

Cover Design: Ranilo Cabo
Layout: Ranilo Cabo
Editor and Proofreader: Gwen Hoffnagle
Book Midwife: Carrie Jareed

Printed in the United States of America

For Sachin and Ashwin,

because the thought of you inspired me long

before you arrived.

Your children are not your children.
They are the sons and daughters of Life's longing for itself.
They come through you but not from you,
and though they are with you,
yet they belong not to you.

You may give them your love but not your thoughts.
For they have their own thoughts.
You may house their bodies but not their souls,
for their souls dwell in the house of tomorrow,
which you cannot visit, not even in your dreams.

You may strive to be like them,
but seek not to make them like you.
For life goes not backward nor tarries with yesterday.

You are the bows from which your children
as living arrows are sent forth.
The archer sees the mark upon the path of the infinite,
and He bends you with His might that His arrows may go swift and far.

Let your bending in the archer's hand be for gladness;
For even as He loves the arrow that flies,
so He loves also the bow that is stable.

—Kahlil Gibran, from *The Prophet*

CONTENTS

FOREWORD

I have been in this conversation since the beginning. Over my 50 years in education, I have participated in every step of the process to improve American education, many of which are named in this book, starting with "A Nation at Risk" (from the National Commission on Excellence in Education in 1983) and culminating with No Child Left Behind and Race to the Top. Woven into all of these was an expectation that we should be explicit about standards; use assessments that are reliable, valid and allow us to disaggregate data; and link the performance of teachers to accountability.

Whether I agreed with the details or not, we all took these efforts seriously. And at the end, after 20 to 30 years of analysis and everything we learned from COVID, it's become clear to many of us that we're long past the point of diminishing returns. We haven't moved the indicators in any way; race and class still predict a student's success better than any other factors. And, if anything, we have sterilized the treatment of the most isolated and underserved students and done things that are totally opposed to true engagement.

So now we are in a moment of rethinking purpose. But whose purpose? From what frame of reference? And how do we approach developing this new vision? If we don't find a way to break through our preconceived assumptions, we will just end up creating a new version of the thing we all know hasn't worked.

That is where *The Future of Smart* comes in. I have been in the movement for racial justice and civil rights since 1963, and yet when I am exposed to the type of rigor and challenge that people like Dr.

Ulcca Joshi Hansen put forward, I see how deep our blind spots are, how institutionalized racism is. Leading programs with her, I have seen Dr. Hansen bring perspective, knowledge and expert facilitation to conversations with stakeholders. Doing all this requires honest community conversations. It means seeking and reaching common ground and articulating difficult issues to various interest groups. And it means creating environments where all voices will be heard and appreciated as part of the decision-making power structure. Dr. Hansen brings an anthropological, cross-cultural perspective about bias, privilege and power, one that is historically anchored, clearly researched and skillfully communicated.

At a moment when we are being challenged to revisit the very purpose and structure of education and reconsider who we talk to and how we engage them, we need a book like this to guide us. For anyone who is really serious about seeing education through a new set of eyes, *The Future of Smart* is almost a handbook of what positions you to be a real listener.

Even for someone who considers himself pretty open and unafraid of new ideas, for me this book was a challenge in the best possible sense. The first time I read something that reminded me of how we've gotten to where we are, it felt like a confrontation—as in, "You need to really think about this." I instinctively reacted because what Dr. Hansen described on the pages is me. You can't be embedded in the culture without carrying it with you.

Every place I had that first response, I made myself stick with it. And the longer I stayed with it, the more Dr. Hansen took me on a journey. By the time I got to the end, questions I had about motivation or perspective in earlier chapters were woven back in and addressed by her compelling story. I was left with a new set of tools for engaging in critical conversations about education, culture and the future of this country.

In this time of COVID-19 disruption, rethinking education systems and social renewal, Dr. Hansen is truly a gifted and purposeful human resource.

Peter McWalters

Peter McWalters is currently a board member and Chair of the Big Picture Learning Board. His expertise in education is extensive, drawing from previously held positions including President of the Council of Chief State School Officers, Trustee of the National Center for the Improvement of Education Assessment (NCIEA), board member of the National Center for Education and the Economy and member of the Council of Great City Schools. He served as Rhode Island Commissioner of Elementary and Secondary Education from 1992-2009. A lifelong educator, McWalters began his career as a teacher of English as a Second Language in the Rochester, New York, public schools in 1970. He became Superintendent of the Rochester City School District in 1985, and in 1987 settled a landmark teachers' contract with the Rochester Teachers Association, an American Federation of Teachers affiliate that introduced the Peer Assistance and Review program, the Lead Teachers program and a model mentoring program for new teachers.

My partner, David TC Ellis, approached me about his vision to create the High School for Recording Arts (HSRA) sometime around 1996. Working with him and some great community people, HSRA was founded two years later. We often say looking back that we just slipped through: a rapper from Minnesota with maybe a year of college and his perceived "slick" New York entertainment lawyer managed to get a charter school application through the system. But these were the early days of the charter school movement. People would say, "This isn't going to work. They're dabbling, trying to build some type of pipeline for entertainers to come up in. They can't possibly be curious about the learning and the pedagogical aspects."

Our other challenge was that our kids were considered dropouts. The general belief was that there was something wrong with them that caused them to be in the position they were in. In the beginning—and to this day—there was a great deal of thinking like that.

But upon reflection, both David and I had experiences that, unbeknownst to us, prepared us for this journey. In college, while working on the Kennedy presidential campaign, I became aware of the fact that the senator took his twelve-year-old son out of school to experience the campaign as school. My immediate reflection was that my experience in school was more of a type of sentence—a prison sentence! I didn't think that one could escape it that easily. This was my first glimpse into the lives of people who had wealth and privilege. I never imagined parents could have the agency to just remove their kids from school to travel abroad for a month or work on a campaign. Where I came from that usually led to a truancy letter to your parents, threats of dragging them into court, then perhaps a visit from child protection. Yet the people who did this saw that these types of experiences, beyond the walls of school, were full of learning and freedom, and a chance to find one's own view and understanding of the world. Whereas I, a black kid from Brooklyn, was like, "Wait, what? You can't do that." Turns out you can—if you are a certain type of person in America.

Recognizing the racist policies and inequalities that led to HSRA's existence, we tried to really reflect on our young people, who were falling through the cracks of the public education system, and what we wanted for them. These were kids whose lives had been marginalized and oppressed by a racist society. As a result of the trauma they often experienced, they had been pushed and kicked out of school because of how they looked and showed up. That showing up at schools often meant active bodies and loud, and at times indignant voices. We asked ourselves, "How do we design a school that provides an open space and an intent to allow for freedom for that?" We were determined to test it out.

We knew that succeeding in this would not be easy; we were serving a group that has little to no power. The educational system has been set up to overlook the full humanity of students; to see them as statistics that need to be improved, fixed or "caught up" within the narrow content areas that drive the system. What is missing from this system helped shape the core values of HSRA: the belief that each of these young people deserves to experience being free within a strong, learning and loving community. Fast-forward 25 years into 2021, and we've made it to this moment, this inflection point. With the COVID pandemic; with the killing of George Floyd; with growing inequalities on environmental, economic, social and political levels; and with our society's inability to address disparities in education, we're newly focused on these questions that deserve new answers from powerful voices:

What are we doing within our educational spaces?

How can we do education in the best way to address these issues—in our schools and beyond them?

The Future of Smart is a deep exploration into these important questions. Dr. Hansen deeply understands the complexity of the type of work done at HSRA and the work our partners and allies around the country are doing. More critically, she has an acute awareness of the ways in which this collective work is moving us toward the equity we say we want, in ways that have been missing in decades of conversations about how to "fix" American education.

From the first time I met her, I have admired her willingness to stand up and recognize that brown, Black, Indigenous, and poor children in America have been denied what other children have been given and barred from the freedom and fulfillment that education ought to represent. She is also wickedly smart, as becomes clear the further you read in this book. She brings clarity of thought and an ability to synthesize all levels of the complex work HSRA and other programs aspire to every day.

I believe this book helps us take note of the current moment and reflect on what got us here. It helps us recognize and appreciate what pockets of innovation are out there; what has allowed them to persist, learn and grow; and what has prevented them from reaching so many of the young people who truly need something different—which is nearly all of them. With this book and the conversations it should provoke, we have an opportunity to put attention and focus on critical issues in a way that creates a transformative path forward. *The Future of Smart* is a big step toward a more equitable and just future.

Tony Simmons

Tony Simmons is the Executive Director of High School for Recording Arts (HSRA), an independent public charter school in St. Paul, Minnesota, that he helped found in 1998, and Director of Development for Studio 4 Enterprises, an educational services and management company. In addition to overseeing the day-to-day program at HSRA, Simmons continues to engage students by facilitating the Business of Music class and mentoring those involved in Another Level Records. He has served as a board member of leading national school-reform organizations including Education Evolving, Reaching At-Promise Students Association (RAPSA), Coalition of Independent Charter Schools, and Edvisions, Inc. He has contributed to critical reports in the field of student-centered, racially just approaches to education including RAPSA's "Seizing the Moment: Realizing the Promise of Student-Centered Learning" and the National Association of Charter School Authorizers report, "Anecdotes Aren't Enough: An Evidence-Based Approach to Accountability for Alternative Charter Schools." He has provided technical assistance to and been a member of the Black Alliance for Educational Options. He also co-founded the New School Creation Fellowship and is Director of Strategic Partnerships and National Faculty at the High Tech High Graduate School of Education/Center for Love and Justice. He accompanied the former lieutenant governor of Minnesota on a trade mission trip to China as the public education representative.

AUTHOR'S NOTE

For someone who's used to speaking to groups and to communicating and sharing ideas in person, writing a book is a unique challenge. First, I had to choose what to include and what to leave out, knowing that there won't be a Q&A at the end during which you, the reader, can give a response or ask for more information. This is it. I have tried to give you enough information to understand it, but not so much that you're swamped by it. I didn't have room to give credit to all the thinkers and teachers whose work I relied on and those who made possible the very fact of my education and my opportunity to write this book. Beyond that I can't know who you are or what experiences, values and beliefs you bring to *The Future of Smart*. And there's much you don't know about me and how I came to these ideas. This author's note is in part my brief attempt to share that with you.

I'm a *third culture kid*. I first heard this term a few years ago. It refers to anyone raised in a culture that's not their parents' native culture, but who also lived in a third culture during a significant part of their formative childhood or adolescent years. My mother and father are ethnically Indian, but were both born and raised in Tanzania by families who migrated from the Indian subcontinent during the height of British colonial rule. My parents, their siblings and their siblings' children were born and identified as Tanzanian. But as African nationalist movements grew in strength and militancy during the 1950s and 1960s, non-black Africans like my relatives were forced to leave the country for reasons of safety and opportunity.

My parents' assets were locked in Tanzania when they arrived in Newark, New Jersey, with two suitcases each and a few hundred dollars. They soon came to realize they wouldn't be able to care for their infant daughter, so I was sent back to Tanzania to be raised by my extended family of Indian-Tanzanian aunts, uncles and cousins, along with ethnically Tanzanian household helpers—an atmosphere fraught with cultural complexities: biases, prejudices, power dynamics and residual colonial privilege. I returned to the US before kindergarten, an English language learner in today's terms. And while I was mostly educated in America, I spent a large part of my life between the ages of six and thirty living and studying outside the US in Botswana, India, Germany, England, France and the United Arab Emirates.

In the literature about third culture kids I read about an experience I had spent my whole life trying to grasp, to normalize. We are people who learned to move between cultures and adapt before we internalized any sense of belonging. We are often referred to as "cultural hybrids" or "global nomads." We are adept at building relationships across cultures and identities, in part because our identities are more diffuse, or more composite, than those of others. The downside is that we essentially belong nowhere. We see and experience cultures differently from those who have lived inside them. My background is no doubt part of why I was so drawn to schools that make identity and belonging a central part of their work. And the lens of cross-cultural nomad is an important part of how I explore education.

Though I live in the United States, my perspective on education is shaped as much by placelessness as by American-ness. Rather than seeking out the debates of the moment, I tend to look for elements of struggle that are common across cultures, across individuals and across communities.

Racism and colorism were a central part of my family's experience when I was growing up. In the 1970s and 1980s, realtors refused to show suburban homes to non-white families like mine. I was about seven when someone burned a cross on the lawn of a local black family, and later that year I was chased home by kids yelling "Go home black girl!" Yet when I was in Germany as an exchange student during my senior year of high school, and I told people I was American, they inevitably asked, "But what *are* you, really?" Members of my own family valued fair skin above dark skin, and rejected cousins in my generation who dated across religion and race. Even at age 11 I saw that my relatives in Tanzania and Botswana talked down to the local African help. By the time I took my first job, I knew something about how the American story of opportunity passes over Black people, Indigenous people and people of color (BIPOC), but when I married into a white family with roots in the Midwest, I also observed that people used to seeing themselves as the backbone of American prosperity were dealing with a sense of irrelevance and a dimming future. My sons' great-grandmother is a Nebraskan child of the Great Depression, a former Rosie the Riveter who will turn 100 this year. When I joined the family, I became one of the few non-white people she'd ever been close to. But the cast at her 100th birthday party will look like those old United Colors of Benetton commercials, with grandchildren and great-grandchildren representing Indian, Dominican, Puerto Rican, Guatemalan, Ethiopian, African-American and Filipino backgrounds—young people loved and raised by parents, aunts, uncles and grandparents who represent the full range of America's social, political and economic diversity. Many of these white relatives are figuring out how to raise and support BIPOC children in a system that is unfair to those children, even as they grapple with a sense that their own identities as Americans are being called into question.

As a child learning English in school well before we had the phrase "English language learner"; as a young Indian girl who grew up navigating white, suburban schools with a weird name; as someone whose parents spent years apart from their daughter in order to establish themselves in a "good" school district, I've seen many facets of America's unequal education system. As a teacher in a Newark, New Jersey, public school, I worked with lots of kids growing up as I did, learning English as they went—kids who didn't see themselves represented in any stories or textbooks they were given. I have seen how decades of reform aimed at increasing equity have actually narrowed our definitions of success in school and life, and how this shift has devalued many of the capabilities people believe they have to offer, including many people in my own family. These experiences inform what I mean when I talk about building an education system that can serve all students well.

If we are honest with ourselves, we can see that our efforts toward educational equity in the past 20 years haven't made much difference. We have documented some types of inequity, and in many cases have raised awareness of them, but we have done little to actually change them. And, in the process, we have created new forms of inequity.

In *The Future of Smart* I trace two dueling forces in education back to an essential conflict in human experience across cultures, a conflict that begins with the two hemispheres of the human brain. Drawing on the work of historians of the science of culture, I cite a massive shift in our experience of the world that began during the Scientific Revolution and became a dominant worldview that changed the very meaning of education.[1] Only by fully understanding this shift, and its legacy in contemporary education, can we ever hope to shift our education system.

Is education a process of molding children to certain economic, social and political systems? Or is it about helping young people become fully themselves and develop their personhood and their most human capabilities—empathy, compassion, collaboration, communication? These two sets of priorities lead to very different ways of responding to learners—different ways of knowing and shaping the world.

Seeing ourselves as part of a larger story, united across time and nationalities, can be empowering. This challenge has been around for centuries. It is larger than our moment, and though we should commit ourselves as fully as possible to addressing it, we cannot expect to resolve it quickly and easily. The first part of this book broadens the question of how to improve education beyond the boundaries of the US and beyond this moment in history. The power dynamic we see in American schools today is not uniquely American. I saw it in Tanzania, Botswana and India, where black and brown children still sit in English-language-medium classes, in schools built by the British in an effort to "civilize" them, teaching them to appreciate and reify English culture as superior. The same dynamic defined American Indian Residential Schools, and it's present in today's curricula in which non-dominant cultures are written out of American history textbooks, and curricula more broadly.

I would like to clarify several terms I use throughout the book. I recognize that some of them have particular meanings in an American or even Western context, but I aim to use them in ways that apply across cultures. My hope in doing so is to help us think beyond our local conflicts and contexts to explore the overarching patterns and themes of our shared human story.

Like many scholars and thinkers before me, I use the term *Cartesian-Newtonian* as shorthand for a worldview that emerged in the 1500s in Europe. Though I focus on the limitations of this worldview, I do not mean to dismiss the contributions Descartes and Newton made to overall human progress, which I believe were substantial. I chose Cartesian-Newtonian over *mechanistic-reductionistic* because the dynamics I'm describing are broader than the latter two adjectives suggest. In education, a focus on correcting mechanistic and reductionistic tendencies has led to superficial changes; we have neglected to address the underlying beliefs and values that give rise to mechanistic and reductionistic approaches, and thus the problems persist.

The term *indigenous* has a broader definition in this book than "those peoples who bore the brunt of colonization in the US and abroad." I chose the term because it refers to "growing, living or occurring naturally in a particular place" and "relating to the earliest known inhabitants of a place." For the story I'm telling, which begins in Europe before mass global colonization, I use the term to refer to ways of being and organizing human life before the arrival of outside religious, political and economic forces—that is, life organized by intuitive, local values rather than values imposed or inculcated from the outside. On balance it appears that human societies were more alike than different before the practice of imposing values on other cultures became widespread, in terms of how people related to the land and to each other. I do not mean to glorify human experience or human societies pre-1500. War, power struggle, human sacrifice, cruelty—these are all constant in human history going back as far as we can know. But something changed fundamentally around 500 years ago that sets the time period since then apart from the tens of thousands of years of human existence before it. I use the term *holistic-indigenous* to describe this preexisting, foundational worldview, and as a counterpoint to the Cartesian-Newtonian worldview.

Finally, the term *liberatory*, which I use frequently to refer to certain approaches to education, has long been associated with Paulo Freire and other leaders in *critical pedagogy* and community-schools movements. My intention in using the term *liberatory* is not to minimize or appropriate their ideas, but to underscore the concept that we can effect social change through education that is based on consciousness-raising and engagement with oppressive forces. There were forebears of what has come to be known as critical pedagogy, many of them European, who were undeniably committed to liberatory education. Their work was a response to the harshness and inhumanity of the first efforts to formalize education for the masses, and they argued for a focus on the inherent value and potential in each child.

The educational thinkers I elevate in Part 1 of this book were white and privileged in their own ways, and their rise to prominence is inextricable from this privilege. Their ideas were not especially popular in their own communities at the time; indeed, they received warmer receptions outside of Europe than in their countries of origin. They were pushing against mainstream beliefs about young people and education, and they put their privilege on the line for ideas and work that mattered to them. While their models often served the more neglected children of their times, the present-day schools that grew out of those models have long been associated with privileged communities—in America and abroad. I am heartened now to see these models embraced (and improved upon) by leaders and communities of color who are recognizing these models for their explicit focus on empowerment.

I believe these schools can be essential parts of a genuine move toward equity in education. To get there we will need to support the codification and expansion of the most promising human-centered/ liberatory models that have emerged in recent years, and of schools designed *with* communities to meet the specific needs of their children. Appendix B provides a list of some such programs, especially those serving BIPOC and lower-income communities.

At a time when fear and anger dominate too many of our conversations, I believe that real change in education will only come through healing-centered approaches. By "healing-centered" I mean those that recognize how certain dominant worldviews have hurt— and are still hurting—all of us by cutting us off from our common humanity. *How* we do this work, *how* we talk to each other about change—educational or otherwise—will make all the difference.

INTRODUCTION

Many teachers looking back at their careers will remember at least one student like Joel. Joel was the one I was still thinking and worrying about when I left my classroom in Newark each night. He was the child whose story—father in prison; single, immigrant mother doing her best to raise three children; early head injury that led to cognitive and behavioral issues—led me to take him and his siblings to my parents' suburban neighborhood for the kind of Halloween night they don't have in Newark. He was the slight, skinny boy who could wear down my resolve with a crooked grin. He was the child who tried to protect me when another student went after a classmate with a pair of scissors.

Joel didn't fit neatly into any box, yet it was my job to build a box and escort him into it. He was the boy I desperately wanted to teach and serve, but simply didn't know how.

This was in 1998. I was a young teacher. I was hopeful. And my first few years of teaching nearly broke me. I didn't have words for the emotions, but I was yearning to do and be something for my students that felt elusive at the time. I felt I was failing in some intangible way.

I was interested in a lot of subjects in college, from economics to international relations to medicine. But whenever I thought about how I wanted to spend my professional life, it seemed to me that education sat at the heart of everything else; that the problems we spend so much time, effort and money trying to fix begin with what we teach our children. It would solve more problems to teach them that each person is valuable; that no one is more valuable than another; and that we should respect difference, take responsibility for ourselves and our actions, and be accountable for our decisions and their effects on others. Systems are made up of people. Education is about shaping young people so that they can go on to shape the world.

I studied hard during my teacher training, completing assignments, learning theories and delivering practice lessons. I also spent months shadowing teachers who had meant the most to me when I was in school, trying to learn from their decades of experience—watching, asking questions, trying somehow to integrate their wisdom into my own practice. But by the time Joel entered my classroom, I knew there was something missing in my work, in my approach, in me.

I decided to take a break for two years to let my heart and body recover. I took a job with the Geraldine R. Dodge Foundation, which supports learning and the arts, and contributed to schools in New York, New Jersey and the New England states. During my visits to some of the schools in this network is when I first *felt it*. I say "felt it" because my first reaction had nothing to do with my intellect. It would take years before I could articulate and explain what I felt in those classrooms.

The first place I remember this happening was at Edgemont Montessori School, a public magnet Montessori school in Montclair, New Jersey, a few miles from the classroom in which I had taught. While doing a site visit for Dodge, I walked into what I thought was a kindergarten classroom to find 35 bodies of widely varying size. There was a buzz of voices and there were pockets of movement, but it wasn't chaotic, and no teacher was intervening to quiet things down. At least four children came up right away to shake my hand and formally greet me. In one corner a child was using a sharp kitchen knife to cut bananas, placing the slices on a table for his classmates.

Nearby a little boy was washing the dirty glass plates other children brought to the sink. Two children were seated together next to a white mat; the girl, who looked to be about five, arranged colored blocks carefully into a large box frame, while the little boy, about three, sat and watched. Another pair was seated at a "peace table" on which were candles, chimes and a single poppy in a vase. One boy was just wandering around the room watching the other children.

The teacher told me that the children were about two hours into their three-hour daily "work cycle," an uninterrupted period during which they were free to work on whatever they chose. I sat down with the little girl with the frame, which she explained was the trinomial cube. I had no idea what a trinomial cube was or what she was doing, but as she looked at the last three blocks on the mat she seemed to realize that she had done something wrong. She removed the blocks from the box and started over as the little boy got up and wandered away to pick up a broom and sweep the snack area.

Later, when I met with the two classroom teachers, they told me about the trinomial cube, a toy designed to help children practice visual and small-motor skills, which in the process subtly introduces them to the concepts of the algebraic trinomial formula. And they described *Cosmic Studies*, an interdisciplinary approach to exploring the connections between science, social studies and culture. They also talked about grace and courtesy and the desire children have at this age to engage with others in a dignified way. The teachers had been with many of the children for several years, and seemed to know them just as well as people as they knew them as students. They knew where each child was socially and emotionally, and their individual interests, strengths and areas for growth, and they could speak about all this in relation to theories of child development that I had studied but had rarely heard discussed in the schools where I had taught. They talked about work, purpose and children's spirits.

I went to another classroom of students who were seven and eight, the same age range I had taught in Newark. But the focus of conversation there was not daily learning objectives, specific subjects or interim assessment scores. Children were talking about interdisciplinary projects focused on their areas of interest. They were teaching each other how to play on dynamic math boards, and solving multiplication problems I hadn't learned about until middle school. They were writing reports on the outcomes of community-based projects that helped them understand local history.

During my two years with Dodge I visited many schools, and most didn't affect me as Edgemont Montessori had. But a handful did give me that same feeling, which I came to recognize instantly upon entering classrooms in the Met School in Providence, Rhode Island; Lake Country Day School in Minneapolis, Minnesota; the Waldorf School of Princeton in Princeton, New Jersey; the Annie Fisher magnet school in Hartford, Connecticut; and the High School for Recording Arts in St. Paul, Minnesota. Over time I realized that what drew me to these schools was the feeling I had the moment I walked in, which I think is a version of what the children and teachers must feel. It is an experience comprised of a thousand dynamic interactions—a sense of welcome, curiosity and openness, combined with deep knowledge and expertise. It's a hard feeling to describe, but it emerges from a philosophy, a plan and a set of capabilities that I explore in this book.

Watching teachers interact with young people in these classrooms also made me feel at once sad and joyful. Sad because it was so unlike what I had experienced as a student, despite having some excellent teachers, and so far from what I had been able to create for students like Joel. Joyful because I knew what I was seeing was quite profound, and that educators were bringing it to students from different backgrounds in ways that honored and celebrated their uniqueness. Sad because I realized I might have been a very different person had I spent time as a child in classrooms like these—not only a better educator but maybe a better friend, sibling, daughter. Joyful because I could see that these students were being engaged not only as learners but as human beings, relating to themselves and to each other in ways I knew would change their paths through life.

Even as I was visiting these schools, the Dodge Foundation was working on a project at the Getty Museum in Los Angeles focused on the role that arts play in education and learning. The foundation brought in a little-known professor from England who had just authored a government report advocating for more investment in school-based arts programming. His name was Ken Robinson. The answer to the question he asked—Do schools kill creativity?—seemed pretty obvious to many of us: Yes. But not all schools. The schools I found so compelling did the opposite. The people in them, adults and students alike, seemed to be alive and mutually engaged in a way I hadn't seen in many schools. However, what Robinson, I and others learned in the coming years is that fostering creativity and curiosity is not as straightforward as integrating the arts or talking about moving beyond the *industrial model* of education—also called the *factory model* or the *factory/industrial model*. Commitment to these ideas alone hasn't changed much in the last two decades. In *The Future of Smart* I explain what has kept us stuck for so long, and describe the next steps we should take.

This book's title was inspired partly by my two sons. They learned the concept of being smart quite early. Each of them began labeling kids in their classes "smart" (and others not) based on associations with the word that they'd learned from babysitters, relatives and, sadly, me. "Smart" meant good at the things most schools tell us are important: reading and writing well, understanding mathematical operations, finishing tests quickly and knowing lots of facts. In different ways, each of my sons measured himself against this standard and found himself lacking. One is a reluctant reader who prefers to access information through audio and video. He was flagged for years in school because he left out words when reading out loud, which he hates to do. The other is a strong student but he is a bit scattered, always thinking about five things at once, often when he is expected to be paying attention. As a parent it broke my heart to see how they internalized the messages they received about all the ways in which they didn't measure up to our society's conception of "smart." I of course see each of them as a unique constellation of potential. My reluctant reader can hold variables in his head visually in a way that lets him see many moves ahead on a chessboard and beat everyone in the family at strategy games. He has a wicked sense of humor and a natural athleticism. His brother taught himself to dissect a fetal pig and mastered the basics of surgical suturing, and launched a baking business a few months later.

Like many parents, I struggle with a painful tension: I know the unique brilliance of my children, but I also know the game of education in America, and what is at stake. And for those from families with less privilege, including Black, brown, lower-income and immigrant families, the stakes are even higher. In this game, much of a child's uniqueness is dismissed as either irrelevant or problematic. The concept of *smart* keeps us from focusing primarily on our children's fulfillment and their development into thriving young people; it keeps them from developing the skills most critical to their developmental stage, and from being who they are for fear of not becoming who the game says they should be. This is a game in which the question is "*Are* you smart?" rather than "*How* are you smart?"

"Smart" has come to represent a flattened, largely dehumanized idea of human capability. It's an idea based on centuries of bias about what matters in people and cultures, and what doesn't. This idea of smart is more than just a foundation for what we do in schools; it's one of the organizing principles of our society. And it poses an existential threat to the development of our children and our communities. This book is an exploration of what *smart* should mean and what our system of education should value most: the complexity and richness of our humanity and the many different ways in which people engage with and contribute to the world. The schools that gave me that feeling, I now realize, were the ones built entirely around an idea of *smart* centered on these latter values.

I left the Dodge Foundation convinced that we shouldn't be building more schools like the ones where I had been a student and a teacher; that we should be building more like Edgemont Montessori School, the Met School and High School for Recording Arts. But I had very little idea about how to do that. Many of the debates about education at that time, the late 1990s, focused on the differences between school governance models—public district, public charter, private and magnet. (We're still hung up on these questions today.)

We talked about magnet schools as though this term, *magnet*, said something meaningful about the kind of education provided— something beyond reintegrating schools that housing, transportation and school-funding policies in urban districts had helped segregate. Nobody was really talking about why magnet schools that adopted the Montessori model, for example, seemed to attract wealthy, educated, white families to urban districts that otherwise serve mostly poor kids of color. Nobody was talking about the fact that the most privileged people seemed to get their kids into schools that prioritized a sense of wholeness, or the inherent value of each child, while those schools were mostly out of reach for underprivileged families.

As charter-school laws were established, ostensibly to allow more diverse approaches to education to exist in the public system, efforts soon converged on opening up no-excuses college preparatory schools that would raise test scores and close academic achievement gaps—"better" versions of the Newark school I taught in. Efforts to design schools that reflect human-centered guiding values, led by leaders like Ted Sizer of the Coalition of Essential Schools and Warren Simmons at the Annenberg Institute, were sidelined by a well-funded rush toward standards-based reform, with its emphasis on high-stakes accountability.

My research and career since then have focused on two intersecting areas: understanding what was different about the few schools that gave me that indescribable feeling, and how to make more of those schools available to more students in the public system. I wanted to understand what values, decisions and experiences made these environments so powerful and welcoming—how they managed to produce creative, independent, well-adjusted young adults who went on to engaged, fulfilled and purposeful lives. Privileged families would pay massive tuitions to send their children to private versions of these schools even though I had seen amazing examples of similar programs that served diverse student populations in the public sector. My intuition was that the differences between these and more conventional schools were far more subtle and far more critical to understand than public education experts were saying at the time. I believed that if we could understand what made these schools unique—what distinguished them from so many schools that were trying to improve how they worked but with less success—we might gain insight into how to improve education as a system.

I refer to these schools as having holistic-indigenous learning programs and as being human-centered/liberatory—terms I describe in detail later in the book. I use "HIL" (for holistic-indigenous learning) as a catch-all term for both labels because I no longer see them as separate; the holistic-indigenous worldview that I describe in part 1 must inform what is called the human-centered or liberatory approach to education, and vice versa, in order for us to find the right path forward.

The last three decades of education reform have been hobbled by biases and blind spots that some call "white supremacy culture," but which I prefer to call "modern-Western supremacy culture." A defining trait of this dominant culture is a relentless sense of urgency—a sense that the best course of action is whatever is quickest and provides the most visible, replicable results. But I believe the best solutions in education are ones that enable us to reflect, engage communities, and work toward sustainable ways of being and organizing ourselves around the education of our children that will, to paraphrase an ancient Haudenosaunee (Iroquois) principle, remain in place for the seventh generation beyond us.

I have tried in my career to learn what it would take to bring these distinctions into the work of transforming American education. I kept hearing from educators in HIL programs that sustaining them within the public sector was getting harder all the time. Even as the field of education began to address questions of equity, we were suppressing or discouraging the very type of education that seemed to be the best solution. Why was this happening, and what could be done about it? What were the specific barriers to change, and what would it take to shift a system as complex and decentralized as American education? How could we bring legitimacy to these programs when the people in power were still communicating in the language of the conventional, factory model?

The Future of Smart is a synthesis of two decades of explorations, conversations, experiences, questions and insights. It is less a how-to guide than a survey of the landscape, one that I hope will help the field of human-centered education coalesce and increase its influence. With this book I don't intend to argue for one right way of doing education, but I do believe the entire system has to change. We need to refocus our energy on cultivating the unique abilities of each young person rather than continue to reinforce largely arbitrary and outdated hierarchies of merit.

The first part of the book examines the history of our education system. It may feel out of place in a book that's ultimately a vision of education's future, but any holistic change begins with a recognition of context. Just as we need to understand every child in terms of where they come from, where they live and how they think, we need to see the present state of education in terms of its origins and the values that underlie it. Chapter 1 is about the big picture—the centuries-long interchange between two perspectives that mirrors the dialogue between the left and right hemispheres of our brains. Chapters 2 and 3 tell the story of a society driven by a left-hemispheric impulse to categorize and quantify that divided school-based learning into discrete subjects and assessed all students against the same narrow criteria. At the same time these chapters trace the history of a more holistic, indigenous, right-hemispheric worldview that has always been with us, though it has often been stigmatized or ignored.

Though these two outlooks have coexisted all along, the left-hemispheric worldview has been unusually dominant in the last 500 years. Before the emergence of modern society and the Scientific Revolution, people lived in small, dispersed communities. Their daily lives were tied to the earth and its rhythms, and neighbors were instinctively and deeply connected. Interdependence was taken for granted. The modern West emerged by emphasizing the individual over the collective; objectivity over felt experience; dominance over symbiosis. The energy of that shift propelled colonization, the establishment of what would become the United States, and the Industrial Revolution. But much was lost in the process, including indigenous and collective ways of being and knowing. There's much more to say about that story than I included; my focus in this book is on the aspects that most influenced the state of education today.

Our current assumptions about school and learning have a long and complicated history, and that history is a burden and a guide. Just as we chose to define learning in left-hemispheric terms when mass, factory schooling began in the eighteenth century, we can now choose to reconceive it. Chapters 4, 5 and 6 explore how that reconceptualization works and what it looks like. You will see how and why educational programs that reflect a holistic-indigenous approach have struggled to find and keep their footing in a landscape dominated by the conventional approach. These programs organize themselves intentionally around relationship, community context, diversity, identity formation, uniqueness and deep, dynamic learning. This approach not only reflects the values of social and racial justice we claim to aspire to, it also aligns with what science now tells us about the human brain, learning, human development, neurodiversity and the future of the working world. For the first time since the advent of mass schooling and the development of the factory model, the goals of human-centered/liberatory education are explicitly aligned with what neuroscience, economics and the social sciences tell us about our children and the world that awaits them. The schools already working from this approach can be our models as we learn what it will take to move forward.

By the time you reach chapter 7, you will have an understanding of the assumptions that underlie much of the recent thinking about what educators should do, what students need and how people learn. You will have seen how a more intentional approach to designing educational opportunities can prepare young people for the future of work, and how it can better respond to the needs of a vastly diverse population whose children have unique abilities and learning strengths. Chapter 7 proposes a pathway—a broader, more dynamic field for inquiry about potential solutions.

An Opening

As a woman of color working on public education in America, I have, over time, found my tribe at the edges of the field—or entirely outside it. This group includes brilliant and generous educators, school leaders, students, parents, researchers and advocates, people who have found a home in Montessori, Waldorf and United World College schools or in the worlds of alternative education, youth development and outdoor education. Some are connected to holistic education, progressive education, unschooling, forest schools, self-directed education—even homeschooling and learning co-ops. They touch the lives of students from truly diverse backgrounds: Black, Indigenous, Latinx, Asian, white; wealthy, middle class, low-income; students all along the continuum of cognitive, affective, social and emotional capabilities; students who have overcome trauma in many different forms and those who have not. It includes many individual teachers who work in public systems and do amazing, life-changing work with the children who are lucky enough to be their students, but who are exhausted by constantly dancing and feinting and fighting against the larger system to do education in the way they know is best for nurturing the humanity and unique potential of the young people they work with each day. Because they often work within different siloes, these educators and advocates can't always see the common goals that unite them, or articulate the shared vision of education they are advancing for the rest of us to consider. I hope *The Future of Smart* will help make clearer why educational approaches that at first glance appear wildly different are actually similar in fundamental ways, enabling these practitioners to see themselves as "sticks in a bundle," able to collectively push for change in new ways.

I've been turning over their stories and thinking about writing this book since 2005, but the moment has never been quite right. In the past few years, though, something has changed; not only for me but for colleagues and mentors who have been in this work since the 1960s or 1970s. At this moment it feels like our nation's choices about how to balance the values of the left and right hemispheres—of individualism and collectivism, progress and sustainability, technology and relationship—will determine a great deal about the future. The choices we make now in education will have ramifications for the climate, the economy, the criminal justice system, the weaponization of race in America, and our definition of human well-being.

The debates we are having in these very different spheres of our nation's life are, in essence, one and the same. They are rooted in a centuries-old choice to disrupt the long-standing dynamics of human connection and community in favor of one view of science, prosperity and expansion. This disruption was birthed in Europe in the 1500s, and it happened gradually. Its perpetuation has not been intentional—not in the sense of conscious choices made by individuals. It is not limited to America, but it is entrenched here in particularly powerful ways for reasons that other scholars have explored more thoroughly than I can.[2]

Mass education is among the last systems to take shape and to change in a society, in part because we use it to pass along the dominant values of the time. When we prioritize individualism, competition and rigged versions of meritocracy, education becomes a tool for preserving privilege and justifying inequality. But when the values we focus on defend every person's right to flourish, education can be a vehicle for individual and collective well-being. Only then do we fully realize that, in Martin Luther King Jr.'s words, "We are all caught in an inescapable network of mutuality, tied in a single garment of destiny."

As I write this introduction, the truth of our global interconnectedness has manifested in the increasing threat of climate change, a world-altering pandemic, and unrest around the world in response to injustice and inequality. America is convulsing as these global events converge with our legacy of genocide, dehumanization and systemic oppression in the wake of a leader who boldly sought to undermine essential norms of democracy and due process.

My hope is that *The Future of Smart*, while focused on education, can provide a new perspective on the roots of these broader challenges and, in doing so, contribute to a new body of work emerging from holistic, ecologically-minded communities and cultures whose voices have long been silenced and devalued in America. Our conversations about education must be driven by our deepest convictions about who we want to be as a people and a nation and who we want our children to become. Such conversations are the only means by which we will commit ourselves to investing in the long-term work needed to provide our children with an abiding faith in their humanity and worth and prepare them to build a world that reflects our highest vision of who we can be individually and collectively.

PART 1

PAST:
(A Brief Overview of)
How We Got Here

CHAPTER 1

Education at a Crossroads

In July of 1989 a team of 23 executives recruited from businesses, unions, industry associations and the US Department of Labor began a year-long project to study the current state and future prospects of America's labor market. The commission interviewed more than 2,000 people ranging from C-suite executives to factory floor line-managers and construction foremen, drawn from 550 American companies and agencies. They studied the dynamics of local labor markets around the country. The study soon expanded to six other nations: Germany, Sweden, Denmark, Ireland, Japan and Singapore. There the work went beyond interviews with company leaders and workers to examine the values and efficacy of social programs that were designed very differently from those in the US, focusing particularly on education, training and labor-market policies. The goal was a composite picture of how systems in other countries work with each other to cultivate a skilled workforce; those lessons could then be applied in the US.

The commission released its findings and recommendations, "America's Choice: High Skills or Low Wages," in June of 1990.[1]

Several years earlier, another paper, "A Nation at Risk," had raised alarms about the state of America's education system specifically, and the consequences for the country's economic, social and political standing in the world if education was not improved.[2] National education leaders, advocates and ideologues mined the "America's Choice" report for recommendations, and one in particular seemed to resonate: the need for an "outcomes- or standards-based" approach to education. The experts reading the commission's report attributed the problems in education to two factors: a lack of clarity and consensus about what schools should actually be teaching, and a shortage of incentives for students, teachers and schools to try to do better.[3]

In 1994 the Clinton administration enacted a comprehensive, standards-based vision for education called the Improving America's Schools Act (IASA). IASA required all states to devise and adopt rigorous standards for all subject areas and grade levels, and to develop uniform, statewide tests for at least reading and math. IASA took a simple assumption drawn from the reports cited above, and used it as the basis for federal law. The assumption was that the key to high-quality education was a set of universal standards.

Once enacted, this vision became the basis for the Bush Administration's 2001 No Child Left Behind (NCLB) Act, which required states to test all students in grades three through eight every year in reading and math. Any school that didn't raise its scores each year risked heavy sanctions. By 2001 a coalition of advocates agreed that for too long the American education system had neglected the needs of many students, among them students of color, students living in poverty and students who have learning differences. In part this neglect stemmed from implicit bias and systemic racism, which led to lower expectations for students from particular backgrounds and circumstances. President Bush, Congress and the thousands of advocates who supported the law believed that with clear learning targets, universal testing and harsh penalties for failure, education in America would be forced to lift up and better serve all children. To that end, NCLB ordered that every student in the country—regardless of disability, English language proficiency or any other consideration— demonstrate proficiency in state tests by the year 2014.[4]

As with most education reforms in this country, the initiative summoned the expertise of smart and accomplished people, generated bipartisan support and was carried out with vast resources at the federal, state and district level. Astounding sums of philanthropic dollars were spent to develop a "Common Core" of academic standards (Common Core State Standards, or CCSS), spanning all subjects and grade bands, that would meet the general mandate laid out in NCLB. States spent millions of dollars either customizing the CCSS to reflect their particular needs or developing their own standards. They developed new standardized tests aligned with CCSS to fulfill the testing requirements of NCLB. States and districts developed new accountability systems that could incorporate student test scores, then ranked schools based on their performance. Forty-three states built their own educator evaluation systems that tied teacher licensure (and sometimes pay) to student test scores. Each of these initiatives required millions of dollars and hundreds of thousands of people-hours to be spent on implementation, training and management. The CCSS cost families and individual students, too: Children were left with less exposure to the arts, science and play. Families who had the time and resources to do so invested in tutoring, test preparation and evaluation, hoping to either game the test system or take advantage of supports and accommodations available to students with diagnosed learning differences or special needs. The latter exacerbated already-existing gaps between kids whose families could afford after-school classes, summer camps and travel, and those whose families could not.

Although NCLB and other reforms helped raise awareness about certain inequities in the education system, the overall outcome was a massive disappointment. Average reading scores for American students in grades four and eight remained relatively flat for 10 years after the passage of NCLB. Average reading and math scores stayed the same at every grade level, while the lowest-performing students ended up doing worse. There were improvements in the top quarter of students, but only between 2012 and 2014.[5]

Regardless of the merits of the definition of success that NCLB laid out, by 2014 the nation's entire public education system had failed according to the law's own definition. Had the law been followed to the letter, almost every public school would have been closed or handed over to new management.[6] In the years since, we've seen cosmetic changes to federal and state law, but for the most part we still live in the same system that triggered all this concern, activism and costly reform beginning in the 1990s.

This plan was not a catastrophic failure because of underfunding, problems with execution or some breakdown among legislators, administrators, teachers, students or communities. This was a massive effort, driven by the best available expertise and funded by the richest government in the history of the world. The experts diagnosed a problem and set about executing a solution.

Their initiative failed because they didn't understand the problem.

In the 1990s the experts—think tanks, legislators and civil rights advocates—were looking at an education system designed during the Industrial Revolution to prepare the children of laborers for factory jobs, rank them, sort the best from the worst and inculcate the values of the time. That was 200 years ago. In 1900, 1950, 1990 and 2010, the system was still running on most of the same basic assumptions about childhood, the workplace, who comes to school and why, and how schools should fit into the larger society (and the mindset persists today). The experts themselves were still thinking in those old terms without knowing it. They looked at the disappointing outcomes and naturally assumed the system had stopped working—had developed flaws. They couldn't see that the system hadn't changed much at all, and that *that* was the problem. The times had changed, our values had changed, and the machine was still chugging along in the same old way.

These experts made the same mistake that educators often make when confronted with a child from a background different from that of their classmates, a child with dyslexia or a child with a history of trauma: Seeing the child struggle or fall behind, they look for a label or diagnosis—some category that will help them know what to do. There's no room to consider that the child's struggles might have to do with the system itself, the narrowness of the categories or the inequalities of the society the child comes from. Just as the educators end up blaming the child for systemic problems, the experts ended up consigning the problems of society to districts, schools and classrooms.

Even though these reform efforts and so many others lit up with failure in every direction, still no one asked whether the education system might contain the problem within its very machinery—within its DNA. They couldn't see that the more force they exerted from outside—the more they tried to bolt on interventions like blended learning; science, technology, engineering and mathematics (STEM); science, technology, engineering, arts and mathematics (STEAM);

science, technology, reading, engineering, arts and mathematics (STREAM); project-based learning; socio-emotional learning; anti-bullying initiatives; culturally-responsive practices; and mental health initiatives—the more the human potential in the system was contorted. While each of these interventions targeted meaningful change, they did very little to alter the outcomes of a fundamentally flawed system. The experts had the best of intentions, but they misunderstood just what it takes for schools to produce healthy, engaged, curious and accomplished citizens.

This misunderstanding is much bigger than just those experts, however. The tendencies to overlook the whole and to see problems through the lens of our preconceived ideas are wired into the human experience and embedded in the very structure and operation of our brains. Just as we struggle to see the whole picture of education, we often misperceive each other, focusing on categories, norms and comparisons rather than seeing the whole person. This tendency is a function of our divided brains, and until we understand our brains we can't fully understand what it means to learn, connect and thrive—and thus begin to reshape education.

Our Divided Brain

The brain—the organism responsible for making all our connections—is itself divided into two distinct hemispheres. We might imagine that human brains would have evolved to integrate the two hemispheres, allowing them to work together more effectively and efficiently. Instead something very different happened. First, the human brain developed a prefrontal cortex that allows us to stand back from the world in time and space and understand what lies beyond ourselves, thus slowing down our most instinctive responses and adding a layer of reflection.[7] The cortex allows a child to breathe and gain control of their emotions rather than dissolve into a tantrum; it enables a teenager full of primal urges to pause and think about what their daredevil actions and possible injury might mean to their future and to the people who love them. This is called having a *theory of mind*—an understanding that we are not alone and that other beings have experiences that are distinct and separate from ours.

The second change was that the division between the hemispheres became even more pronounced. One of the theories of this book, based on the work of psychiatrist Iain McGilchrist, is very different from the common assumption that each hemisphere "does" different things; that is, that the left "does" math, logic and thinking while the right "does" art, music and feeling. We now know that both hemispheres of the brain are involved in everything we do, including high-level activities such as reasoning, imagining and creating.[8]

The difference between the two hemispheres, McGilchrist found, lies in how they engage with the world. The hemispheres work both individually and in concert, allowing humans to do two critical things at once. On the one hand, humans have learned to make use of the world, manipulate our surroundings, locate discrete entities and figure out their behaviors and their utility. In order to do that the brain creates a simplified version of reality—something like a map. A map isn't reality, but for many purposes it works better than the real thing because the real thing is simply too complex to survey and analyze every time we need to, say, drive to the beach. So to navigate the world we conjure abstract, narrower versions of it; we create categories, maps, rubrics, comparisons. This is the work of our left hemisphere. On the other hand, we exist in the world as embodied beings, moving through space, flooded with sensory input, interacting with others, interpreting clues about how to engage—in short, having experiences that don't fit into neat categories; that immerse us, surround us, move through us. This embodied way of experiencing the world is associated with the right hemisphere. It's an intuitive, body-based and timeless way of being. To take just one example of the dual experience that's happening in us all the time, our left hemisphere allows us to recognize the little person sitting across from us in the airport as belonging to those categories known as "family" and "child," someone who must not be ignored or left to fend for themselves. Our right hemisphere elicits the complex emotions of caretaking, disciplining, cuddling and playing. Our right hemisphere allows us to not only know the world but to experience it in a visceral way.

Right Hemisphere	Left Hemisphere
Holistic Processing	Sequential Processing
Contextualized	Decontextualized
Embodied Sensations	Abstractions
Implicit Meaning	Explicit Meaning
Large Flows of Information	Linear
Images and Patterns	Reductive and Familiar

In more concrete terms, the left hemisphere pulls things out of context to identify features and give them names, while the right tends to see things in context—to experience connections between things as much as the things themselves. The left tends to make things abstract while the right makes things vivid and concrete. The left seeks to know what to do and what things mean, while the right is attuned to how things feel and how they simply are.[9]

To come back to the example of the experts seeking to reform education in the US, consider one particularly relevant difference between the two hemispheres: the left hemisphere cannot process information that does not comport with what it already "knows"— with categories it has already created. It is programmed to search for information in terms of similarities and differences. If we favor the left hemisphere (which, as you'll see in this book, we Westerners tend to do), we end up missing the forest for the trees, seeing things from the outside without understanding them from the inside. We see education in terms of outcomes and quantifiable data, but forget that learning is an experience full of subjective experiences. You could say that the left hemisphere is prone to seeing the world as either/or. The right hemisphere is more of a both/and entity; because it considers experiences as a whole, it's less equipped to exclude information (and less prone to know what to do with it). Our comprehension of the world begins in the right hemisphere, with input from the senses. That data is then passed to the left hemisphere for technical functions like analysis, measurement and codification, especially through language. Information is then passed back to the right hemisphere for a full synthesis—an integration of our experience at all levels that leads to decision and action.[10]

By its very nature the left hemisphere's "way of being" is more culturally contagious than the right hemisphere's.[11] The left wants to turn the dynamic and complex into the simplified and systematized; it tends to bypass what is unique and unknown, searching for whatever can be standardized and described. This simplicity—this quick and discrete problem-solving—is inherently seductive to human beings, who are constantly trying to make sense of their environment in order to be safe and productive. The more we are drawn to the left-brain's categories and systems, the more we lose sight of the complexities all around us. The left hemisphere's engagement in crafting precise language and reducing complexity into data points and descriptions stands in contrast to the right hemisphere's capacity to perceive the complexity of the whole of a situation or person, even as it sacrifices what some might consider a level of perfection and precision in how and what it perceives.[12] Once the left-hemispheric way of being takes firm root, it shapes culture in such a way that the culture begins to respond to this way of being as the known and therefore the "correct" one.

Taken to the extreme, left-hemispheric human experience is like living in a hall of mirrors: a constant search for comparisons, practicalities and solutions, but disconnected from any intuitive, felt sense—or physical embodiment—of what matters. In a world dominated by the left hemisphere, the big picture is lost. Bits of discrete information dominate our attention, but true wisdom eludes us. We focus on specialization at the expense of general practice and understanding the whole. Craftsmanship, acumen and intuition are replaced by "expert" knowledge based on theory and qualifications rather than experience. Technocratic solutions flourish even as we become disconnected from true democracy and engagement. We experience the world ever more through simulations rather than through experiences of ourselves and others. Speed and volume supersede quality. Cultural history and context are confidently dismissed in favor of a future *driven* unwittingly by data and technology rather than intentionally mediated or enhanced by it.[13] We're not entirely left-brain-oriented yet, but we're moving in that direction. The question is what to do about it.

Education has a major role to play. The field sits at the intersection of the social, psychological and political spheres. At its core, education is about teaching people how to live, find fulfillment and meaning, and form meaningful relationships to the world. Unfortunately, when we look at the reform efforts undertaken over the last few decades from a hemispheric perspective, left-hemisphere dominance is unmistakable. The experts were often people who had already thrived in an individualistic, standardized, efficiency-oriented system. They looked around them and saw schools that were underperforming and required more stimulation, higher expectations, more urgency. They saw unmotivated or "ineffective" teachers, low standards, bad tests, inadequate accountability systems, inferior technology and disorganized classrooms. In trying to understand education, they pulled learning out of the context of living, broke the richness of knowledge out into discrete subjects and envisioned schools as optimized machines for measurable learning. They were doing what they knew how to do—what many of us are taught to do. They saw a system that was deeply flawed and did their best to identify glitches, inefficiencies and opportunities for better performance. It didn't seem to occur to them to question the system itself or to look inside at the essence of what we mean by *learning* and what we value in ourselves and our society. Their recommendations pushed us further toward left-brain priorities—more measurement, more abstraction, more comparison.

To take just one example, when more kids were failing the tests we gave them, we simply broadened our definition of *special needs* rather than asking ourselves whether the tests might be measuring the wrong things or whether there were different ways to know about and be in the world that ought to count as ways of being smart and capable.[14] As a result of our efforts to improve the system, we now have two generations of students whose learning is even further removed from the context of their lives than that of previous generations. We still haven't found a way to teach young people how what they learn in school relates to the lives we want them to live and the lives *they* want to live.

This left-hemispheric way of being doesn't dominate only our schools; it reflects the values of our culture as a whole. And as the left hemisphere is on the rise, the right appears to be in decline. Educators describe having to help ever more children learn how to read the human face, a difficulty that used to be associated mostly with those who have autism-spectrum disorders.[15] Indeed, autism-spectrum disorders and anorexia nervosa are on the rise; both of these conditions mimic deficits in right-hemispheric processing.[16] Children are struggling to sustain their attention, unable to complete tasks that 10 years ago would have been standard for their grade level. Some research suggests that children are now less empathic than in previous generations.[17] Each of these faculties—the abilities to read faces, to empathize and to sustain attention—relies on the right hemisphere of the brain. And each is essential to surviving in the human world as we know it.[18]

Our well-being and survival have always depended on a balance between these two modes of being. McGilchrist notes, however, that in the past the right was the master and the left its servant.[19] Everything we know about human evolution and the health of individuals, communities and society at large suggests that our experience, while informed and strengthened by the capacities of our left hemisphere, should be governed by the right hemisphere, overseen by an awareness of connection, wholeness and embodiment. What we're seeing now, and what we're reproducing in our schools, is a dangerous reversal.

Our Big Misunderstanding in Education

Human well-being results from being engaged in meaningful pursuits that are grounded in a sense of purpose. This may sound intuitive, but it's easily forgotten in our society. The narratives we teach our children about what it means to be smart and successful; about what they should be learning and achieving in school, and why they should do so; and about what options they have to build fulfilling lives, are based on how we understand well-being and fulfillment. These messages—implicit or explicit—stay with them for the rest of their lives. Unfortunately, one metric has fundamentally changed over the last three decades as we rolled out our billion-dollar efforts to improve education: children's overall well-being. And it's declining. In other words, not only are we failing to improve academic outcomes, but our efforts to do so have now made our children measurably less happy in a span of just 20 years.[20]

In general terms, student engagement in school has dropped drastically over the last decade and a half, and the longer young people stay in school the more their engagement declines. Only a third of high school students report being engaged in their learning.[21] As engagement drops, disruptive behaviors emerge and we see an increase in punishment, expulsion and the operation of the school-to-prison pipeline. From 2001 to 2012—as more schools implemented "no excuses" policies designed to improve academic performance—disciplinary action, suspension, expulsion and drop-outs increased.[22] For years Black and brown children, mostly poor, have been harshly disciplined and dehumanized at schools described as having "successful" college preparatory environments—schools to which few white or middle-class families choose to send their children. While there have been improvements in recent years, large gaps remain in the treatment of students of color and those who have learning differences or disabilities. [23]

The education system as a whole—including many private and independent schools—has gotten very good at pathologizing and even criminalizing young people who deviate from narrow definitions of normal: children who have experienced trauma or adverse childhood experiences, children who are not white and middle class, and children who are dyslexic or whose brains are wired to experience the world differently. At least partly as a result, we have record-breaking levels of anxiety, self-harm, depression and substance abuse beginning at younger ages than previously. Health researchers now widely declare that we have an epidemic of youth "unwellness" in this country:[24]

- Each year more than one in five females and one in seven males between the ages of nine and sixteen engage in self-injury.[25]
- More than 30 percent of students who seek mental health services report that they have seriously considered suicide, up from 24 percent a few years ago.[26]
- Between 2006 and 2016 the suicide rate among children younger than 13 rose 114 percent, and the rate for all children rose by 64 percent.[27]
- One in five teens has abused prescription medications; and rates of vaping are increasing, with about 37 percent of twelfth graders reporting vaping in 2018.[28]

The US has some of the highest rates in the developed world of stress, depression, self-harm, substance-abuse, bullying and youth violence. These high rates show up in children as young as eight, and cut across social and economic backgrounds. They are getting worse every year.

If that's not reason enough to question an approach to education that was at least partly driven by a desire to prepare young people for the working world, employers continue to complain that young people come out of school lacking the skills they need to contribute to a rapidly changing workforce. One of the criteria for the success of any education system in twenty-first-century society must be preparation for an uncertain work and professional future, one in which artificial intelligence will be increasingly capable of replicating some aspects of human cognition and capacity, many of them left-hemispheric in nature.[29] In that regard we are failing. Most of us cannot even imagine the world our children will graduate into. Many of the jobs they will apply for don't yet exist. Most of us didn't know what an app was 20 years ago, let alone that in 2019 there would be over 1.7 million jobs available in imagining, funding, building, selling and improving them. We didn't know 40 years ago that the skills and mindset associated with moderate autism—attention to detail, pattern recognition and strong task-orientation—would be a driving force in Silicon Valley's success.[30] The skills our children need in their adulthood might not be defined until a year or two before they enter the workforce. Chances are almost zero that they will remain in the same job for their entire career.[31]

Whenever the future looks uncertain, people latch on to simple narratives. Lately we've been telling ourselves that our economy will soon be dominated by "highly skilled" (read: college and graduate-school training required) jobs in science and technology. This is a comforting narrative, since our education system is already geared toward preparing students for college. But this scenario ignores the fact that the working world is evolving *away* from what our schools are currently teaching. The "highly skilled" individuals we need are more likely to emerge from schools that allow them to learn by doing—by engaging with the community around them and following their interests—than from schools that compel them to follow a preset curriculum.

It's certainly true that technology will continue to play a big role in our lives and that the sciences will always be a driving force in our economy. But a look at labor markets and demographics suggests a more nuanced picture.[32] The "senior Tsunami" of baby boomers entering their retirement years invites a surge of human-services jobs across many fields, particularly medical and social care, nursing-home care and live-in care. We will need more skilled technicians in automotive technology, electrical technology, engineering and computer science. The push over the last few decades to devalue and eliminate training in vocational and skilled trades in our schools and colleges has led to a huge shortage of skilled craftspeople.[33] Along with those skills, workers will need interpersonal and communication skills, even in fields defined by specialized knowledge and technical skill. All indicators are that the future of work will continue to demand the exact capabilities—learning to learn, self-motivation, collaboration, adaptability and flexibility, to name a few—that the conventional system was never designed to cultivate.[34] We now have a practical reason as well as an ethical one to cultivate diverse minds and interests, human-specific skills and professional pathways in our schools. That, too, will begin by reconsidering our entire approach to learning.

The Journey Ahead

At moments like this in our society, when large and long-standing systems have proven inadequate to our present and future needs, we have the chance to look for something new and to reconsider things we've taken for granted. For decades we have debated whether or not our economic, health, criminal justice, and social welfare systems reflect the values of our society as a whole and our aspirations for equity, justice and opportunity. Education represents the convergence of all these systems. To fix inequities and oppressive systems in our society we must be willing to embrace the inherent values and the interconnectedness of all these elements. If we truly want to change, we can't continue to bolt solutions onto the existing system and expect radically different outcomes.

This is deep work, collaborative work. It cannot be imposed from above or outside. It cannot be implemented technocratically. It requires a change in our relationship with both the idea and the practice of education. For a long time there was no room in the mainstream conversation for this holistic way of thinking about education—only a reform agenda. But something is shifting now, and a window has opened. We need to recognize it for what it is: a conscious choice point.

For many of us this choice emerges from the gap between the values perpetuated by the dominant system in education and our intuitive, deeply felt sense of what our children need. For educators it's the gap between what young learners plainly need in order to thrive and what the conventional approach to education provides. For students it's the gap between who they want to be in the world and what our education system tells them they should care about. In many cases we can't describe exactly where the tension comes from, and we don't have words to make sense of it. But we should trust our intuitions—and what our young people are telling us.

That's where this book comes in. *The Future of Smart* is a guide to that kind of change; to how it might proceed and the dynamics of its progress, if not the map. Our brains allow us to learn about, understand and exist in the world in complex ways. Many of us believe, in the abstract, that education should be focused on the whole child—on developing the range of knowledge, skills and dispositions they will need to thrive in life. But we don't know how to start pushing for that. We look around and find only left-brain solutions—new rubrics, new change models, new assessments and new language. But these changes don't draw on our intuitions, and they don't move us toward the dynamic, holistic experience that can truly cultivate our full humanity.

However you have come to this book, and wherever you are in your relationship to holistic learning, *The Future of Smart* is an invitation to consider the fundamental questions that rarely get asked in the public conversation about education in this country: Why have our efforts at reform been so disappointing? How did we actually arrive at our basic assumptions about what school-based learning should be? And do those assumptions still line up with what we know about our children and the world that awaits them?

Einstein is quoted as saying that when confronted with a challenge, he spent 90 percent of his time defining the problem and 10 percent of his time finding a solution. Before we can change the education system we must come to a new definition of the problem—a new understanding of what's actually going wrong. The next few chapters trace these issues back to their source: our collective past and the origins of our most deep-seated and influential beliefs—beliefs that hold us back in ways we barely understand.

Applying These Ideas

- We often talk about the significance of brain hemispheres in behavior, referring to people as "left-brained" or "right-brained" to suggest a tendency toward more logical or more creative approaches. But the neuroscience about brain hemispheres has evolved significantly in the past few decades, and we now know that the role of the hemispheres in thought and experience is more complex. The neuroscientist Iain McGilchrist, whom you met in this chapter, created an animated video entitled "The Divided Brain" that further explains his ideas about how brain hemispheres work. *Watch it on YouTube and consider what is new to you about his approach. If he's right, what are the implications for how we engage with the world?*

- Young children cannot help but explore and take risks—so much is new! But research shows that the longer children are in school, the more they internalize what they perceive as their "limitations" based our society's definitions of *good, smart* and *successful,* and the less willing they are to try new things and risk failure or embarrassment. *Think about the societal definitions you might have internalized that limit the way you express yourself or try new things in the world. Think of a way to challenge those definitions, and rather than worrying about the outcome, simply enjoy the process.*

- When we encounter something that makes us feel uncomfortable, our brains are wired to flood our bodies with chemicals that put us on full alert. Most of us instinctively try to think our way out of the sensation of discomfort or push the feelings aside. As a result we don't give ourselves the opportunity to move *through* the uncomfortable feeling by navigating it, investigating it, and learning from it. According to Harvard brain researcher Dr. Jill Bolte Taylor, it only takes 90 seconds for the chemicals to flush out of our bodies, which means we have 90 seconds to observe ourselves as this process plays out, to feel it and to watch it dissipate. Without consciously engaging in this process, we can unwittingly enter a cycle in which our own thoughts, rather than any external stimuli, cause us to have this physiological reaction over and over again. *When you next experience a moment of discomfort or a negative reaction, just pause and scan your body to see if you can locate the sensations that make up that negative feeling. Then try to breathe into that part of your body, holding the breath for three seconds, then exhaling for three seconds. Do this a few times, paying close attention to whether you feel subtle shifts in the emotion and the sensation. This can allow you to move through the feeling rather than avoiding or dismissing it.*

CHAPTER 2

The Origins of the Divide in Our Modern Worldviews

A few years ago I went into the living room to find my family divided on a question of profound importance: "Laurel or Yanny." Science class had apparently introduced my two sons to the world of optical and auditory illusions—the classic images that can read as an old woman or a young one, or a face or a vase; and sounds that register differently for different listeners based entirely on the listeners' biases and sensitivities.[1] Laurel or Yanny had gone viral in May of 2018, posted by a 15-year-old student from Atlanta, Georgia. My son played the short audio recording about 100 times in the next few hours, and I learned that I was among the 53 percent of people who heard "Laurel" along with my younger son. My older son heard "Yanny." These arguments were all over the internet as #teamyanny and #teamlaurel fought it out in message boards and comments sections. How was this possible? And, even more fascinating, how was it possible that what I was hearing could change? Sometime after the seventieth listen, on the same computer, through the same speaker, I suddenly heard "Yanny." And after that I could hear nothing else for the rest of the night.

Over the next 10 days our extended family launched a competition over WhatsApp to see who could introduce the most baffling illusion. We also experimented with what it took to shift our perception—to reorient our minds from Laurel to Yanny, face to vase. It turns out optical and auditory illusions are known to scientists as *perceptually ambiguous stimuli*, experiences that can be meaningfully altered in the process of perception. The stimulus itself is not a definitive signal, but a set of clues that the mind can assemble in different ways based on a large set of variables.[2] With Yanny and Laurel, for example, a key variable is the listener's sensitivity to frequency. The clues in the recording that made me hear "Laurel" were lower than the clues that led my son to hear "Yanny." It turns out that as we age we lose our hearing at higher frequencies, a fact that amused my sons immensely, especially after they located a version of the clip in which the lowest-frequency elements of the sound had been removed, and I heard "Yanny." For others the word switches when they change headphones, stand in a different position while listening or see one word or the other projected on a screen along with the sound.[3]

To some extent everything we hear is influenced by our particular sensitivities, prior experiences and expectations. Whatever you actually hear, your brain ends up filling in the rest. At a concert you can more easily discern the sound of the violin, for example, if you watch the violin player. Our brains have learned to expect certain sounds based on certain visual cues. In another example, known as the Tritone Paradox, people can hear the exact same pair of notes but have different perceptions about whether the notes are ascending or descending, based on their native language and where they live.[4] Our perceptions, then, are often at the mercy of unconscious tendencies. When presented with confusing, ambiguous or unsettling clues, our brains often fill in the information most convenient to our presumptions and biases.

As we consider how our education system arrived at its current state and what it will take to make real change, it is worth considering what assumptions we bring to the issue and what blind spots we have inherited. When we consider the assessment-driven approach to education of recent years—the factory/industrial model—we focus on disappointing data points. We try to trace low performance back to some correctible flaw. We fill in the gaps based on our left-hemispheric biases and miss all the planning and intention that went into the development of the factory model. Our modern brains struggle to see that the current problems result from a tradeoff made long ago, at a time when the left hemisphere was first ascendant. This was the dawn of the Scientific Revolution, a relatively short period during which people's sense of their place in the world was profoundly disrupted. While many good things came from the discoveries of that period, something just as important was lost.

Two Worldviews

The Indigenous Worldview

Contrary to what most of us were taught, back in 1492 there was a dominant worldview that was fairly consistent in cultures across the globe. In the Americas, about 75 million people were spread across 16.4 million square miles. The Aztecs, Incas, Mayas and the people of Cahokia had built monumental cities with huge plazas and mounds of earth arranged for communal living. Outside the cities, most people lived in small, migratory settlements and kept few private possessions. They hunted and gathered for food, and kept only small animals like pigs and chickens. They spoke hundreds of languages and practiced many different faiths, which were conveyed orally from generation to generation and almost never written down. They believed in goddesses and gods; in the divinity of animals and the earth. Their origin stories often began with a primal darkness pierced by deities, who then separated earth and sky, brought forth water and light and created life. Across cultures, people understood themselves to be part of a unified creation: they were both takers and givers, hunters and hunted, and entirely dependent on the earth for survival.[5]

In that same year, 60 million people lived in Europe, a landmass of barely four million square miles. They built magnificent cities, and castles, cathedrals, temples, mosques, universities and libraries that were open only to the privileged few. Most people lived off the land, raising crops, small livestock and cattle, all within fences demarcating individual property. They spoke and wrote dozens of languages, recording their religious stories and tenets in illustrated manuscripts and books. They were Catholic, Eastern Orthodox, Jewish, Muslim, pagan and witches, and for long stretches of time these different faiths coexisted peacefully. When they didn't, they decimated each other, torturing and killing in the name of their true god. The members of the prevailing faith thought theirs was the one and only truth—the word of God revealed through prophets and interpreted and enforced through institutional hierarchies. Their origin story also began with a darkness pierced by an all-powerful creator, but this god commanded his creations to "be fruitful and multiply, and replenish the Earth, and subdue it, and have dominion over the fish in the sea, and over the fowl of the air, and over every living thing that moveth upon the Earth."[6] By the end of the fifteenth century they had only just begun to achieve this dominion.[7]

These premodern peoples didn't know a lot about how the world operated, at least by today's standards. They had stories to explain what was, and why—stories that reflected the learning of their forebears, passed down through elders and wise women and shamans of each generation.

Though they lacked scientific theories and empirically tested knowledge (by today's definitions of those terms), by the end of the fifteenth century societies in other parts of the world had achieved more than any European society. The Maya knew enough to navigate across the ocean as early as 300 AD. The ancient Greeks knew a great deal about cartography. The western African civilizations of Ghana (700–1200), Mali (1200–1500) and Songhy (1350–1600) developed empires that could rival any in the world in size, power, scholarship and wealth. The Chinese invented the compass in the eleventh century, and were already exploring the coasts of Asia and eastern Africa.[8]

The same Europeans who had dismissed indigenous cultures during the twelfth through fifteenth centuries were about to be dismissed themselves as continuing to reflect the ignorance of what we now call the Dark Ages. Between 1540 and 1690 the foundational idea of an organic, living and spiritual universe would be displaced in Europe by the vision of the world as a machine, a metaphor that has influenced the Western world and its socio-political and economic systems ever since.

The Rise of the Cartesian-Newtonian Worldview

The Scientific Revolution in Europe laid out a world that could be truly known only through rational thinking, empirical data and an organized scientific method. The brilliant work of three men— Nicolas Copernicus, Johannes Kepler and Galileo Galilei—essentially overthrew the belief that the Earth was the center of the universe and that religious texts described the one true history of humankind. While these discoveries were complex, rarefied and carried out by educated men, their implications altered the worldview of Europeans at every level of society.

Galileo was the first in Western science to formulate universal laws of nature based on scientific experimentation and mathematical language. He argued that scientists should consider only measurable and quantifiable properties of material bodies—shapes, numbers and movements. Other properties—color, sound, taste and smell—were merely subjective mental projections and thus should be excluded from scientific study.[9] Through employing Galileo's perspective, the world of the average European went from being one meaningful, unified experience under the eye of an all-knowing God to a set of fractured, irrelevant experiences, fleeting and unobserved.

While Galileo worked in Italy, England's Francis Bacon set forth a method for conducting experiments and drawing verifiable conclusions. Bacon led the charge for humans to dominate and control nature—in his words, to "torture her secrets from her."[10] While Christians had already been commanded by their God to gain dominion over the earth, Bacon gave an intellectual and scientific mechanism to that pursuit.

His approach gained force with the work of René Descartes and Isaac Newton. Descartes held three main beliefs with respect to the natural world: it was made up of matter, it had a few fundamental properties and it interacted according to a few universal laws. He spent his life trying to describe the world in terms of these three beliefs and thus to banish the superstition and mystery that had enchanted the world for most of human history.[11] Descartes's natural world did, however, include an immaterial mind—a mysterious human entity that was directly related to the brain. In this way Descartes formulated the idea that humans exist within an abstract world of the mind while at the same time living as embodied creatures in the knowable world—a concept known as the *mind-body problem*, which was an early parallel of the brain's left-right hemispheric divide.[12]

Descartes's method was to doubt everything he could until he reached one thing he could not doubt: the existence of himself as a thinker. ("*Cogito ergo sum*," he wrote: "I think, therefore I exist.") He believed that the essence of human nature lies in thought; that anything we can conceive of clearly and distinctly is true. The ultimate meaning of something—an object, a person, an experience—lies not in its inherent qualities but in its parts and their relationship. Every entity could be reduced to parts. The material universe was nothing but a machine holding no purpose, life or spirituality. Nature worked according to mechanical laws, and everything in the material world, including living organisms, could be explained by those laws. The whole thus becomes irrelevant, as does the quality of an experience. Descartes's methodology made the brain's analytic work life's ultimate aim and purpose. No longer was the left hemisphere working in service of overall knowing. This was his most important contribution to science, and it became an essential characteristic of the modern scientific approach.[13] Newton provided a complete mathematical formulation of this mechanistic view, synthesizing the works of Copernicus, Kepler, Galileo, Bacon and Descartes, and seeming to confirm the Cartesian view of nature: The universe is indeed one huge mechanical system operating according to exact mathematical laws.[14]

As these ideas proliferated, they altered the average European's sense of their relationship to the world around them. No longer an organic, living, familiar-yet-mysterious earth influenced by the pagan gods and goddesses of the ancient Greeks, it was a soulless machine. The people had no precious place in the natural order; indeed, they stood completely apart from it. This new worldview did not encourage a healthy respect or awe of the natural world. In fact it said the opposite: The earth is a resource—a set of objects to be studied, understood and controlled.

Knowledge itself meant something different now. What had been a mysterious, ongoing revelation of gods, goddesses and myths, the world was now completely knowable and explainable, its fundamental nature and behavior accessible to all. And just as knowledge changed, so did the tools people could use to "know" their world. The real world was that which could be seen, measured, categorized. The smell of rain, the taste of berries, the joy of birth, the sorrow of death—these were considered soft and subjective, losing part of their relevance and their power to define the known world. The world could be taken apart, counted, calculated, sorted and valued—its value was the sum of its parts. And once the parts could be separated and measured, that assessment became the driving force of daily life. No longer did a farmer merely ask whether his crop was enough to feed the village; now the yield could be measured, now it could be compared to that of the next village over, and compared to last year's. Humans would learn to define their lives and each other in terms of competition and relative status.

All of these changes took shape in just over a century, with scientific discoveries and practices coalescing into a worldview that still dominates today. And as the scientists were redescribing the natural world, intellectuals were redefining human life by the same new principles.

From Science to Society

Eighteenth-century thinkers took hold of the Scientific Revolution and asked why these laws couldn't be used to better the lot of those who had been denied the spoils of progress in the past. This question resulted in the creation of the social sciences, which shaped new debates about the economy, governance and education.

A dominant influence in this development was the thinking of the seventeenth-century English philosopher John Locke. Applying the approach that Newton had taken with physics, Locke developed an atomistic view of society, describing the human being as the basic building block. He traced large-scale patterns of behavior back to individual behaviors, applying ideas about human nature to economic and political problems. He believed that, like the universe itself, humans could be explained through universal laws. Just as the atoms in a gas could achieve a balanced, stable state, Locke argued that human society could ultimately arrive at homeostasis. If we could understand the principles that drive people and their interactions, we could guide society toward a better end. Human beings were withdrawn from context and relationship and considered as discrete and purposeful elements, like chess pieces on a board.[15]

As the eighteenth century unfolded, Locke's ideas about the manipulation of social dynamics appealed to a new generation of economic and political leaders who were observing patterns of increasing mobility and unrest. Workers were reacting violently to the disruptions of the Industrial Revolution. Economic and social reformers in Europe saw an opportunity to rally workers against the upper class, an effort that culminated in the French Revolution.

In the wake of the French Revolution, James Mills and Jeremy Bentham, two leading political and economic thinkers of the early nineteenth century, devised a theory that the value of a thing—a person, activity or idea—is determined by how useful it is. This came to be known as *utilitarianism*.[16] Industrialists prized efficiency, and sought to maximize efficiency in their factories by standardizing workers' value. They divided complex tasks into small, discrete actions. They designed conveyer belts to move the process along between stages, while training workers to function as efficiently as these new machines. This vision of human value, in which people could be assessed in terms of their efficiency, performance and productivity, would come to shape the mindset of the modern world, perhaps most prominently in our definition of school-based learning.

When Worldviews Clash

It was not inevitable that Europeans would be the ones to cross the Atlantic and "discover" the Americas. Many non-European societies flourished through trade and exploration of Africa and Asia during the thirteenth, fourteenth and early fifteenth centuries. They preserved the knowledge of antiquity, and it became the foundation of their technologies. They established booming trade routes throughout the Mediterranean and into Asia and North Africa.[17]

On the other hand, a series of disasters had befallen Europe in the fourteenth century: invasions; famine; the Black Death; the collapse of the great Italian banking houses; and increased costs of warfare as emperors and popes lost control, feudal states declined and the region divided into city-states and principalities. Facing scarcity and violence, the poorest and weakest Christian monarchs sent explorers off in the late fifteenth century to expand the reach of the Christian faith, establish new trade routes and improve their fortunes.[18]

When they landed in the New World, European explorers found largely migratory communities that had learned over millennia to live off the land, even in cold climates. The inhabitants' indifference to ownership and property rights made them immediately suspect to Europeans, whose lives had been shaped for centuries by wars fought for control of land. These indigenous people lived by myths and rituals that tied every facet of their lives to the earth. They lacked a "sophisticated" written language, whereas the Papal regime in Europe had recently increased its power through the widespread distribution of religious texts and laws.[19] Thus a crowd of desperate, displaced and traumatized travelers searching for gold and glory encountered a population of interdependent people living in relative harmony with the land. This is yet another clash of worldviews—one abstracted, disembodied and held by people looking outward and reliant on language and theories; the other intuitive, ritualistic and held by people immersed in their surroundings.

There is a connection between the left-hemispheric approach to the world and the *scarcity mentality*. If we relate to the world primarily through what we already know—an abstracted representation of what we have experienced—then we are already limited in our ability to take in and connect to the actual reality around us. On the other hand, by its very nature, a right-hemispheric way of being in the world sees the whole—sees the living and dynamic nature of what is and how it changes and evolves. It is connected to what is local, real, communal and attached to place. It is not operating out of representations but out of reality, and the very ability to accept the fluid and emergent nature of reality opens the door to a mindset of possibility and abundance.[20]

Add up the realities of scarcity—the violence and trauma inflicted on European peoples over the course of centuries in the name of threatened Papal regimes and monarchies—and the influence of the Scientific Revolution, and what came next is less surprising. Over time the priorities of expansion and the ascendant values of the Cartesian-Newtonian worldview could not allow for the survival of the indigenous way of being. The conquest of America was a violent mission for land and property, to be sure. But it was also a clash of left- and right-hemispheric perspectives in which only one would be allowed to continue and thrive.

Could it have gone differently? Must one worldview overtake the other by driving it into hiding or submission, or can the two coexist in the same culture and in the same minds? For this we can look to what happened in China at about the same time. China had its own scientific revolution in the seventeenth century. Western mathematics and mathematical astronomy had been introduced a little after 1600. Chinese scholars soon began to reshape astronomy accordingly, and came to believe, for the first time, that models could explain and predict astronomical phenomena. This was as revolutionary in China as it had been in Europe. However, the revolution in China did not generate the same all-out conflict. It did not burst forth in a fundamental reorientation of humankind's position in the natural world. It did not cast doubt on traditional ideas about the heavens.[21]

The most striking long-range outcome of encounters with European science during that period was, in fact, a revival of traditional Chinese astronomy—a rediscovery of forgotten methods that took on new life when integrated with European mathematical principles.

Why didn't this conceptual revolution in China have the same social consequences as in Europe? For one thing, Chinese astronomers who made sense of the new ideas were fundamentally attached to the traditional values of their culture. The most influential first-generation champions of Western astronomy were men of the lower Yangtze region who had lived through the Manchu invasion of the 1640s. They were grounded in their cultural values and in their communities and their particular geography. When they learned this new astronomy they immediately turned it toward the neglected techniques of their own tradition. In other words, rather than seeking to transcend the local, intuitive, spiritual values they had inherited, they sought to fortify and enrich those values with science. [22] They were the opposite of Descartes, for whom every ancient institution had to justify itself by the new criteria or else be cast aside. And China's recent history was the opposite of Europe's: Whereas European societies had been torn apart and reshuffled during the Middle Ages, leaving their people in search of new realities, China maintained a great deal of its coherence during the same period. Thus leaders and citizens alike saw the new ideas of science mostly as a gift, something to be incorporated into an existing whole.

While I've shown in this chapter how the Scientific Revolution initiated an unhealthy reliance on left-brain thinking, there can be

CARTESIAN-NEWTONIAN	HOLISTIC-INDIGENOUS
Classical physics	Quantum physics
Classical economics	Behavioral economics
Euclidian geometry of perfect shapes	Fractal geometry of nature
Domination of nature/extraction	Ecology/conservation
Unrestrained capitalism	Social capitalism
Colonialism/enslavement	Indigenous existence
Hyper-individualism	Collectivism
Paternalistic systems	Liberatory systems
Patriarchy	Intersectional feminism
Hierarchical managment structures	Flat/networked organizations
Health as intervention to prevent death	Alternative medicine/ health as wellness

no question that it also transformed the world for the better in many ways. The ability to comprehend and predict the natural world led to much of the technology, convenience and material prosperity we enjoy today. But along with that growth came a narrowing of everyday experience for the average citizen. The inclusive whole that most people had long felt themselves a part of began to crumble—to atomize; and the world was diminished as surely as it was explained.

We are now living out the long-term impact of this shift toward scientific, abstract knowing. But just as China in the seventeenth century managed to balance the new empiricism with its heritage and cultural values, we can choose which ideas to embrace and which to abandon. If we remain committed to interconnectedness, seeing each other as elements of an interrelated system, we can revive indigenous ways of knowing without discarding science or technology. That integration can begin in schools. But first we need to understand how this "worldview divide" already influences our education system as we know it, and what it would take to build something truly different.

Applying These Ideas

- I thought a lot about which terminology to use in this book to describe the different worldviews, and I struggled particularly with the term *indigenous*, which I use to describe a worldview based on values very different from those of our dominant culture. I considered using the phrase "holistic-ecological," but it didn't quite capture the breadth and depth of this perspective. What does the term *indigenous* evoke for you?

In your mind, were or are there indigenous cultures or groups in Europe? *As you engage with the remainder of this book, track your reactions to the term. Do they shift or stay the same? Does the term's meaning change as you read? Does the link between the educational concepts and the indigenous populations of the world feel apt? Does it feel fair? What other terms might we use instead?*

- The ideas in this chapter are meant to challenge long-standing assumptions about the links between modern European history and education in the US today. *Think about what was new for you in this chapter's version of history and how you reacted to these ideas. Were some harder to accept than others? Can you trace any of your reactions back to your essential beliefs or assumptions?*

- In his book *My Grandmother's Hands*, Resmaa Menakem suggests that racism and *white-body supremacy* have their roots in the same period of European history I discussed in this chapter. He argues that these constructs traumatize all of us, including white people. *Looking at Image 2, think about the characteristics of systems designed to reflect primarily Cartesian-Newtonian values. What would systems grounded in holistic-indigenous values prioritize?*

- The young graphic designers who designed the images for this book helped me "untable the table" that was my original format for presenting the Cartesian-Newtonian and holistic-indigenous worldviews. We wanted to invoke a both/

and versus either/or approach to considering these values. There are strengths associated with a Cartesian-Newtonian approach to understanding the world and designing systems; I'm not arguing to disregard or discard this perspective but rather to ensure that it works in service of something greater and more supportive of the communities we want to build. *How does intentionally considering this image with a both/ and frame inform your reaction to it?*

CHAPTER 3

The Worldview Divide in Education

Pediatrician Dr. Gopal Gupta's office, about 15 minutes from Children's Hospital in Boston, feels remarkably homey for a Western medical setting, even a pediatric one. The waiting room is furnished with deep, squishy chairs and the walls are lined at eye level with toys meant to soothe and distract nervous patients waiting for the doctor. Gupta's wife helps manage the office, taking calls and greeting patients in the lilting accent of their native Rajasthan. Dr. Gupta was trained and practiced for a decade in India, where native Ayurvedic medicine coexists comfortably with Western medical practices. He has worked at Children's Hospital for nearly 20 years, often with seriously ill children. But his private practice is made up largely of perfectly healthy children cared for by chronically worried parents.

"The first couple of times parents call I tell them to give things a few days or a week," he said. "If they keep calling sometimes I prescribe something for their child or suggest a technique to try. And if they *still* call I prescribe something for *them*." He's joking—mostly—to make the point that American medicine tends to pathologize things that are considered perfectly normal in other cultures such as India's. Rather than beginning with diagnosis, he asks himself first whether or not his patient's issue can be worked through by their body's natural capacity for resilience, healing and growth.

When asked about peanut allergies, for example, he leaned forward in his chair. "Look," he said, "what do you think people around the world do? Have always done? They take what they eat, they mash it up and they give it to their children. Indian food, think of it—spices, peanuts. The children eat it and they are fine." He sat back and shrugged. "You do the rice and oatmeal, but you can also give them a bit of whatever the family eats, including peanuts. You watch them the first couple of times to make sure they don't have a bad reaction. But most children are just fine."

For a long time this advice went against the recommendation of most of those in the American medical establishment: to keep children away from common allergens until age two. But lately things have been shifting in Dr. Gupta's direction. Healthcare practitioners have been slowly integrating what indigenous communities have always known into the research-based, pathology-driven Western model.

Dr. Gupta is, of course, a medical doctor, well-versed in journal articles and conventional wisdom and sensitive to the concerns (and litigiousness) of the culture he serves. But he's also held on to the intuitive, anecdotal wisdom passed down through generations in his native culture. He moves freely between the two, with no need to choose or invalidate one or the other. Like the Chinese astronomers, he is a model of left-right balance, of compromise between the holistic-indigenous and the Cartesian-Newtonian approaches.

Even as the principles and practices of the Scientific Revolution expanded beyond Europe in the eighteenth and nineteenth centuries, displacing indigenous ways of knowing the world, this indigenous knowledge did not disappear. Often it just went underground. When the formal medical establishment in Europe passed laws intended to limit what kinds of healing were allowed and by whom they could be practiced, many people who practiced herbal folk medicine were singled out as witches and prosecuted. In response, these healers transferred their knowledge into "spellbooks," using poetry and carefully crafted narratives to conceal their remedies from the establishment.[1]

This period also saw the beginning of mass education in which, again, the goal was to replace the informal learning that had historically been conducted within the spheres of families, communities and churches with something formalized, measurable and answerable to the economic, social and political priorities of the time. As you'll see in this chapter, what emerged was the factory model of education—the template that survives to this day. Holistic ways of teaching and learning didn't disappear, but they were withdrawn for a while before reemerging in the early twentieth century through the work of several pioneers in education whom we'll meet later in the chapter.

The Rise of the Industrial Model of Education

It was a time of crisis. Dramatic changes in technology and immigration patterns were shifting the economic, social and political landscape of the country both at home and abroad. Members of the business community and social and political advocates came together out of concern for the country's economic and social stability. They determined that the only way in which to ensure the continued stability and security of the country, its economy and its civic society was to improve the country's system of education. It was vital that educational content be identified, organized and delivered to students in the most efficient and effective way possible. Regular testing would ensure that students were mastering content and skills. There was a push for teachers to be evaluated on their performance and rewarded monetarily based on the performance of their pupils.

This description is as relevant to America during the early 2000s, the era of No Child Left Behind and Race to the Top, as it is to Europe during the early 1800s. In the wake of the Scientific Revolution, conceptions of people and society were changing to reflect a more mechanistic, reductionistic, technocratic reality. This was true in education as well. As in most indigenous societies, European children had long been educated entirely within their families and communities. The content of their education was life—whatever they needed to know to take care of themselves, contribute to the family and maintain a role in their community. Girls learned to acquire food, cook, sew, care for younger siblings and livestock, and keep the home in order. Young boys learned to hunt, farm, chop wood. This learning was inextricable from daily life in the family and community; it was embodied, contextualized and inherently meaningful in the sense that it was relevant to the lives they lived. Formal education—reading, writing, history, literature, etc.—had until that time been reserved for wealthy land-owning males, a tiny portion of the population in Europe.

The move to establish schools for the masses in Europe during this period was not an act of generosity or populism; rather it was guided by the priorities of industrialists and political and social leaders intent on uniting the middle class against the existing oligarchy, specifically the landed gentry. They decided the shortest route to that goal was to provide an education to the children of their workers. This would achieve two goals at once. First, it would secure the allegiance of the workers; and second, it would provide a venue in which the workers' children could be taught to support changes to the existing social order. Social reformers hoped that if workers learned early on that their future prosperity depended on private property and the free movement of capital, they would join the push for an empowered middle class to displace the historical dominance of landed gentry.[2]

At the same time religious leaders were unsettled to find that scientific discoveries had undermined the Bible's status as the one and only truth—particularly with regard to the Creation and the workings of the physical world. Religious and community leaders worried about moral decline—that children of the working class would lose their way or forget their place. The Christian belief in original sin taught that children tended naturally toward evil; left to themselves, they would fall into vice and crime. Religious leaders hoped formal education would instill some righteousness and judgment and help shore up the social order. They felt that the children of the poor, in particular, must learn compliance, industriousness and a sense of contentment with their place in society and in the eyes of God.[3]

With the various parties aligned, the challenge became one of scale—very much the domain of left-hemispheric thinking. Abstraction, compliance and efficiency drove the design. Children were seen as blank slates upon which the priorities of the leaders could be impressed. No one knew about child development at the time, nor how learning happens. Learning was limited to reading, writing, math and religion—

enough knowledge for students to question the existing social order and assume roles in the factories, but not so much that they would fantasize about having meaningful lives. No attempt would be made to adapt the content to individual pupils. Material was broken down into small, discrete units to ensure ease and consistency of delivery. Discipline would be rigid and severe, to teach compliance. An idea known as the *distraction prevention principle* dictated that windows be high enough to keep children from looking outside. Walls were covered with instructional materials so that students idly looking around the classroom could find nothing to look at but more lessons.

Students were organized by age and sat together in large rooms. When one group completed a unit, the teacher would examine them, and those who passed would be moved to the next unit. Competition was encouraged between groups and within them—it was thought to be an incentive. As in the factories, attention was focused on measurable outputs, with an emphasis on quantity and, secondarily, quality. Outstanding performance was rewarded; lapses punished. Schools soon established standards for performance in each subject so that students and classes could be compared and teachers' salaries could be linked to student output. This approach was known collectively as the *monitorial system*, and it was essentially a factory for knowledge acquisition: precise division of labor; an assembly-line progression through sequential stages; incentives for good work; an impersonal system of inspection; and strict attention to efficiency and the economic use of space.[4]

The model was a triumph of left-hemispheric thinking. It translated the infinitely complex process of human beings' learning about the world into a grid of discrete, measurable transactions. And this is why it has survived for so long. None of our major efforts at education reform in America have addressed the nineteenth-century template of the system itself. Schools still answer to the mechanistic, reductionistic tendencies that informed their development. And many of us still hold beliefs about who children are, how they learn and what it means to be smart that allow the industrial model to survive despite all the changes and discoveries in the world since the nineteenth century.

Dissenting Voices in Education

In response to the trends of nineteenth-century society and the development of mass schools, voices emerged throughout Europe that warned of the limits of scientific reason, urban life and the utilitarian view of human life. Deeply aligned with right-hemispheric experience, Romantic thinkers like Jean-Jacques Rousseau and Friedrich Froebel argued that vital human qualities were being suppressed; that Europeans were sacrificing their inherent freedom and losing contact with the natural world. The Romantics saw people as linked to the past by an unbroken flow of experience and as manifestations of a divine, creative source. They rejected the dominant intellectual/religious perspectives of the day—materialism, original sin, the split between humans and the divine—that drove educational practice in the direction of compliance. They believed that children are born naturally good and will remain so if they are protected from the corrupting influences in society.[5]

The Romantics' more expansive views of science and human nature foreshadowed discoveries of the late nineteenth and early twentieth centuries that would redeem the holistic worldview in the domain of science. First, the theory of evolution, which presented life on Earth as endlessly adapting rather than a fixed entity perfected once and for all by the Creator, took on a new complexity. Evolutionary holism argued that the theory of natural selection ignored the interconnectedness inherent in all complex systems.[6] Second, physicists developed the theory of relativity, which described a fluidity in the concepts of time and space. The world, we would learn, is a living, evolving entity—a network of relations, just as indigenous people had always believed it to be. Time cannot be understood independent of an observer, and no living creature can be explained without an understanding of its environment and the survival adaptations that make it what it is.[7] And third was the introduction of fractal geometry, the discovery of which enabled people to finally see and measure the predictable irregularity of holistic systems in nature—the jaggedness and symmetry that manifests in non-human-made systems. This was a complete contrast to Cartesian-Newtonian measurement, which was based on a presumption of flat planes, straight lines and perfect circles.[8] These discoveries would challenge the concept of objective knowledge and complicate our vision of the natural world. No longer could everything around us be divided into discrete, knowable and perfectly measurable parts. The right hemisphere began to assert itself in science.

The ideas of the Romantics unfortunately didn't catch on with leaders in education, and nineteenth-century education systems in Europe and America sustained the factory model relatively unquestioned until the arrival of three pioneers—three educators from different backgrounds unified by their sensitivity to the whole child and alliance with right-hemispheric perceptions of the world: Maria Montessori, Rudolf Steiner and Jiddu Krishnamurti.

Born in 1870, Maria Montessori trained in Italy as a physician and an anthropologist. Early in her career she visited the asylums in Rome, where she first encountered the so-called "idiot" children housed there alongside the insane. The children in these asylums, she noticed, had no toys or materials of any kind, nothing to play or experiment with. As she observed them scrabbling desperately on the floor for small crumbs and pebbles, she interpreted their behavior as a hunger for stimulation and engagement rather than any organic defect. She broadened this hypothesis into a theory about the types of social and intellectual engagement that were essential to every phase and aspect of child development. As embodied, living beings, she argued, children need to engage with the world in order to learn and to grow into healthy adults.

The Montessori method of education was based on her observations that children absorb knowledge effortlessly from their surroundings; that they naturally manipulate whatever materials they can find in order to support their engagement with the world. Every piece of equipment, every exercise, every method Montessori developed was based on what she saw children do "naturally," by themselves. She observed children drawing from their right-hemispheric experiences to build left-hemispheric conceptual frameworks, which in turn informed the ways they engaged with the environment—and all of this happened without any assistance from adults. In other words, children teach themselves. This simple but profound truth guided Montessori's work on educational design, psychology, teaching and teacher training— always centered on the process of children's self-creation.[9]

Rudolf Steiner was an Austrian philosopher and teacher committed to rebuilding culture in the wake of the First World War. Steiner was deeply influenced by the German Romantic writer Johann Wolfgang von Goethe. Bolstered by Goethe's explorations of materialism, Steiner argued that a strict reliance on knowledge gained only through sensory data and the particular type of scientific thinking that had prevailed for much of the previous two centuries prevented people from fully understanding themselves and the world. He believed that in order to grow and thrive as human beings, everyone must learn to think spiritually as well as scientifically. By "spiritual" he meant that aspect of the human experience that transcends the material world and is inaccessible through our physical senses.

As the First World War neared its end, Steiner worked to renew life and culture by connecting people to spiritual experiences. He recognized that people felt torn between the search for community and the experience of individuality, which created anxiety. Community, he thought, involves material interdependence, a condition that defines our daily lives as much as it does the world economy. Yet individuality and independent thought and speech are essential to any creative endeavor or innovation. Without spiritual engagement, he wrote, a culture will wither and die. He felt that individuality and community must be maintained and balanced as dual priorities in any human life.

Steiner found ways to apply these ideas in social, artistic and scientific endeavors, including education. When he spoke to the employees of a factory in Stuttgart, Germany, in 1919, the nation was on the brink of chaos. He was asked to start a school for workers' children that could seed some kind of renewal, and thus the Waldorf method was born. This method reflected many of the same principles of human development as Montessori's. The Waldorf curriculum encouraged young people to use their intellectual, emotional, physical and spiritual capabilities to become better members of their various communities.[10]

Jiddu Krishnamurti was born in India in 1895, but spent his life travelling and working around the world, initially through the Theosophical Society, which sought to form a Universal Brotherhood of Humanity and encourage the study of comparative religion, philosophy and science. As he was being groomed to lead the society, Krishnamurti became skeptical of systematic philosophy and institutionalized religions. On the day he was intended to become its leader, he ordered the Theosophical Society dissolved and reminded his followers to question all assumptions and listen to themselves above any authority, including him.

Krishnamurti believed that from the moment of birth we are conditioned to see ourselves as separate from others. We are taught to focus on the differences between us. These perceptions become our reality and our "cage," he said, preventing any real understanding of the world. Political, social and religious allegiances only strengthen this illusion. To be free, then, he argued that we must learn to observe the world anew; to shake loose of our conditioning and perceive the reality of our interconnectedness.

Like Montessori and Steiner, Krishnamurti's primary concern was reconnecting people with themselves—with their essence—which is an extension of truth, ultimate reality or God (though he did not use either of the two latter terms). He felt that this essential "self" is eternal and incorruptible, a balanced and pure state of connection with all other beings. The high schools he started were designed to provide tight-knit communities in which students could challenge their conditioning while developing the skills and dispositions they would need to build a solid identity and a place in the world.[11]

Holism in Education

Despite having very different backgrounds, Montessori, Steiner and Krishnamurti shared three important characteristics that made them foundational figures in the movement for a human-centered approach to education that they saw as the alternative to factory-model schools. First, all three had deeply spiritual and mystical experiences early in their lives that left them skeptical of the aspiritual Cartesian-Newtonian worldview. Montessori, a devout Catholic, recalled several mystical experiences and encounters in her early life that attuned her to a higher purpose in the world. Steiner described experiencing moments of clairvoyance, starting when he was seven and continuing into adulthood, that connected him to his spiritual nature. Krishnamurti's mother died when he was 10, and he reported several mystical experiences soon after her death that awakened him to the illusion of separateness and the ultimate unity of reality. Each credited to these early experiences their belief that the world was fundamentally bigger and more meaningful than everyday observation would suggest.[12]

Second, all three lived through massive political and economic upheavals in the late nineteenth and early twentieth centuries. Each saw these events as the inevitable results of an oppressive, reductionistic and mechanistic approach to life, and believed that people must reorient themselves toward interdependence and holism. In this they were supported by emerging trends in science being synthesized in the work of Albert Einstein.

Einstein entered the field of physics at a time when holistic thinkers in the sciences were using discoveries in electromagnetism, biology and evolution to articulate a more nuanced vision of the world than that of the Cartesian-Newtonian worldview. These scientists pointed to the newly discovered phenomenon of energy fields and observed that they were not material bodies out in space, but networks affecting our natural world in ways that we cannot fully comprehend through our senses. This did not make them unreal, which would be the conclusion of a strictly Cartesian-Newtonian way of thinking, but rather elements of the physical world that the Cartesian-Newtonian conception of the world could not adequately explain.[13]

Darwin's original theory of evolution described organisms and a natural world that evolved and changed according to fairly straightforward rules that maximized reproduction and survival of an individual organism's genes. Holistic thinkers argued that he hadn't accounted for the ways in which elements of a living system work together to benefit the collective more than the individual. These thinkers proposed that the natural world operated according to principles that were far more complex, dynamic and emergent than Darwin's conception of evolution had accounted for.[14]

Einstein believed in the inherent harmony of nature, and his general theory of relativity ultimately revealed the limits of the Cartesian-Newtonian explanation of physical reality. This "new physics" introduced profound changes in concepts of space, time, matter, object, and cause and effect. Its effect on conventional scientists was as earth-shattering as the Cartesian-Newtonian worldview had been on indigenous perspectives three hundred years earlier.[15]

These new scientific discoveries affirmed three critical aspects of holistic-indigenous beliefs about the world. First, the world is indeed a network of relationships, not discrete, individual parts. Harm done in one part of this network has consequences for other parts. And viewing nature as ours to be dominated and extracted from can cause both specific and generalized harm. Second, truly objective knowledge is not possible. If all natural phenomena are interconnected, then to explain any one thing we need to understand everything else. This is impossible in a dynamic system because the system is always changing. Rather than searching for absolute truths, we should deal with limited and approximate descriptions of reality. And third, the world cannot be reduced to constituent parts. While the properties of the parts contribute to an understanding of the whole, the parts cannot be understood separately from the whole.[16]

Just as the mechanistic view of nature had led to mechanistic views of human beings, holistic beliefs will lead to treating people holistically. Montessori, Steiner and Krishnamurti saw an education system that entirely misunderstood children, treating each child as an identical blank slate ready for the impress of knowledge. Their human-centered/liberatory approaches emerged as a response to the Cartesian-Newtonian, industrial approach to education. Indigenous learning had always happened within families and communities, preserving holistic, contextualized, embodied values and ways of being; while the industrial model of education was intentionally designed to promote abstraction, decontextualization and efficiency—a deliberate, forcible departure from education as it had been before. These three thinkers saw children as individual, complex, emergent and entirely connected and responsive to their environment. They also believed that society could only be transformed through the transformation of the individual.[17]

This leads to the third shared characteristic of Montessori, Steiner and Krishnamurti: all three applied right-hemispheric attention to the challenge of educating vast and diverse populations. Each immersed themselves in the communities and groups of children they wished to serve. Their approaches to education emerged from that participation— from their own experiences of joining and empathizing with children— rather than from a desire to determine what children need from the distance of authority and bureaucracy.

Human-centered/liberatory education is complex and nuanced work. It requires changing not just the structures of education, but our entire understanding of the endeavor's purpose and who young people are in relationship to the work of learning. Einstein and other holistic thinkers' work in the sciences revealed limitations of the Cartesian-Newtonian worldview, and in the process called into question many of the values that grew out of that worldview. This, in turn, required scientists to rethink important elements of their work. Similarly, the educational models developed by Montessori, Steiner and Krishnamurti do not simply approach education differently; they require us to rethink the basic assumptions that have driven education for centuries—assumptions that structure much of our society as well.

Applying These Ideas

- Populace and Gallup found that less than 10 percent of Americans define success for themselves in terms of status, comparison to others, or competition for resources, yet the vast majority believe that *other* people define success in those terms. *Think about how you understand that gap. What did school teach you about what it means to be successful? What does the world tell us? Consider how those align with what you actually believe today.*

- A left-hemispheric worldview often leads to a scarcity mentality. In the dominant culture of North America, that mentality suggests that resources, time, success—even love and acceptance—are limited; that we must compete for them; and that some people inevitably lose out. Practicing gratitude can help us refocus on everything that's *already present* in our lives, priming our minds to focus on what we have rather than on what we lack. People who regularly take time to notice and reflect on what they are thankful for experience more positive emotions, feel more alive, sleep better, express more compassion and kindness, and even have stronger immune systems than those who don't. *For one week, write down three good things that happen each day. And each day, tell someone—your child, your partner, a friend or a co-worker—that you appreciate them. Be as specific as you can. See if at the end of the week you feel less scarcity in your life.*

- Think back to your most memorable learning experience, or your favorite teacher (in the broadest sense of the word). How old were you? What was happening? How did the experience make you feel? Many people remember experiences of engagement or curiosity, or learning something new about their capability; yet our conversations about education and teaching tend to focus on statistics and numbers. In *Street Data*, Shane Safir and Jamilla Dugan challenge us to think about what it means to "know" more broadly and to honor the lived experiences, stories and potentials that can't easily be expressed through numerical data. What were you taught about narratives being less valuable than data in the form of numbers? When a young person brings home a test or report card, what if we first asked them what they learned, where they struggled and what most interested them? *Think of a few adults you know casually. How would you describe each one to a friend? What details about them would you emphasize? Are those the most important details about who they are? Are some related to accomplishments, status and comparison to others, while others are related to interests, character and idiosyncrasies?*

CHAPTER 4

Holistic-Indigenous and Ecological Values in Education

My family was embarrassing to me while I was growing up. We ate strange foods, guided by the *ayurvedic* belief that the bacteria in fermented foods and yogurt would keep my mind clear and my body in balance. We were given turmeric and honey at the first sign of a sore throat instead of the Robitussin I saw on TV. My aunt's morning yoga and meditation practice was supposed to move energy through us to promote mental, physical and emotional health. My uncle tried to persuade me that human beings have two nervous systems: one in our head and one in our gut. Never mind the *Encyclopedia Britannica's* entry on the matter; he insisted the gut was at least as important as the brain.

Not until the late 1990s did an American doctor named Michael Gerson rediscover the findings of two German doctors who, in the late 1880s, located nerve cells in our gut that act as a brain.[1] Yet somehow my uncle, born in Tanzania and raised in an Indian-African culture, had known this 20 years earlier. The inherited dietary wisdom in my family and many other Indian families had embraced as truth what Western medicine had discarded.

It might seem strange that the scientific establishment could have simply *forgotten* the existence of this second brain for more than 100 years. But remember, the Cartesian-Newtonian worldview privileges top-down hierarchy, sees the mind as master of the body and relies on mechanical metaphors to describe living systems. Most likely the discovery of a gut-brain just didn't align with these basic premises, so it was ignored.

A mathematician named Benoit Mandelbrot happened onto a similar crossroads of belief systems while studying naturally occurring cycles on Earth such as the rhythm of the flooding and subsiding of rivers. Mandelbrot found that though clear patterns existed, most of them could not be described by the geometry he was taught, known as Euclidean geometry, which describes the world in terms of lines and planes, circles and spheres, and triangles and cones. Mandelbrot pointed out that all these figures are imaginary, their "perfect" dimensions existing only in theory. He believed that beneath the complexity of natural systems and phenomena, a much richer set of symmetries and patterns was waiting to be revealed—patterns we overlook because our observations are conditioned by the geometry we're taught in school. "Clouds are not spheres," he wrote. "Mountains are not cones; lightening does not strike or travel in a straight line. The new geometry mirrors a universe that is rough not rounded, scabrous not smooth. It is a geometry of the pitted and the broken up, the twisted, tangled and intertwined."[2]

Mandelbrot's ideas put him at odds with centuries of Western mathematical tradition. Traditional statistical modeling presents formulas that "smooth out" the unevenness of data, creating perfect curves that make for tidy, readable graphs. Smoothness is the standard and the goal. Mandelbrot's ideas opened the door to rhythms, patterns, cycles and complexities that had been ignored for centuries. Beyond that his work revealed that the tools we use to measure things determine what we end up perceiving.[3]

The term *architecture* does not just describe the inherent structure of something; it refers to the *intentionally designed* structure, whether of manmade objects or natural entities. Thus the architecture we refer to in natural systems—the structure of DNA, for example, or the arrangement of cells into tissue—is not the essential thing itself but the patterns we've identified in it, the patterns we've learned to detect. All our descriptions, just as all our designs, are influenced by our worldview, vocabulary and values. The Cartesian-Newtonian worldview values linearity, smoothness and efficiency, so these are the terms in which we design and assess systems when we operate with that worldview. We've seen how this translates into the architecture of social systems like education. The factory model includes our assumptions about human growth and learning: that the process is linear, sequential and uniformly-paced, for example; and that order and work must be imposed from the top down, from teacher to student, drawing a line from external accountability to individual behavior.

With the advent of Mandelbrot's discoveries we can see that the architecture of natural and ecological systems share certain key design features. First, the patterns within them tend to recur at several levels of magnitude—a phenomenon known as *self-similarity*. In holistic-indigenous learning (HIL), for example, the dynamics between young people and teachers are similar to the dynamics between the adults in the system. Second, although the dynamics and processes within a system might not be linear and uniform, they can still be measured. Natural processes like learning and human development do not follow linear progressions, but we can still find meaningful patterns within them. Finally, natural systems are organized so that each individual part of the system has what it needs to operate independently, even as it is attuned to the needs of other parts and adapts as necessary to ensure the well-being of the whole, a phenomenon known as *emergence*.[4] For example, when starlings fly together in a vast, unified group known as a *murmuration*, we see hundreds of birds flying at up to 40 miles per hour and turning 180 degrees within milliseconds, in unison, in an acrobatic movement that emerges from the collective behavior of individual birds; no single bird is leading the group. The pattern of their flight emerges entirely from the interreacting shifts in the collective.

People who have a worldview that allows them to understand and value such complex dynamics in a system such as a school, a family or a child's psychology will design structures that correspond to the dynamics of that system. These designs often represent a radical departure from the traditional and introduce an entirely new vocabulary for the values, relationships and goals of the system. This is why it's often so difficult to change how schools are run, which is why we must design new structures intentionally and consistently so that the new values and dynamics are reinforced at every level of our education system. We will explore this imperative in various ways over the next few chapters.

I will note here that in our time, *holistic-ecological* is a more relevant term to use when discussing the holistic-indigenous worldview generally because it has become much more commonplace to reference natural (ecological) structures and systems in fields ranging from economics to medicine and business. In the past, in the absence of an understanding that indigenous communities organize themselves in ways that reflect a larger ecological reality, we labeled the worldview "indigenous." Using the term *ecological* helps us understand the relationship between this worldview and the broader context in which we exist as human beings. I will continue to use the term *holistic-indigenous* to reference the worldview as it pertains to education, however, because the term *indigenous* better reflects the values that drive these learning environments and systems.

Education and the Holistic-Indigenous Worldview

In previous chapters you saw how the Cartesian-Newtonian worldview gave rise to the factory model of education, a model that still dominates today. In this chapter we consider the essential elements of a holistic-indigenous worldview and see how this worldview translates to the design and practice of learning. You'll see how a few essential differences in defining the purpose of education and in defining personhood, community, growth and knowledge end up creating entirely different types of schools. And you'll see why this so often leads to the failure of schools in which reforms have been bolted on. To affect a real change in values, educators must rewrite a school's DNA by reorienting its values at every level of experience.

Holistic-indigenous learning programs reflect the self-similar dynamics of natural systems, with each level reinforcing wholeness, connectedness and embodiment. The individual student's experience is shaped by the classroom dynamic, even as the classroom dynamic is shaped by the individual—as in the murmuration of starlings. This same pattern plays out in the school as a whole, and in the school's relationship to the community. Everyone is attending simultaneously to the process and the outcomes. They learn to see human experience as dynamic, non-linear and jagged, whereas students in factory-model schools are moved along a straight line, from ignorance to knowledge, in discrete, progressive stages.

In this chapter we will also look at two main properties of HIL models: how they support the development of children as people, and what their practitioners believe about the growth of knowledge and understanding. In each area HIL schools are fundamentally different from their Cartesian-Newtonian counterparts. Though we'll consider these two properties of HIL models separately, they are completely intertwined in practice. And while I will describe them as happening in school, HIL approaches to education can and do exist outside of the conventional classroom. (In fact the classroom itself was an innovation of the factory model.)

The Purpose of Education

The priorities of factory-model schools were heavily weighted toward political, social and economic ends that had almost nothing to do with an understanding of young people's experience. Students were to acquire factual knowledge and adopt values that helped promote and support these ends. The development of the child as an individual, let alone as an individual spiritual being, was not considered the work of education. The dominant view that emerged from the Scientific Revolution was that children were nothing more than young specimens of *Homo sapiens*. They were empty vessels into which society should pour whatever was needed to shape them into socially and economically useful units.

In the holistic-indigenous view, the world is not divisible into material and non-material; what some people refer to as the "spiritual" is not distinct from the physical. The non-material—the spiritual—is as real and fundamental to existence as the substances we can touch, see and measure. Whereas in the Cartesian-Newtonian view we use the separateness of things to measure them, describe them and predict their behaviors, in the holistic-indigenous view we see this separateness as a useful illusion and we see growth as coming from the recognition that we are part of a whole and part of many networks within that whole.[5]

This mystical view of human experience is a hallmark of the holistic-indigenous worldview and informs the spiritual element of education that Montessori, Steiner and Krishnamurti often referenced. *Mystical*, however, is very different from *religious*. Most religions are oriented to a deity (or deities) and a belief system that describes the relationship between the higher being(s) and humans, often with a formal religious institution mediating between the two. Mysticism, on the other hand, is simply the belief that anyone can connect with a higher power, or a deeper reality, without employing the vocabulary or the rituals of religion. An education based on a mystical view of human existence, then, helps learners move toward a clearer understanding of themselves and their relationship to the larger world.[6]

For Montessori, Steiner and Krishnamurti, the purpose of education was to teach children to understand themselves and each other as independent from external expectations and definitions, and at some remove from the political, social and economic agendas that mass education systems typically serve. They felt that this freedom and self-understanding would enable each child to find their role in their community and to be accountable to something larger than themselves. Instead of becoming what the world sees as useful, they could discover who they wanted to be as individuals and in relationships. It was most important to these thinkers that the aims of education not be derived from external influences and that they should not be separated from a sense of who the child is. The phrase *liberatory education* refers to this ideal.[7]

Becoming People

In this section we'll consider the most fundamental work of human-centered education: young people's growth into personhood. What does it mean to be a person? First, we are conscious and capable of thought. We can grasp concepts that allow us to make sense of our experiences. We are intentional; we can consider what we want and make choices accordingly. Societies the world over have generally recognized that, perhaps most important, persons are not born *fully* into a state of personhood; that these singular abilities evolve through interaction and experience.[8]

This last point is essential to the holistic-indigenous perspective. Each child is born with unique traits, and the cultivation of that particular human energy should be central to the child's development. Whatever is unique in the child connects them to the divine, and it should be protected and nurtured in the learning process. Hence the significance of naming-ceremonies and vision quests in many indigenous cultures: each is a recognition of the child's particular essence.[9] Helping a young person grow *as themselves* by attending to the physical, intellectual, social, emotional and spiritual aspects of their being is the collective work of families, schools, communities and societies.

The definition of personhood as a continuously evolving expression of uniqueness related to one's connection to the larger world defines every phase and moment of human-centered education. It invites into the classroom facets of spiritual development, self-knowledge, wisdom and morality alongside the more conventional focus areas of discipline, citizenship, practical skills, knowledge of facts and intellectual excellence. The mixture of these elements varies across cultures, but all are present to some extent in holistic-indigenous learning.[10]

Many in American education today believe that the conventional system has begun to focus on the whole child, but the reality often falls far short of the "whole child" slogan. True attention to the whole child requires a deeper understanding of personhood: our human development, our relationship with others and our evolving understanding of the world.

Supporting Healthy Human Development

The Cartesian-Newtonian worldview focused on mechanical, linear and static modes of operation, so its factory model of education included no understanding of child development. The child's life at school was driven by the curriculum with no consideration for what the child's brain was capable of at the various stages of human development. The holistic-indigenous perspective embraces the importance of human development. The educational environment and programs are matched to a child's development at each stage of growth. The life of the child drives the work of the school at all levels.

Maria Montessori, Rudolf Steiner and Jiddu Krishnamurti all identified broad planes of development during which children are most receptive to certain types of social, emotional, physical and cognitive engagement. For example, Montessori and Steiner noted that in the earliest stages of development children do and know things through embodied activity—the ways in which they relate as physical beings to the world around them—before they are consciously aware of feelings and emotions. Emotional life emerges next, and with it intuition. If intuition is not trusted and cultivated at this stage, the child's capacity for judgment and reason can suffer later on. Intuition must be integrated into the child's character, capabilities and approach to the world in order for their development to advance naturally. Montessori and Steiner also both found that there are sensitive periods of development in areas such as oral language skills, symbolic representation and interpretation, visual/ perceptual capabilities and emotional development. These sensitive periods are windows of opportunity during which children can learn specific concepts more easily and naturally than at any other time in their lives; the period between age one and age seven, for example, is a sensitive period for the acquisition of language and vocabulary. They noted that as children transition from late childhood to early adolescence, they have a growing need to immerse themselves in their broader community and peer group and to find a sense of belonging and significance beyond their immediate family. During this period they can move from the concrete into the abstract, engaging with ideas and concepts. Krishnamurti noted that as young people transition into middle adolescence they can do more of the conceptual and self-reflective learning required to create an independent sense of identity. All three theorists urged educators to capitalize on these developmental openings.[11]

Montessori's, Steiner's and Krishnamurti's observations, which have since been borne out by academic research, reflected generations of indigenous wisdom about childrearing practices.[12] This wisdom informs every choice made about curriculum and classroom materials in HIL environments, which center on human developmental needs and allow young people the flexibility to engage in the areas of growth and study that best meet their needs as they navigate their unique developmental pathways.[13]

Personhood through Community

In the Cartesian-Newtonian model, individual property rights, individual freedom and individual privacy rights were central to the idea of citizenship, and thus were written into the foundation of America's legal, political and economic systems.[14] But the holistic-indigenous conception of self emerges from interconnectedness rather than from separateness. There can be no self without the other, and we learn to be ourselves by relating authentically to one another. In holistic-indigenous learning, relationships and connections are central; whereas the Cartesian-Newtonian model prizes categories and distinctions.

Every school must find a balance between structure and the autonomy of the student, and the dangers of too much of either are familiar to anyone who has ever spent time with children. An overly individualistic view of self leads to relationships defined by competition and power struggle. Conversely, subjugating one's identity and needs in deference to the needs of others leads to relationships defined by dominance and compliance. Instead, learners in the HIL model are taught to understand their well-being as tied to the well-being of their teachers and classmates. Collective satisfaction is the path to individual contentment. In order to be in relationship with another, they learn to exchange strict independence for mutuality.

In this way equality and freedom condition each other reciprocally. Equality is a condition of freedom in human relationships; if we do not treat each other as equals, we exclude freedom from our relationships. But freedom also conditions equality; if there is constraint between us, there is fear, and fear leads to the imposition of control, the exertion of power and the loss of equality.[15]

At a practical level, viewing a school as a community changes the way in which it operates as an organization. Relationships are no longer purely functional, based on the exchange of knowledge and the maintenance of discipline. Encouraging personal relationships in schools leads to flatter and more networked organizations with less power at the top. Respect, self-discipline and recognition of mutual responsibility reduce the need for authority figures. The nature of the relationships determines the overall strength of the organization.[16]

The notion of community in HIL schools extends beyond the school grounds. Whereas the factory model is a closed loop—a sequestered setting for the transfer of knowledge—the holistic-indigenous approach places the school inside a larger whole and extends learning to all relationships in the child's life. Since education is not concerned merely with academic subject matter, activities such as play, practical work and non-structured time are explicitly and deliberately valued. Children are taught to respect the external world, and the boundary between the broader community and school is more porous. Community, in these schools, is a way of being and a way of relating to one another.

Shifting Conceptions of Knowledge

Educators in HIL schools reject the idea of knowledge as an absolute and bounded set of data that students can master. They are skeptical of the Cartesian-Newtonian worldview's tendency to make knowledge and learning the sole domain of the rational mind, and of its push for "objective" truth, both of which further support the idea that knowledge can exist independent of context. Because the brain's left hemisphere is highly self-referential and values things that align with what is already known, "rational" and "objective" perspectives tend to devalue right-hemispheric kinds of knowing: embodied, experiential and relational.

In HIL settings the world is presented as complex and constantly changing and growing. Teachers guide students to understand how various events and entities affect each other, and that those relationships are constantly evolving. No attempt is made to separate what students learn from their personal experiences, beliefs and biases. Instead, they are encouraged to be self-reflective and aware of how contingent and changeable their perceptions are. Subjective experience thus becomes an important type of knowledge, worthy of study. After all, human experience originates in the right hemisphere as immersive, undescribed, unsynthesized information; it then passes to the left hemisphere where it's mapped into an increasingly sophisticated framework of abstractions.[17] A child sees a thing. The thing has two legs. The child's brain searches a database of abstractions to distinguish whether that two-legged thing is a person, a dog on its hind legs, or a rabbit hopping. Once the child has determined which it is, the information moves back to the right hemisphere to determine how they should engage with this person. Thoughts alone won't allow us to understand our experience; feelings enable us to determine what the experience means. HIL educators teach children to value that right-hemispheric information and to attend as much to meaning as to information.

In practical terms, allowing for students' different approaches to acquiring, demonstrating and assessing knowledge transforms the everyday experience of a school. Students are organized into multiage learning communities in which they practice the social, emotional, intellectual and cognitive skills required to trust themselves and their relationships and to contribute meaningfully to their communities. Time is given for walking, building, daydreaming, playing, bickering, taking things apart, planting, drawing and being still. Students access information through videos, podcasts, conversations, interviews, observations and reading. Teachers aim for depth of learning as much as breadth of coverage. Student projects emerge from the students' own questions about their lives and surroundings. They are allowed to work at a pace determined by how they best engage with the world and new ideas. Students who dance and perform are celebrated as much as those who read and write well. In math, equal credit might be given to a student who applies the principles of geometry to build a birdhouse as to one who shows conceptual understanding of geometric proofs on a written exam. Children leave their education having mastered different subjects and skills than others based on considerations including their interests, aspirations, family background and community.[18] And finally, assessments are conducted primarily to give students meaningful and ongoing information about how they can improve their learning process.

By implementing all of these practices at every stage of the education process, HIL approaches displace traditional definitions of learning, capability and success that were designed for a world totally unlike the one our children will inherit.[19]

From Equitable to Liberatory

Our education system is an embodiment of our deepest values. What we choose to teach our children, and how we want them to interact with each other and the world, paint a portrait of those values. This is as true now as it was when the left-hemispheric worldview that facilitated the Scientific Revolution and brought schooling to the masses also facilitated the expansion of empires and the decimation of indigenous cultures and indigenous wisdom. In their drive to know, measure, categorize and conquer, Europeans of the nineteenth century abandoned generations of intuition, ritual and interconnectedness. Ultimately this commitment to individualism and reliance on the technocratic at the expense of the relational has resulted in the world's wealthiest citizens being lonelier and more alienated than ever, and led us to abuse our planet to the point that our very existence is threatened by climate change.

Montessori, Steiner and Krishnamurti developed the holistic-indigenous educational approach in response to similar alienation and similar crises. They saw education as a force for the liberation of individuals, societies and the planet as a whole, and as a response to educational institutions that had ignored the richness, diversity and vulnerability of childhood experience.

We find ourselves at another pivotal moment, a moment when what the world needs and what holistic-indigenous learning models can provide our children are even more closely aligned than they were when the approach was first advanced. The presence and impact of these models have waxed and waned over the decades, but their practitioners have always positioned themselves against dominant economic, political and social systems that alienated people from their world. Now the balance between left- and right-hemispheric thinking—between the Cartesian-Newtonian and the holistic-indigenous—is shifting once again. The themes and threads of the age-old dialogue are playing out prominently in social, political and economic spheres.

We hear demands to preserve our planet, consider what we produce and consume, live sustainably and honor the cycles of the earth as an organism in ways that indigenous cultures always have. We are drawing on our increased understanding of the nature of ecological and biological systems to change our approach to health and wellness. We are attempting to honor and reintegrate cultures and communities that were subjugated and displaced by slavery and colonialism. We are questioning economic systems that generate value and success at the expense of human well-being. Beneath the specific terms of these debates is an acknowledgement that something went wrong— that somehow our actions have not aligned with our values, our commitments or our hopes for the future.

In the next three chapters we will consider what it takes to address this misalignment with our values through HIL education and to actually put the ideas we've been exploring into practice. The work of creating and sustaining HIL schools is incredibly complex. It is already underway in pockets of practice around the country, but expanding it requires new initiatives, new structures, new policies and a deep commitment at every level of society.

Applying These Ideas

- Many of us have heard about the importance of early childhood, a period of profound growth and change in the brain that should be attended to in our social and educational policies. People at the Center for the Developing Adolescent at UCLA are working hard to share the science showing that adolescence—early adolescence especially—is a comparable period of brain plasticity when neural pathways can be shaped in profound ways through active engagement with the world and the development of social and emotional capabilities, including self-regulation. *Consider how these discoveries might influence how we structure learning experiences for young people.*

- I have been involved with dozens of focus groups that asked parents and community members to focus on the question *What do we want for our children?* The answers are rarely about GPAs, standardized test scores or college acceptance letters, yet these kinds of metrics still largely define popular definitions of success. *Think about one thing you could let go of in your power/wealth/status expectations for yourself or your child in order to create room for experiences that provide a sense of purpose and fulfillment.*

- In this chapter we explored what it means when education honors and centers the uniqueness of each person. Feminist author Regena Thomasheur challenges people to share "a brag." The word has negative connotations in a culture in which we're taught to compete for resources, and that having more is better and having less is shameful. Thomasheur's point is that the unique aspects of ourselves are gifts to be shared, and therefore to brag is not to gloat or push others down but to allow oneself to shine. Greatness is an infinite resource. By owning our strengths we invite others to celebrate theirs. *Try sharing a brag. You can start with something small—maybe a little accomplishment or a physical feature of yours that you like. "I brag that I have beautiful eyes." Once you're comfortable with that, you can go further: "I brag that I hold on to my beliefs and act in ways that align with them even when the world tells me I'm wrong." Or "I brag that I negotiated hard for a salary that represents my value to my organization." It gets easier the more often you do it. (And as I learned by bringing this exercise to my book club, it's even better when you do it in community and affirm each other's brilliance!)*

PART 2

PRESENT:
Shifting Our Gaze

CHAPTER 5

From Theory to Practice: The Instructional-Model Framework

Challenges Faced by Holistic-Indigenous Approaches to Education

In contrast to what we might believe based on the level of partisan rancor in America today, there are actually many examples of social, economic and environmental issues on which Americans agree that there is a problem that needs to be addressed and on the broad contours of how to address it. However, because we are so entrenched in Cartesian-Newtonian values, we can't get our collective minds around possible solutions; can't even see our way toward them.

There is broad agreement that our planet, our communities and many of us as individuals will benefit from a transition toward cleaner energy sources that will help us preserve the quality of our air and water and the health of the earth.[1] Americans also agree that the government has a responsibility to ensure that everyone, regardless of age, working status or current health condition, has access to basic healthcare.[2] And as a nation we are near universal agreement on the idea that workers should be provided the flexibility and supports necessary to care for their children, aging parents and sick family members.[3] Yet our energy, health and economic systems are not shifting to deliver these changes; instead they operate to satisfy conceptual ideals of free markets, maximum choice, limited government and individualism. They were designed this way. The systems we are trying to change are driven by a left-hemispheric, abstracted set of values embedded in their DNA. They are fragmented, profit-driven, extractive systems that resist humanistic, holistic, collectivist efforts at reform.

And education is no exception. Students, parents, educators and civic and business leaders agree that our education system fails to prepare students for the working world they will actually meet as adults. In the 250 years since the Industrial Revolution we've invented technology and artificial intelligence that can better handle and even replicate the abstract cognitive skills that were the backbone of the curriculum in those times, yet those skills are still the focus today. We continue to pathologize and marginalize minds that operate differently, more holistically, more intuitively, at the exact moment when the world needs creative problem-solving, the kind that emerges from just such unconventional minds. Beyond failing to prepare young people for the realities of adulthood, the pressures of a stratified, competitive, alienating and highly unequal education system have accelerated an epidemic of youth unwellness. We are actively causing harm, yet nothing is changing.

Change in human-centered systems like schools does not happen in response to increased pressure from the outside or by tweaking this or that element in hopes of creating comprehensive results. It happens by creating conditions that invite change from within. These deeper changes then radiate outward at all levels, ultimately changing the very nature of how the system as a whole operates. But the systems and structures we built to support, evaluate and improve our conventional, factory-model schools—schools still operating with the DNA of a mechanistic worldview—were unfortunately not designed to implement this type of emergent change.

Educators who try to adopt an HIL model have to contend with many elements of our system that aren't aligned with HIL values, such as college admissions requirements, reliance on grades and GPA rankings, and discrete subject requirements. So the vast majority of HIL schools and programs exist outside of the public education system.

Evidence suggests that HIL programs struggle for other reasons, too. A large percentage close soon after losing a founding principal or key staff members. Many have been justly criticized for poor administration or for structures so relaxed that they only work for children whose families help them learn foundational skills at home or through tutoring. Most HIL schools that survive follow the prescriptions of specific models such as Montessori, Waldorf, Krishnamurti, Expeditionary Learning and Big Picture Learning; yet many implement such models inconsistently and/or produce inconsistent results.

The question is why. Is there something inherent in the HIL approach that makes it more difficult to launch and sustain? What can we learn from the struggles of these schools that will help us shift education more successfully and sustainably toward holistic-indigenous/liberatory practice?

The Unintended Costs of the Quest for Educational Equity

For a period of about 10 years after the widespread passage of charter-school laws in America, it seemed like HIL programs might have a shot in public education. Charter public schools were conceived to provide unconventional education programs some freedom and flexibility within the public school system. Districts like Milwaukee and a few in California focused on opening public Waldorf programs, and other regions saw a surge of interest in public Montessori schools.[4] The initial findings regarding student engagement and academic performance in these schools were positive.[5] But then came No Child Left Behind (NCLB).

NCLB was aimed at improving educational equity and access, and in terms of elevating awareness of the fact that America's education system was not serving all students well, it was arguably successful. Nevertheless it was a death knell for the vast majority of public HIL programs in the US, regardless of whether they operated in public districts or public charter sectors. The complexity of the work and the adaptations that HIL education required of educators and families were already challenging. Then NCLB doubled down on the Cartesian-Newtonian values of standardization, linearity and efficiency. How could programs designed to honor the unpredictable nature of children's natural development contort themselves to ensure that every child hit grade-level reading benchmarks at exactly the same time? How could they force all children to cover the same science and math standards in the same order and on the same timeline? They couldn't.

NCLB also made it very difficult to study what was happening in HIL schools in the US, since it essentially hamstrung them and left them to collapse. So at that time I looked to England for answers. The culture and the education system there were similar to ours, but England was slightly behind the US when it came to implementing standards-based reform and high-stakes accountability. Instead there was a government unit called the Office for Standards in Education (Ofsted) that conducted site visits and reviews that were the foundation of England's accountability process. Ofsted inspections involved a visiting team of experts spending days at a school observing teaching, meeting with educators and students and developing a nuanced understanding of what was actually happening. There was a lot more room for out-of-the-box models, including HIL programs, to gain support.

I spent about two years embedded in a new high school in a former industrial town on the coast of England, a school that intended to adopt an HIL approach. I'll call it King's Green School (KGS) to protect the school's identity. KGS was in its first few years of planning and operation when I arrived, and it had not adopted any established or specific HIL model like Montessori or Expeditionary Learning. Thus I was able to witness the development of an HIL program from scratch, and engaged in candid conversations about the work and challenges with the school leader, educators and students. I also spent time at two well-established English HIL schools as points of comparison, one a Steiner-Waldorf school and the other a Krishnamurti school, both of which served students in the same age range as KGS.[6]

Case Studies; Divergent Experiences

King's Green School

King's Green School (KGS) ran from seventh grade through high school. It was the third high school to open in an economically depressed area and served a racially and socioeconomically diverse and highly transient student population. At least a third of the school's 260 students had one parent who had been in prison for drug use, drug dealing, theft or assault. Nearly 30 percent had special educational needs. Many had already been expelled from the two other local schools. Because of these challenges, and because of his interest in social justice and equity, the founder of the school, who I'll call Tom, was committed to trying to make KGS a non-traditional public school. He had worked in education for decades with some of the foremost practitioners in progressive education, and he wanted KGS educators to apply the best available knowledge about teaching, learning, student success and personal growth.

When I arrived, Tom had hired a core staff of six teachers and five teaching assistants to support about 120 students. By the time I left the school in late autumn of its second year, it had fourteen teachers, nine learning assistants and 260 students.

KGS was guided by five main principles common to HIL programs:

1. **Respect for students:** All students would be respected as people. Their particular potential and needs would be at the forefront of teachers' engagement with them.
2. **Development of community:** Educators would work to create small learning communities in which teachers and students would come to know each other well.
3. **Integration of the curriculum:** Teaching would not be divided into subject boxes, since learning is most successful when information is synthesized and connected to prior knowledge.
4. **Inclusion of all students:** Suspending or expelling students from the classroom or school was unacceptable; their needs

would be met at a level appropriate for them. This would be the responsibility of the adults.

5. **The "how" matters as much as the "what":** How education was done—the experience it created for students and teachers—would be as important as the outcomes achieved. Organizational design and school structures would intentionally support, not hinder, the school's goals.

Tom and his team had translated these broad principles into several non-conventional ways of working with the schedule, the students and the curriculum:

- **"Schools within a school" model:** The school was divided into three teams: Lighthouses, Windmills and Towers. Each team consisted of a third of the students and a group of teachers who worked with only those students for multiple years.

- **Alternative ways of working with time:** They eliminated conventional design elements like 45-minute subject periods and subject-based planning meetings, which encouraged teachers to identify primarily as subject-matter educators. Instead they instituted common planning and teaching time in the hopes that teachers would begin to design interdisciplinary units of study and teach as integrated teams, identifying primarily as facilitators of learning as opposed to subject-matter experts.

- **No suspensions or expulsions:** Administrators held teachers accountable for developing educational approaches that best suited their pupils. Teachers could not simply send students out of the classroom because they were challenging to work with.

The themes of the HIL approach to education are present in the above policies: wholeness, interconnectedness and, above all, embodiment/contextualization. The KGS educators believed that young people needed to be seen as whole human beings with social, emotional, intellectual and spiritual needs. Everyone was focused on building a community and a sense of shared responsibility. The approach to teaching, and to learning—for teachers as well as students, was interdisciplinary, with topics and lessons arranged in ways that suited the students. Learning blocks were designed to offer students different ways to engage with content and to demonstrate what they learned.

Tom was a compelling advocate for what he believed KGS could be, contrasting it explicitly with the industrial model and how it has evolved to support narrow ideas of education and success: imparting formal and informal rules, teaching specialized knowledge and skills, keeping children contained and screening individuals for occupational pathways. He talked to educators about "developing a sense of community, mutuality and shared responsibility"; "encouraging a sense of self-worth, contribution and personal dignity"; "acquiring a set of strategies/competencies for life-long learning, living and earning"; and "promoting global awareness of contemporary issues."

The teachers were excited about this radical approach. Many had come to education in the first place thinking they could teach this way, only to find themselves stuck in factory-model schools. By the time they reached KGS they had sat through some version of Tom's pitch often enough to be hearing it in their sleep. One said she felt constantly "preached at." Another admired Tom's "vision and passion" but felt that his "head was in the clouds." One expressed admiration for his constantly pushing them to go farther: "I feel like I am on the same page as him but then I lose it…I intuitively understand what he is getting at but making it work moment to moment is hard. I often wonder if I'm doing the right thing."

Tom could be relentless with teachers he thought were not on board with the KGS mission. He was creating a school for students who had already been let down by the system, and he had little tolerance for teachers who placed blame on the kids. Many of the teachers were committed, but even over the course of the school's first year their exhaustion was apparent.

They had been called upon to create an organizational structure that would support a human-centered school: organizing students and teachers into the three separate teams; selecting an interdisciplinary, thematic curriculum that would meet the requirements of the national curriculum without being reduced to disjointed lessons in isolated subject areas; setting up the schedule to allow creative teaching and collaboration among teachers; and designing an environment that would nurture community and mutual responsibility. All this on top of planning and teaching lessons that would engage a broad selection of students from a range of backgrounds, and keeping up with the readings and suggestions from Tom.

Tom was visionary, but even he acknowledged in conversations with me and his staff that he had an undisciplined management style. The organizational culture was constantly in flux. He would have an idea and send teachers off to work on it, only to change his mind soon afterward. And the teachers themselves realized they had very different definitions of a "person-centered" school culture. One new teacher, aiming to give students more autonomy in the classroom, gave open-ended and vague assignments intended to get students to pull together content across disciplines. Students could work alone or together; in the classroom or elsewhere. The teacher collected work but did not grade it. The result was not the hoped-for classroom of independent learners; it was something close to chaos. Down the hall a veteran teacher kept on with a fairly traditional approach of lectures, homework and grades, but she was such a skilled educator that students thrived in her class. Her success reinforced her belief that "person-centered" was more about caring about her students than shifting her approach to the work.

Some of the school's challenges seemed natural for a new program, and some might have been endemic to the HIL approach in its early stages; but in such an unstructured environment it was hard to tell. The two more established schools described below provided comparison.

The Rudolf Steiner School

The Rudolf Steiner School (RSS) is a long-standing public Waldorf program that adheres closely to Steiner's vision in which children are encouraged to, in Steiner's words, "root themselves in their humanity as they live and grow through childhood." The campus occupies about 10 acres of an elevated site overlooking a rural landscape. The buildings are old but the grounds are well tended, and lively murals on the courtyard walls brighten the atmosphere. Inside, the dark walls are decorated with student artwork. RSS has a nominal head of school, but the organizational structure is very flat, mostly because responsibility for teaching and learning devolves to groups of educators, sometimes including students, organized by discipline or student age. Most administrative and financial decisions are made by a rotating committee of staff members, students and parents. Changes in policy or practice are presented to the community at large before being discussed and decided by the committee. In most cases the views of the community align with those of the committee.

The Waldorf approach sees people as three-fold in nature: mind, spirit and body; and strives to prepare that entire person for a life of meaning and purpose. Educators in Waldorf schools approach education as the interplay between art and science, and tailor their teaching to each student's unique developmental stages. They intentionally integrate the arts—music, dance, painting, weaving, sewing, woodworking— into all academic disciplines at all ages, believing that the arts keep students grounded in wholeness and attuned to their internal intuitive responses to the world. Waldorf teaching is not based on a fixed syllabus or established curriculum. Each teacher is responsible for creating and recreating the curriculum for each group of students using a broad outline developed by Steiner. Children remain with the same teacher for the first eight years of school so that teachers can cultivate security and community among the children and get to know each student deeply as a person. The curriculum and activities for grades five through eight are geared toward developing memory and providing a foundation of background knowledge and intellectual constructs. Teachers present interdisciplinary lessons covering science, culture, history, mathematics and literacy in a lively manner, often integrating images and visual aids into lessons. Students also learn practical subjects such as farming, building, gardening, woodworking, painting, drawing, music, drama and movement.

By the end of eighth grade, students are considered to be entering a new phase in which they will no longer depend primarily on their right-hemispheric capabilities to think and learn. They are encouraged to develop an inquiring mind by using left-hemispheric strengths that enable a more exact understanding of the world. Steiner believed that at this stage education should foster clear, independent thinking. Adolescents long for someone to respect and to go to for help, so in high school each class is provided an advisor who is available to any student for consultation. Though lessons in core subjects focus on intellectual activities, games, arts and exercise remain part of the curriculum throughout high school.

Brockwood Park School

Brockwood Park School (BPS), based on Jiddu Krishnamurti's teachings, is located in the farmlands of southern England, two hours from London. The sprawling house and grounds were originally donated as a retirement home for Krishnamurti. BPS reflects the standards, policies and practices that Krishnamurti felt were essential to creating a school with the "right" type of learning atmosphere—a place where a whole community can inquire together into the perennial questions of humankind.

Krishnamurti believed that all things are part of a sacred, integrated whole, and that the bridge from secular to sacred is the ability to see things as they are. This "right" perception, he believed, transcends the illusion of ego and separateness and frees us of society's efforts to bind us through expectations and constraints. Krishnamurti was very focused on the human tendency to fragment the whole—that is, to be dominated by the left-hemispheric tendencies of our brains. Resisting this, he said, requires participating in life and in the world around us at many different levels. In his view, human beings have the capacity to venture to the limits of thinking both generally and particularly, understanding the world through both hemispheres at the same time.

BPS follows the model of all Krishnamurti high schools in bringing together a relatively small co-ed student body—in this case about 60 students, many of them on scholarships. The school draws students from as many as 20 countries, and at meals I heard students and teachers talking in at least five different languages. The main building is a large, well-maintained manor house on beautiful grounds, with an interior that feels more like a luxurious home than a school. And indeed, most of the students and teachers live there, in an intentionally developed and thoughtfully maintained community that blurs the line between education and life. This is true particularly for older students, who experience the freedom of being away from family as they build new relationships in this highly personal and interconnected community. Each prospective student is sent a statement of the school's purpose and is required to write a personal message to the school about themselves and their particular interest in the program. Students agree to follow a completely vegetarian diet and to abstain from drugs, alcohol, tobacco and irresponsible sexual behavior on school grounds.

As with RSS, there is a head of school, but the vast majority of decisions are made at the interpersonal level or delegated to committees of educators and students. The staff and student-body meetings have an improvisational, democratic interplay to them, but the school day is fairly structured, running from 7 a.m. to 10 p.m. and operating with a sense of order, regularity and efficiency.

Although BPS claims not to overemphasize academic work, students are expected to study for a minimum of 30 hours per week if they are under 16 years of age, and 20 hours if they are older (as they spend more time on unstructured learning). There is a focus on what most people would consider fundamental academic knowledge and skills; however, subjects are organized thematically based on areas of enquiry, and stem more from student interests than from a standardized checklist of state-mandated content. Students and staff are asked to participate in various work teams to accomplish tasks such as cooking, gardening and building maintenance, reinforcing the school's ethos of shared participation and responsibility.

The weekend at BPS runs from Tuesday afternoon till Thursday morning, a schedule designed to put students slightly out of step from the mainstream rhythm of society. The goal here is to help them see things in a more detached and critical light, something Krishnamurti considered especially important for adolescents. One silent meal is held every week. Fridays are reserved for a school meeting open to staff and students, at which any topic can be raised for discussion.

At first glance the code of conduct appears strict, but the difference is in the enforcement. As you read in chapter 4, deep personal relationships and close communities allow for very different approaches to discipline and authority. BPS emphasizes voluntary adherence rather than sanctions. The intended lesson is that choosing to live in harmony with others is not the same as sacrificing one's freedom. Within true community, freedom is responsibility in cooperation.[7]

Some students described having pushed the boundaries at first, testing the commitment to self-discipline. They talked about how their growing relationships and the modelling of older students and teachers eventually taught them to appreciate their shared responsibility for building and sustaining the school community. Many recalled meetings during which they debated the meanings of terms like *authority* in order to come to an understanding that worked in the BPS environment. When students recalled times when their behavior fell outside accepted norms, they described learning to feel and accept the impact their choices had on other community members, take responsibility for making others whole or making things right, and integrate what they had learned into their subsequent choices and behaviors. As Krishnamurti predicted, these types of restorative practices enabled students to see the rules of their community as empowering them to live with others rather than as impositions on their autonomy.

The Unique Needs of Ecological Systems

Going back and forth between the three programs over the course of the nearly two years I spent on this study was incredibly illuminating for me. Beyond all the differences in curriculum, setting and structure, the most powerful impression I had at the Steiner and Krishnamurti schools was simply the feeling I had when I stepped into a classroom or meeting. There was a contained liveliness in the air—a sense of welcome, curiosity and fluid connection. It's difficult to describe, but unmistakable. And it was one of the most glaring differences between these two schools and King's Green School. When I walked back through the doors of KGS after a visit to one of the other schools, the energy felt frenetic and unstable, and therefore stressful, much like the unmediated adolescent energy of the students. The adults were navigating a maelstrom of shifting emotions, from joyful excitement at some small win to frustration at some disapproving response from Tom. This energy flowed into the multiple levels of the system, influencing Tom's mood and his interactions with government officials in preparation for an Ofsted inspection, and amplifying the unrest of the students, who had the usual complaints about things like cliques, teachers and favoritism.

The difference in energy at KGS turned out to be highly consequential. The other two schools contended with the usual range of disagreements, joys and frustrations, but there was a settledness in the more established programs that touched everything. It was most notable among the educators, who seemed far more grounded in their expectations and their day-to-day work. Even those in their first year or two of teaching seemed more confident and fluid than the veterans at KGS. Conversations at the Steiner and Krishnamurti schools were more measured, whether among adults or between adults and children. When there were debates, the energy didn't seem to be aimed at authority figures but rather at exploring and understanding the community rules in question. Even middle- and high-school-aged students at those two schools engaged in mostly mature, non-accusatory reflections about academics, social dynamics and even the operation of the school as a whole. They talked about these things like people who were on a journey together. When things didn't go as planned, there was a calm atmosphere in which community members could cope and adapt rather than constantly struggle to figure out what had gone wrong and what that might mean for their next steps.

So how to account for the difference? It could not adequately be explained just by the backgrounds of the students being served, because all three schools had fairly diverse student populations. Interviews with both students and educators seemed to point to reasons that had to do with the structure and organization of the programs themselves. For one thing, both the Steiner and Krishnamurti schools had much flatter, more democratic structures; students called adults by their first names, teams of teachers led the schools, and students and teachers collaborated on administrative decisions. At KGS, Tom was clearly in charge. He spoke about preserving teachers' autonomy and encouraged them to try new ideas, but he was the ultimate decider—in the words of one teacher, "an autocrat." In spite of the HIL framework,

Tom's leadership was typical of a school in the industrial model. But this difference, it turned out, was only a symptom of the lack of an underlying structure. The problem was not the chaos itself, but something under the surface that was not as it should be.

The Steiner and Krishnamurti schools operated through a dynamic described earlier as emergence, which describes how collective behavioral changes develop in natural systems. Instead of a structure designed for authority descending from the top or being dictated by an outside force, emergence allows new structures to arise from repeated interactions between the individual parts of the system in order to meet a particular need. An ant colony, for example, achieves things as a whole that no one ant could ever do on its own. Each individual ant operates individually, going about its own business and processing only the information available to it. However, the interactions between individual ants often result in collective shifts in behavior that allow the colony as a whole to find food or avoid attack. There is no centrally distributed message, rather the behavior emerges from the interactions of the individual elements of the system.

The neurons in our brains, the dynamics of forest ecosystems— even the behavior of dynamic economic markets responding to the choices of human actors—show that in dynamic or living systems the whole comprises far more, both in its essence and its capabilities, than the sum of its individual parts. In the two more established school programs discussed above, the vision, culture and responsibility for the whole had been internalized by adults and students. They engaged in their own work and learning while very aware of their role in the larger community. As issues arose, their autonomy, combined with their capabilities, allowed for dynamic and fluid responses that were consistent with the overall culture of the program. In this way the programs were sustained through the collective efforts of the individual members of the school.

My experiences at the Steiner and Krishnamurti schools suggested to me that without emergent energy, HIL schools won't develop systems strong enough to sustain the model. This theory was solidified in my conversations with a teacher I will call "Elizabeth," a senior teacher at KGS who seemed to struggle the least. Elizabeth had embraced the interdisciplinary curriculum and the flattened authority structure. She had helped many of her colleagues teach their students how to *be* in the school—how to assume and make use of the responsibility they were given. She pointed out to her colleagues how hard it was for students to adjust to a system that wasn't governed by conventional forms of authority, and that it required each student to learn something new about agency, self-management and mutuality. She talked a lot about "scaffolding," her metaphor for the temporary, basic structures we all need in order to transition from one way of being to another. In construction, scaffolding allows workers to build a roof before a staircase exists. In medicine, a scaffold works as a temporary stent, allowing the body to rebuild internal structure before the scaffold dissolves into the bloodstream. Elizabeth taught her colleagues to create temporary scaffolding for their new students, providing enough structure to empower and support them but not so much that their learning and observing was constrained.

As you read in chapter 4, the architecture of a dynamic system enables self-similarity at various levels of the system so that what is happening at one level mirrors the dynamics at other levels. How students relate to one another and to the educational program, for example, should mirror the dynamic among the adults in the system and the adults' relationships to the work. In the Steiner and Krishnamurti schools I observed that this scaffolding enabled self-similarity between the students' adjustments to a new school and the teachers'. Though it may seem counterintuitive, RSS and BPS were able to successfully construct a relatively flat, fluid set of community relationships *because* of this underlying structure—a scaffolding passed along from one community member to another and customized to each relationship. Emergent systems require robust structures to grow and to maintain their complexity. Lacking this underlying structure, KGS struggled to create a sustainable dynamic within the HIL framework, and the disorder was particularly hard on the educators.

In HIL programs, educators are of central importance because they are the units of the learning community that interact with and shape various other levels of the ecosystem, including students, other teachers and community members. The teachers at the Steiner and Krishnamurti schools spent a lot of time working on their personal development as part of their initial educator training. The founders of both models, along with Montessori, believed that in order to guide students on the intellectual and personal journey that is education, and in order to provide opportunity for young people to become themselves, teachers must undergo and continue to reflect on their own processes of personal transformation. They need to become aware of and accept their backgrounds, assumptions, conditioning and challenges; only then will they be equipped to create community and learning for students in authentic and embodied ways.

This scaffolding for teachers begins in their HIL training. Many established HIL models include adult-preparation programs specifically aligned to their model. In addition to personal work, teachers engage deeply with the topics we explored in chapter 4: human nature, theories of knowledge, the purpose of education, child development and theories of learning. They also learn about and analyze specific classroom approaches. Many conventional teacher-training programs bifurcate theory and practice, and the practical student-teaching opportunities they provide don't enable aspiring teachers to be deeply and consistently immersed in the dynamics of daily life with students for months on end. In HIL programs, new educators don't just learn how to decide *what* to do; they learn to embody the logic behind these decisions. Before taking on their own classes, they often work in programs alongside experienced teachers, often full time, and for at least a full year. The apprenticeship coincides with their theoretical training so that right- and left-hemispheric learning—the embodied and the abstract—are constantly integrated. Aspiring teachers get to experience the ebb and flow of learning that is non-linear, jagged and sometimes unplanned. They process their discomfort with ambiguity and uncertainty so that when they encounter these feelings later they are better equipped to accept and transform them rather than falling back into old patterns of behavior.

When an HIL system is working well, its HIL community provides the supports and experiences that each person—whether teacher or student—needs. The staff is deeply connected to one another. Teachers describe their colleagues as partners and collaborators in a community that benefits everyone. They talk to each other candidly and authentically about the work and challenges, motivated by their commitment to strengthen the community, which they know intuitively will take care of them in turn.

The educators at RSS and BPS had everything they needed for their work to succeed. They were clearly grounded in the same ideas, language and values. Thus when a problem or disagreement arose, no single person had the responsibility (or the right) to provide the answer; everyone in the community was invested in the school's guiding principles and could refer to them when contributing to discussions and solutions. At BPS, for example, when I asked teachers about the communal living atmosphere, their responses usually included some version of Krishnamurti's idea that students need to experience an environment that is separate from the people and places that conditioned them. Students were just as likely to refer to these ideas.

None of this was happening at KGS. As one teacher phrased it, educators weren't "singing off the same song sheet."

Instructional Models for Learning

The main lesson I took away from these two years of research was that every HIL school needs a coherent theoretical model, something I came to call an "instructional model." An instructional model is a clear, thorough and consistently applied set of theories and practices that answers the questions below and guides educators and students continuously toward the values of wholeness, interconnectedness and embodiment.

- What are we doing, and why? (What is the purpose of education here?)
- What are the developmental needs of students during the stage(s) of development we are designing for?
- What do we believe and/or know about how learning happens?
- In light of development and learning, what skills, knowledge and dispositions are we going to teach, and how will we teach them? How will we assess students' learning and growth?

- How do we prepare and support adults in understanding this content and set of practices?
- What other systems do we need to support this work?

By grounding the design and the work of a school in a stated purpose, and building on that groundwork, educators create a coherent and consistent structure that facilitates the complex work of learning and community-building.

It might seem that every school should be able to answer the questions listed above. But as I learned at KGS, and as you'll see in chapter 6, most educators don't have the opportunity to stand back and conceive of their program as a whole, theorize about their objectives and help those in the program figure out their relationships to one another. Like the commission of experts we met in chapter 1 that was summoned to address America's failings in education, they aren't given the space, the time or the context necessary to really see the whole picture. Instead they're forced to work largely from deeply entrenched left-hemispheric assumptions and patterns of behavior, a process that never enables them to be free from their past conditioning.

An "instructional-model framework" allows us to intentionally design programs that serve as richer, more comprehensive alternatives to the approach taken by the industrial model, which oversimplifies learning as a linear process that moves students through successive categories and levels and encourages teachers to measure their success by linear, usually quantitative metrics. An instructional-model framework helps us organize HIL programs into progressive layers that are grounded in clear conceptions of what personhood and human development require us to provide to young people, and in what theories of learning tell us about the types of experiences we want to create for them. Every successive iteration should be informed by the choices made at the level of purpose, such as what knowledge, skills and dispositions will be addressed through the curriculum; what types of learning experiences will be created; how learning through those experiences will be measured; how adults will prepare for supporting students; and what other systems will be put in place to support the work.

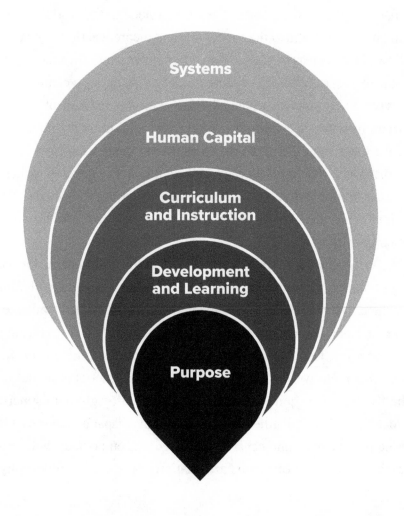

The most durable HIL programs are based on specific instructional models, including the Montessori, Waldorf and Krishnamurti programs. These founders didn't simply write theories of development and education and send them out into the world; they built intentional practices that reflect these theories at every stage, made the programs operational and dictated the spirit in which they should be carried out. All three oversaw the actual development of schools. In other words, each was able to navigate successfully between right- and left-hemisphere orientations. They saw a need in the world (right), took it into the realm of the conceptual and theoretical (left), and then allowed those ideas to shape living programs in which the ideas could come to life (right). Each of these models, now nearly a century old, survives today almost unchanged. Every educator and student in these programs knows the theories behind the work, knows the relevance of the theories to their own development and understands what the theories look like in practice. Thus the cultures that develop in these schools are quite durable and allow the institutions to become self-perpetuating, absorb newcomers and send graduates out in the world to embody their ideals.

As the founder of KGS, Tom believed in the ideals but he skipped over building an instructional model. He had no template to offer his teachers. The stacks of annoying memoranda that filled their mailboxes and the rigid lectures on discipline and communication were Tom's ad hoc effort to purvey his theories of learning and his vision for the school. He was trying to be a one-man instructional model on the fly. He never quite completed the right-left-right hemispheric process; he hadn't distilled and organized his disparate theories and principles into a comprehensive, consistent and embodied whole. His teachers needed an organized articulation of the overall philosophy, but they also needed a scaffold—a way to bridge these ideas into lived experience—and time to internalize the changes this would require in their relationship to the work. Tom expected them to create this on their own while they were already working with students. This created an ecosystem with no underlying structure, and the chaos took a toll.

As we saw in part 1, instituting holistic-indigenous approaches to education requires a fundamental shift in thinking, which is a herculean effort for teachers. To build out a school, structure curricula and design assessments, all while adapting your personal way of working in the program, is more than most people can handle all at once. When teachers at KGS were overwhelmed, they reverted to familiar methods of practice based on their past experiences, which of course eroded the consistency of the school's mission.

Instructional-model frameworks not only benefit teachers and leaders; they also make the work visible and accessible to students, families and the broader community. When students understand where they're going and what will be required in order to get there, they feel safe and invested enough to take ownership of the journey. This allows teachers to let go of control and relinquish authoritarian discipline. It enables families, caretakers and neighbors of the school to understand the work of the school and what it would mean to play a role. All schools want to engage families, but Montessori schools, for example, teach the parents their theories of child development and model ways to organize their homes to promote independence for young children. Waldorf programs explain to families that children need ideas brought to life in concrete ways, and facilitate connections between students, families and community organizations. Thus the school community expands constantly outward into the world.[8]

Instructional-model frameworks also help educators decide what does and does not work for their programs, which keeps their programs from sprawling, or from bolting on solutions that don't align with the model. Many education reforms in recent years, for example, have led to adding another hundred pages of academic standards, or to legislation that requires schools to offer anti-bullying programs or career counselling or service learning. These were all efforts to bolt on something that would mitigate the shortcomings of the industrial model or close the gaps between what young people need and what the schools were actually providing. Any honest educator or administrator will tell you that they cannot and do not actually cover everything that these mandates require. They can't. There simply isn't time.

All educators have to make hard choices about where to direct resources. More art and music might mean less math and literacy. More time spent building and sustaining relationships might mean less time spent on content. Instructional-model frameworks provide rationale for these decisions. If what we know about human development tells us that six-year-olds are at a prime moment to develop socio-emotional skills, then why not spend more time on that than on academic content? If the science of learning tells us that making connections across content areas helps students develop the skills associated with deep learning, then perhaps we should design for fewer discrete-subject-area classes and leave more time for interdisciplinary ones.

Being clear about the experiences and learning we want for students, and why, also enables educators to be thoughtful about their choice of specific design elements. For example, "looping" a teacher with the same group of students for multiple years (or within advisory structures) furthers the goals of developing deeper relationships between young people and educators; attending to student outcomes, like a student's ability to self-regulate or to organize complex tasks, that can take multiple years to become visible; and tracking student learning and growth over multiple years. The process of creating an instructional model enables educators to consider and incorporate design elements like these as ways to address multiple goals across various levels of the system. Just as complexity in nature tends to be achieved through the iterative application of fairly simple rules, instructional models enable complex work to be done without needlessly adding complexity to the program's design.

Finally, instructional-model frameworks ensure that for each choice made about what a program does and why, there are systems in place to support that choice. A program that keeps students with teachers for multiple years likely has a different hiring cycle and different hiring criteria than a conventional program. The same is true of programs that use advisors in roles that are different from the conventional role of teachers.[9] Interdisciplinary programs often require unique schedules and a higher level of collaboration. Programs guided by a belief that adolescents need to understand the relevance of their learning might want to set up work and internship opportunities; a sound instructional model anticipates this goal and provides a clear justification for the expenditure of time and money. In a school without a clear model, any of these programs might become siloed and have to fight against other program elements for consideration and resources, arguing for the value of, say, human capital versus community engagement. Designing for these programs up front takes a huge burden off the everyday work of teachers and leaders. As a result they are freer to spend their energy on actually meeting the needs of students and adapting the model to the specific needs of their students and the unique experiences of a given day.

Creating New Structures to Enable Different Work

Our existing social and economic systems are so deeply—often invisibly—grounded in Cartesian-Newtonian values that it's often difficult to see how they prevent the emergence of right-hemispheric thinking. By providing a formal, coherent and consistent strategy for a school to *embody* HIL values and theories, instructional models provide a bulwark. They empower schools to build a coherent, self-sustaining environment and to expand their values purposefully into the surrounding community.

The HIL endeavor is inherently complex and dynamic. In this way it mirrors much of what we see in nature, from the functioning of human tissue to the mysterious workings of the universe. But we must be careful not to mistake *complex* for *impossible*. Complexity simply requires a more intentional design. Instructional-model frameworks play that role for HIL education, and they provide the best chance of doing the work successfully.

In the coming chapters the instructional-model framework will help us consider what it takes to operationalize HIL education in the larger educational landscape of America today. Too often our education debates are focused on governance models—whether a school is a public district school or a private school or a public charter school—without recognizing that the defining factor is the school's orientation toward learning, whether it remains invested in a factory model or designs itself from the bottom up according to holistic-indigenous values.

Applying These Ideas

- Most of us have never experienced the type of education described in the case-study schools in this chapter. The foundational values of a holistic-indigenous approach to education push adults to cede power to young people— even very young children. *How did you feel about the level of autonomy students were given in these examples and the adult-student relationships in these schools? What is inspiring about them? What makes you uncomfortable? Can you trace those responses back to core beliefs you have about learning, education, society and hierarchy?*

- We assume that communities simply exist. But they are constructed, individual by individual and relationship by relationship. In a culture that emphasizes individuality and competition, we have seen communities weaken in part because we rarely teach people how to be in genuine relationship to others. We often hear the phrase "holding space for others" in therapeutic contexts, but it is incredibly difficult, particularly across lines of cultural differences, to truly hold space for others, be present for them and be in relationship with them. *Think about the skills adults need to enable successful holistic-indigenous learning environments. What are the best ways to prepare people to hold space for each other and themselves?*

- One school network I admire asks every new student, "What do you do when no one is telling you what to do?" "What are you interested in?" and "Who do you want to be in the world?" *Ask the young people in your life how they spend their time at school, during extracurricular activities and with their mentors or coaches. Consider where they seem to find happiness and fulfillment, and how much of it comes from being at school.*

CHAPTER 6

How the Worldview Divide Lives On through Educational Orientations

In 1969, as the original *Star Trek* neared the end of its third season on NBC, the network was considering canceling it for low ratings. America, it seemed, was not quite ready for a futuristic drama about spaceships, computers and aliens. At the same moment, a small American program called the Advanced Research Projects Agency (ARPA) was developing a secret network of computers that could communicate with each other over vast distances. Developed by men who called themselves "mad scientists," this little network soon broadened into a digital network for transferring packets of data around the world. Even as Americans were making up their minds about Captain Kirk, using stationery and telephones for communication and searching encyclopedias for information, ARPA's work on the internet was underway. At that moment two versions of the world were operating in parallel—one science fiction, one accepted reality—but they were on their way to a thrilling convergence in the near future.

The most striking feature of ARPA—and of its successor, the Defense Advanced Research Projects Agency (DARPA)—is that this very right-brained, emergent group of experimenters works within one of the most technocratic, compliance-oriented, left-hemispheric agencies in American government: the Department of Defense. Small, nimble and free to think and experiment wildly, DARPA exemplifies holistic, interdisciplinary, cross-functional work, sitting always at the edge of what's known and possible. And the agency's success has justified this freedom. DARPA is charged with developing radical new systems and incubating them for as long as it takes until they can be introduced and accepted into the mainstream. The agency wouldn't be able to function were it not kept completely separate from the dominant systems and structures of the Defense Department; the ideas are too radical and the methods too unorthodox to be monitored and approved by a traditional bureaucracy. So DARPA is allowed to have its own rules regarding personnel, operations and financing. The agency is guaranteed independence and encouraged to create the future at its own pace and in its own idiosyncratic ways without interference from overseers who think more conventionally.[1]

The education system we have now is as unprepared for the broad introduction of HIL systems as the Defense Department is to integrate the radical genius of DARPA. There will be a lag time—a long phase of introduction and adjustment. We will need to keep improving the existing education system, working within its existing framework, even as we build and spread HIL ideas throughout the country. This requires using a very clear set of criteria to distinguish elements of the existing model from truly human-centered/liberatory ways of teaching and learning. If we allow the two to be confused along the way, the Cartesian-Newtonian system will simply co-opt all efforts to create real change. This is the natural tendency of any dominant system: to preserve the status quo at all costs. To pick one of many examples in the recent history of the US, consider the idea of "clean energy." The term originally referred to energy created entirely without carbon emissions. Then the dominant system got hold of the concept and slowly transformed it. Clean energy now includes "clean coal" and "clean burning" of natural gas, both improvements but neither of them carbon-neutral.

In education, "individualized learning plans" and "personalized learning" used to mean customizing a curriculum to a particular learner's interests, strengths and aspirations. Now students who have individualized learning plans get essentially the same content as their mainstreamed peers, just with different frameworks or different time frames. "Personalized learning" is used to refer to online programs that have simply converted conventional academic standards into a format that allows students to move through them at different paces and in different orders than their peers. Rather than ripping out the industrial-model assembly line, we created separate conveyer belts that operate at slightly different speeds or take a different route through the factory. "Formative assessment" used to mean focusing on *how* students were progressing and learning; now it means evaluating them in order to rank them and divide them into groups, often using nothing more than the standardized tests that formative assessments were originally designed to replace.

So how can we make sure that HIL ideas and practices are preserved intact while we work to integrate them into the dominant system?

Educational Orientations

In the 12 years since I visited King's Green School, I have traveled around the US visiting programs; interviewing hundreds of educators, administrators, students and families; and researching the essential distinctions between schools. I observed daily operations—not only in classes but during the time in between—to see how members of an organization interacted with one another and how they oriented themselves to their work. My goal was to cut through the categories that group schools based on their governance model (such as district-run public, charter public, independent) or theme (such as STEM, arts, alternative, college prep). None of these categories really tells us how a program approaches the work of teaching and learning. A Montessori school, for example, can operate as a district public, charter public or private school. A STEM-focused program can approach its work in a fairly conventional, lecture-based way, or can organize itself entirely around real-world projects that enable young people to learn about science and math while contributing in meaningful ways to their communities, such as designing artificial limbs or energy-producing toys. I wanted to see how programs' instructional models addressed or neglected the central elements of the HIL approach: supporting personhood, fostering relationship and community and adapting forms of knowledge to individual learners.

With respect to personhood, I asked educators what they saw as the primary purpose of education, or the main objective of their program, listening for answers that went beyond the usual academics or social and emotional well-being. How did programs incorporate the developmental needs of each age band (early childhood, elementary, middle and high school)? To understand their approach to relationships and community, I looked at discipline, instruction in morals and character, and how programs addressed challenges in focus, attention and behavior. I also examined the collection of knowledge, skills and dispositions that were considered essential as reflected in the program curricula. How were these organized to reflect the school's purpose as well as the students' needs? What were the basic theories of learning, and how did they translate into pedagogical practice, student assessment and overall accountability for the program? How did the school deal with all the different cognitive profiles that learners present?

We now know from cognitive psychology that people arrive at school—and often move successfully through life—with many different sets of cognitive skills. Some have a strong verbal capacity. Others lean on visual/perceptual skills, which help them orient in space and organize visual perception into patterns and meanings. Some learners have a gift for mental imagery, which plays a role in thought processes, dreams, problem-solving, reasoning and anticipating events. Some process things at atypical speeds. Some have more working memory capacity and some less. Some have already developed the abilities to sustain and shift attention, engage socially and manage emotions; and some have not. Every student falls along a continuum of each of these indices. Students who have dyslexia, for example, might perform poorly on sequential-processing tasks (highly associated with left-hemisphere functioning) but excel in holistic and visual processing, pattern recognition and inductive reasoning, all of which are linked to right-hemisphere functioning.[2]

Industrial-model schools, of course, emerged out of a highly left-hemispheric approach to the world. They're designed to focus heavily on specific cognitive functions: verbal processing, quantitative abilities, the written word and mastery of material within limited time frames, often heavily skewed toward written forms of learning and assessment. These schools are also designed to favor compliance, stillness and the ability to pay certain kinds of attention. In other words, they offer nothing like a comprehensive appreciation of young people as they actually show up in the world. They are not designed to allow students to learn in accordance with their natural cognitive capabilities. In fact they are designed to force students to learn in one particular manner. My question became how a school's overall design elements and its educators' approach to the work of learning further (or do not further) our stated desire to serve all students well.

I found that schools tended to fit into three categories—three broad educational orientations that capture the most common patterns in teaching and learning: conventional, whole child/innovative reform and human-centered/liberatory (HIL). Broadly speaking, schools with a conventional orientation are direct descendants of the industrial-model school in terms of their overall aims, their theories of learning and the ways in which their designs reflect very little about human developmental stages and needs. Educators in schools with a whole child/innovative reform orientation recognize ways in which the conventional orientation falls short and attempt to mitigate those shortcomings by bolting on solutions, often in the form of initiatives and programs aimed at addressing specific gaps. Programs with a human-centered/liberatory orientation have been designed intentionally to embed and reflect the holistic-indigenous and ecological themes we have been exploring thus far, weaving them throughout the content and process of their work.

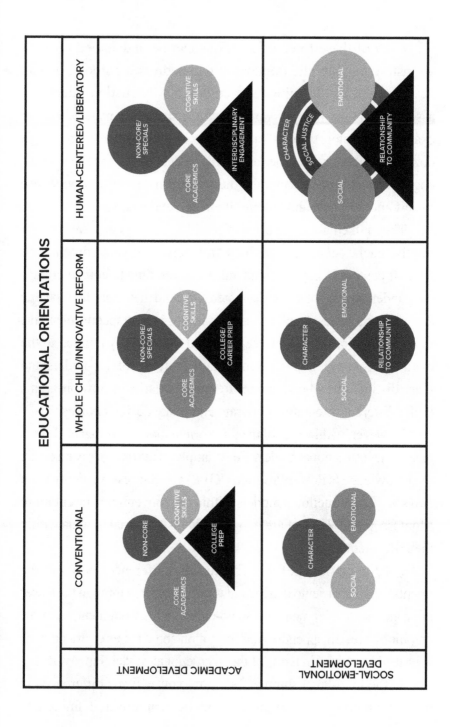

Each of these three orientations can be understood through an instructional-model framework that addresses purpose, human development and learning, curriculum and instruction (including assessment), and human capital (see the image on page 133). For example, educators talked about the purpose of education referencing a dozen specific categories such as helping students develop academically, cognitively, socially and morally; helping them develop a strong sense of self and purpose; and helping them achieve equity.

They talked about theories of learning in ways that were either highly teacher-centered (such as "a teacher delivers content") or student-centered (such as "students are given time to construct their own understanding of ideas and material"). And they identified specific approaches to assessment. It was the patterns in how specific elements of an instructional model were clustered that initially pointed to the distinctions between the three orientations. It is useful to understand these distinctions when it comes to the granularity of how programs in the different orientations operate and make design choices.

However, within each of the three orientations there can be dozens of specific instructional models. For example, at the time of my research, the Knowledge Is Power Program (KIPP) and Success Academy were two specific instructional models within the conventional orientation; Montessori and Waldorf are two specific instructional models within the HIL orientation.

For the purposes of this chapter, the differences between the orientations are easier to understand when considered through the lenses of academic development and socio-emotional development, as in the graphic above. (In appendix A, information about the three orientations is instead organized in terms of the instructional-model framework.)

In the high-level summaries below you will see differences in how programs across the three orientations approach defining and supporting personhood, fostering relationship and community, and providing access to knowledge. (In chapter 7 you will see why and how seemingly different school models actually reflect the same educational orientation, and that new policies and systems are needed to support current HIL-orientation programs if we hope to increase their viability and availability, especially for those programs that operate within the public education system.[3])

Conventional Orientation

Conventional schools are the modern-day versions of industrial-model schools. Their overarching feel is left-hemispheric, with a strong sense of urgency around closing the gaps between students' achievement levels as measured primarily by standardized tests in literacy and math. Their primary focus is on getting kids ready for college. Educators in these schools prize efficiency and work hard to limit experiences that distract students from this goal. They use timers to count down activities, enforce strict dress codes, require silence in the hallways and publicly reward students who adhere to established codes of behavior as an incentive for other students to comply with rules.

The model is consistent across age bands; educators at conventional schools do not take the stages of development into account when developing curricula. They prefer to view all students as scholars rather than focusing on individual or developmental differences or human complexities. In this sense conventional schools reflect the industrial model of children as miniature adults. Even in elementary schools where young children are taught to socialize and collaborate, this teaching is highly structured and often transmitted through lessons or specific protocols rather than through free-form play and interaction.

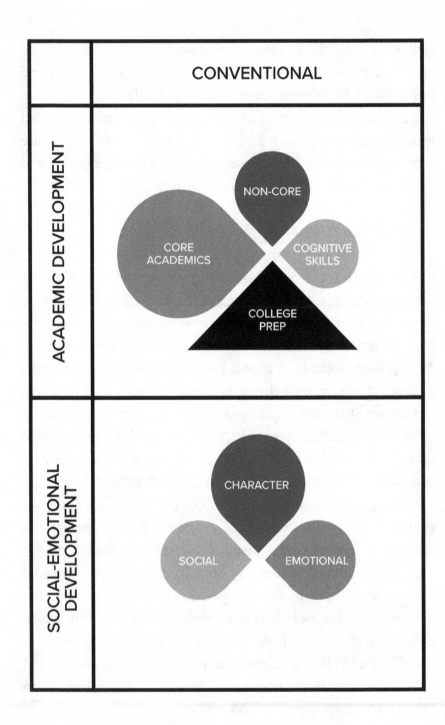

Academic achievement is the primary focus of these schools at every grade level, with a strong emphasis on core academic development (particularly literacy and math, and secondarily science, social studies and history). The fact that students are referred to as "scholars" hints at the value placed on academically related aspects of identity.[4] In terms of cognitive development, educators at these schools value thinking, reasoning and recollection, and academic activities are oriented mostly to reading and writing. They are not likely to spend much time on emotional regulation, for example, or developing visual-spatial skills through art, dance or free play. Although most conventional programs have non-core academic classes such as arts and music, these are often seen as means to an end—a way to keep kids engaged or to provide a break for those who struggle academically. Indeed, these "non-core" activities are often described as supporting the development of academic skills.

Conventional programs reflect teacher-focused theories of learning and pedagogies aligned with these theories; the teacher is considered the conduit for learning. They place a high value on lesson-plan design and delivery and classroom-management skills that keep lessons running efficiently. Teachers strictly organize learning time, determine how students engage with content, and drive the process of assessment.

Almost all conventional schools use some type of external curriculum designed to align with core academic standards, or specialized programs such as Advanced Placement and Core Knowledge. One common reason for this, particularly in the charter school sector, is that teachers in these schools often come into the profession through alternative certification pathways like Teach for America. Many have never studied child development or educational theories and approaches. Based on interviews with school leaders it appears that the most straightforward way to ensure instructional quality is to provide a specific curriculum and scripted lessons.[5]

Conventional programs are driven by standardized summative and interim data, and often include elaborate processes for collecting and analyzing quantitative data on student performance and growth. Although leaders often talk about what the school values beyond academics, data collection and analysis seldom focus on qualitative data, and very little data is collected regarding non-academic outcomes.

Schools with a conventional orientation address socio-emotional learning and character-building, but mostly as a way to further academic performance or prepare students for college. Educators and students are seen as working toward a common goal: academic success that correlates to college readiness; and their interactions are mostly perceived through that lens. Thus social and emotional development are steered toward a set of values sometimes framed as "habits of scholars"—*scholars* being a ubiquitous term in these programs. Educators work hard on developing protocols, processes and systems that enforce student behavior that is consistent with the values of a scholar. Critics argue that many of these values are associated with white, dominant cultural norms like sitting still with hands folded and eyes tracking, following scripted behavioral protocols and dressing in certain ways.[6]

Discipline in conventional-orientation schools is often "zero tolerance" or consequentialist. Strict rules govern what happens when a student commits an infraction, and there's rarely any consideration of extenuating circumstances, individual history or even culpability. If a student forgets their homework, for example, they have violated the expectation of responsibility, and thus should expect a consequence.

Consequences often involve a public apology as a way to promote taking responsibility and to discourage transgressions by other students.

From a cognitive perspective, these schools work well for highly verbal students whose working memory or processing speed falls at the high end of the continuum. The academic programs rely heavily on students learning information that is provided either verbally by a teacher or through written materials, and efficiency and speed are built into classroom practices (such as using timers during lessons).

Verbal proficiency, fast processing and a strong working memory are, of course, the primary traits of those who score well on timed standardized tests.[7] Thus the same students who do well in conventional schools tend to perform well on those tests, and the test scores, in turn, aggregate into high ratings on public-school accountability measures. As you will see, conventional schools are set up to be judged as superior to schools with other orientations.

Because they do relatively little work on the social and emotional development of students, these schools aren't well suited to serving students who have experienced adverse childhood experiences and trauma, struggle with executive functioning and emotional skills or need help with social skills, anxiety or depression.

Taken as a whole, the conventional orientation is limited in terms of supporting students across the spectrum of cognitive profiles. While there has been no formal research into this limitation, the hypothesis is borne out by two key trends. First, standards-based reform and high-stakes accountability have pushed education as a whole in the direction of the conventional orientation, and we find more students labeled as "special needs" or as needing accommodations.[8] Second, in districts that have tried to close the achievement gap through the proliferation of programs with a conventional orientation, there seems to be a plateau in the trajectory of those programs' success. Once they hit a certain market share of students, test-score performance no longer increases at the same rate. And these programs often pivot to provide more special-education support, essentially transitioning toward a whole child/innovative reform approach.[9]

Whole Child/Innovative Reform Orientation

The bulk of US schools fall within the whole child/innovative reform (innovative-reform) orientation, including the vast majority of district-run public schools. Since these tend to be neighborhood schools, and include large, comprehensive high schools that are required to accept any student who enrolls, they must accommodate students with diverse abilities and dispositions. In contrast, a small charter or magnet program can attract a more specific subset of students by offering a particular curricular focus, providing certain specialized supports and/or conducting aggressive marketing efforts.

Schools with the innovative-reform orientation vary widely in their design, curricular focus, size and governance model. They are bound together by their efforts to address the shortcomings of conventional schools without fundamentally abandoning the industrial model. They attempt to mitigate the shortcomings of the factory model by bolting on solutions wherever they can, adapting in all kinds of ways to address the needs of students and educators. Sometimes this means adding a socio-emotional curriculum, an anti-bullying program or a new family-engagement effort. It might mean training teachers to use a project-based learning approach, or developing new learning-management systems. The list of possible bolt-on solutions is long, so the programming at these schools looks incredibly different from one to the next.

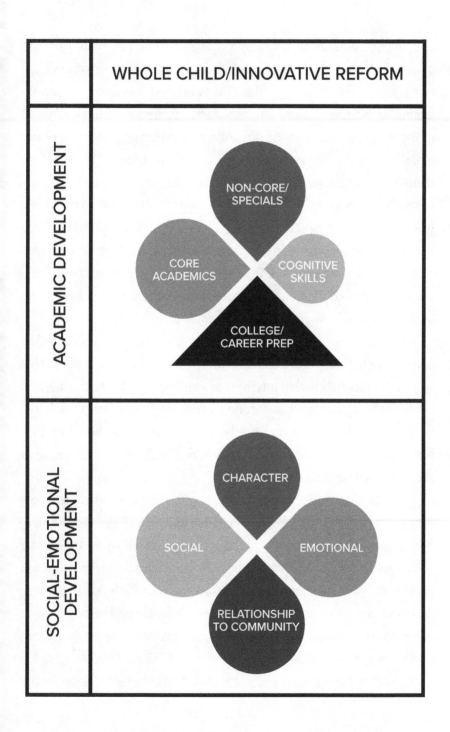

In general, though, these schools can best be described as being caught between worldviews. Some innovative-reform schools try to be human-centered, but the efforts are too scattered, or run up against opposition from administrators, teachers or families. Some of these schools move in the direction of transforming learning under a particularly visionary leader, only to have that leader leave before the overall culture of the program becomes robust enough to be self-sustaining. Others are hamstrung by state and federal policies that make transforming their practice very challenging, if not impossible. This is often in the case with Title 1 programs that serve high percentages of low-income students. Other schools simply lean more toward the conventional orientation, by design, even as they adopt some aspirational HIL language and elements.

One way or the other, though, these schools focus on broad academic readiness more than on college-readiness specifically. This is a subtle distinction that attempts to validate the idea that college is not the only legitimate post-secondary pathway. In elementary schools particularly, developmental needs are more likely to be taken into account, and more resources are made available for programming in areas like arts and music.

The theories of learning in these schools are still mostly teacher-focused, but with some room for teacher-guided lessons and enquiry-based methods. Teachers in these schools, especially in the public sector, are also more likely to have gone through traditional preparation programs where they learned about constructivist theories of learning, which promote the idea that learners need to construct their own sense and meaning in regard to learning in order for deep learning to happen.[10] Even when project-based learning or enquiry-based pedagogies are brought into these classrooms, the work is still largely driven by the teacher rather than emerging organically from students' interests.

Innovative-reform schools are still at the mercy of state academic standards or beholden to an externally designed curriculum rather than guided by founding principles or particular student needs. Because they are more likely to have formal programs for students with learning differences, they're more likely to have students with related diagnoses or Individualized Education Programs (IEPs) on their rolls, as well as more educators trained to meet those students' needs. Just as their academic focus is generally broader than that of conventional schools, they do slightly richer work in the socio-emotional realm, often adopting some type of socio-emotional framework or curriculum.

These schools are more flexible than conventional schools in terms of curriculum, instruction and assessment, and thus have more room to negotiate between student needs and school performance targets. Of course, this flexibility and openness means their students often perform slightly below those in conventional schools on standardized testing, and therefore are sometimes rated lower on accountability frameworks.

Educators in innovative-reform schools are scrambling to correct the shortcomings of the industrial model and therefore rarely have an opportunity to step back and make intentional, coherent choices. They're often compelled to satisfy requirements that have no regard for who their students are or how they're trying to teach. Many of these schools have so many different initiatives happening at once that teachers, leaders and even students easily become overwhelmed. It's not uncommon to see operations buckle under the weight of too many efforts at improvement, many of which are underfunded, misdirected, or contradict some other initiative in the same school. Despite the best intentions of educators, their efforts can result in inconsistencies in the program.

Human-Centered/Liberatory Orientation

Perhaps the defining experience of my time in HIL schools is the feeling I get when I first walk into the building or classroom. These programs embody a sense of wholeness and consistency that can be felt in different ways throughout the building. I can hear it in the open, gentle way a teacher reminds a student of some community expectation that the student isn't meeting; in how students and adults of different races and backgrounds speak critically yet thoughtfully with each other about issues such as white privilege and identity, which tend to be avoided in other schools; in how little adult management is needed in order for students to do their work; even in how natural it feels to come in as an outsider and engage in conversations with students about their experiences. Students and adults talk often about "belonging." People feel seen, known, valued and accepted. Their identities and differences are regarded as strengths, not problems. One high school student told me, "Everyone isn't my best friend, but we all know we belong here and that everyone here is your family."

In general these programs tend to be small, with fewer than 200 students, due to the central focus on development and the sense, borne out by research, that deep relationships are difficult to sustain when the student body exceeds 180–200 people.[11] Like everything else in HIL schools, relationship-building is conducted with attention to students' particular developmental needs. In preschools and elementary schools, the guiding need is independence. Children are granted considerable freedom and autonomy. They can move around freely, go to the bathroom without permission and enter and leave classrooms without a formal process. In middle schools, relationships help students develop a sense of belonging along with independence. In high schools, relationships focus on developing identity—"Who am I and who do I want to be in the world?" In HIL environments, emotional development and emotional regulation are understood as cognitive achievements. Students need support from teachers as they align their emotional growth with their overall development. A great deal of time and attention is paid to helping students self-regulate.

HIL schools encourage the creation of multiage cohorts in which students stay together for several years, often with the same teacher. In older grade bands students are grouped into *advisories* under the guidance of an adult advisor who knows each group member deeply. Because advisors' roles are structured differently from those of teachers, advisors are often not required to meet the same credentialling requirements as formal educators. As a result, HIL programs are typically able to recruit more diverse staffs than other schools, and can include people with ties to the local community and its students. These adults often take primary responsibility for engaging families and caregivers in a student's overall development—though family involvement is inherently more common and more substantial in HIL programs than in others. These are the schools where I most often saw parents coming and going freely and greeting staff members they knew by name.

The character work in these schools is subtle. Many of them formally adopt an approach to community and discipline that centers on restorative justice and restorative connections.[12] Behavior that falls outside accepted norms is not necessarily viewed as grounds for punishment. It is first addressed as a disruption between the student and the community or an obstacle to the student's learning. In response to missed assignments, a student might be asked, "You didn't do your homework. Why? What happened? You're responsible in many areas of your life, but not this one. How can we help you be responsible across all the areas of your life that matter right now?"

Conflicts are addressed quickly in these schools. While there might not be formal punishment, someone who has violated a rule is required to own the impact or consequence of their action, and some kind of corrective action is initiated as soon as possible. This reinforces everyone's sense that the community is looking out for all its members and that problems in relationships will not be downplayed or ignored.

Themes of social justice come up naturally and consistently in these schools, emerging not from a political agenda but from a core focus on community. Students are constantly interacting with the larger world in their learning, and thus they're regularly exposed to the larger issues that define the surrounding community, such as racial injustice, environmental issues, poverty and inequity. Students are not shielded from the gravity of these problems, and the adults are unusually comfortable with and skilled in providing time and emotional space for candid discussions about them.

Academics in these schools are aligned with student development. For elementary-aged students the focus is on understanding connections across subjects and forming a schema that enables them to comprehend the world. Teachers use whatever subject or issue happens to be the focus of a student's interest to expand that student's engagement with the world. The focus shifts evenly among core and non-core subject and cognitive-development areas without much concern for moving through a specified curriculum. This is the age band about which there is far more uniform agreement in regard to the specific outcomes most students need because this is the developmental stage during which most children are expected to achieve fundamental human capabilities.

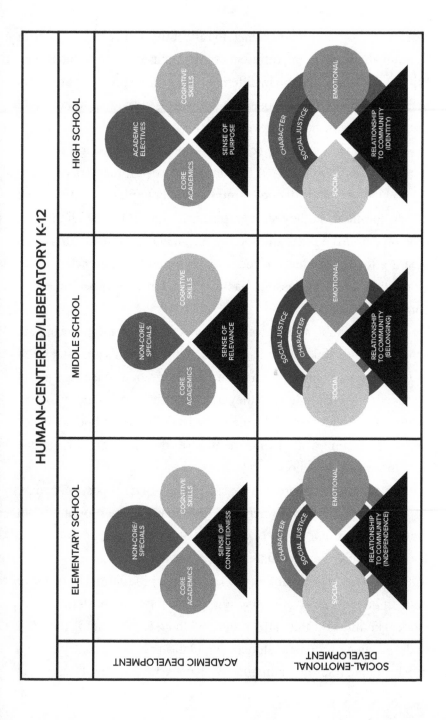

However, programs are designed to reflect the reality that from birth through about age eight, different children master these foundational skills at different rates and in different orders based on a host of factors including personality, exposure to the world, individual interest and the jaggedness of human development.[13]

Academics in middle school are understood through the lens of the student's question "Why should I care?" Educators candidly acknowledge that academic learning is likely to plateau at this stage of development, so they shift emphasis accordingly, spending more time on cognitive skills and socio-emotional capabilities. This often means allowing students to focus on community-based activities or work, then building lessons backwards from that experience into content and competencies.[14]

In high school, academics are grounded in a sense of purpose, and programs begin linking academic work to the student's growing sense of identity. A student beginning an HIL program at this stage might be asked to think about who they are, what they enjoy and who they want to be in the world. The answers drive the scope and sequence of their academic work, and in many cases dictate an entirely unique path through high school.

Students are supported in considering all kinds of post-secondary options. Immediate enrollment in a four-year college program is not viewed as a primary goal or a mark of success. HIL graduates are far more likely than graduates from schools with other orientations to take a gap year or find a job right after graduating in order to hone in on their motivation and purpose in pursuing post-secondary work. Having said this, HIL programs that serve some of the most underprivileged, diverse student populations in the country have a much higher rate of graduating students who eventually enroll in and complete post-secondary programs than do comparable non-HIL programs.[15] From an equity perspective, this is an achievement that has generally eluded the public system for decades.

HIL schools rarely adhere to an established curriculum. When they must, as with those in the public system, educators try to organize students' progression through the curriculum around age-band competencies. Rather than expecting students to follow a specific curriculum progression from sixth through eighth grade, for example, educators, students and, in some cases, caregivers take responsibility for knowing the broad sets of competencies—knowledge, skills and dispositions—students will need to demonstrate at the end of a three- or four-year period in order to meet the requirements of the public education system or post-secondary programs. They ensure that whatever projects and learning experiences students undertake over those few years allow them to meet these broad targets; but students have the flexibility to progress through these competencies in ways that align with their interests, capabilities and aspirations. Some of the learning may happen in a classroom, but external camps, work experiences and family responsibilities are all viewed as legitimate ways in which to engage with, master and demonstrate what is learned. On the other hand, these schools often use formal programs like Khan Academy or one available at a local community college to ensure that students learn the types of specific academic skills that can be harder to acquire solely through interdisciplinary or real-world learning.

HIL educators believe that if students are not strongly engaged with the subject matter and able to connect it to some personal sense of relevance, no meaningful learning will happen. Enquiry-based, project-based, play-based and situational learning are meant to generate that engagement and give students the freedom to direct the order and pace of their learning.[16] If a student prefers to listen to a story via an audio book that other students are reading in hard copy, they'll usually be allowed to. The focus is more on engagement with learning than on specific modalities.

In true right-hemispheric, both/and fashion, these schools don't eliminate direct- or teacher-guided instruction. Some students need more of this approach than others, and some subjects are best learned through a teacher-delivered lesson, a university lecture or an online video. Educators in these environments view teaching methods as tools, and choose among them based on the situation. HIL schools rely as little as possible on standardized and interim testing. They emphasize teacher observations, student self-assessments, authentic work products, portfolios and exhibitions. Each of these helps reinforce the focus on the process and progression of learning.

HIL schools work with the widest ranges of learners in terms of cognitive profiles. By integrating close relationships and socio-emotional work throughout, they effectively reflect *trauma-informed* or *healing-centered* practices. This enables them to engage productively with young people who have affective, socio-emotional, attentional and other developmental issues as well as with those who have a history of trauma or adverse childhood experiences. Strong relationships allow every student to be known and their particular needs to be addressed and incorporated into their everyday work. If this means finding a way to feed them or get them to school or accommodate a job or childcare, the school helps with that. This consideration strengthens each student's sense of belonging.

Rather than framing a student's learning difference as a weakness and trying to remediate it, HIL schools take the full measure of a student's capabilities in shaping their work. This is not to say that these schools don't provide students with opportunities to learn what many people consider to be fundamental skills that most people need to thrive in life and education. Rather, they are organized in ways that allow them to determine on an individual basis which skills should be considered basic in the first place, and then to approach the development of those skills in an individualized and flexible manner. It is accepted that outcomes will look different for a student who has severe cognitive challenges and might never work or live on their own than they will for a student who is deeply interested in a skilled trade or a student who is *twice exceptional*, meaning they need more stimulating academic work to remain engaged even though they have some type of learning difference. There is no need for any of those three students to be labeled in regard to their special need since the program itself is flexible enough to adapt to those differences. The amount of variation in learner outcomes generally increases with age. Students in the elementary age bands are expected to engage with a consistent set of learning experiences, while high school students pursue specific learning experiences that match their interests. For example, we would expect most students in the elementary age band to learn basic mathematical operations, while high school students would develop their quantitative skills through very different courses— calculus, statistics or math for everyday life—based on their interest and post-high-school aspirations.

While most HIL schools are private or independent, there are some in the public system. Elementary and middle school HIL programs tend to be in higher-income communities where parents' education levels and socioeconomic status result in their kids performing better on standardized tests; under local and state accountability systems, these schools are rated well and remain open. (There are several reasons why student test scores are better in these communities than in poor and urban areas: there are biases in test questions, affluent parents are more likely to provide their children with supports such as test accommodations or private tutoring, and the parents of students who have the most challenging learning needs can afford to instead enroll them in private schools removing them from the rosters of public schools.[17] Thus test scores indicate that these are "good" schools regardless of whether or not the schools themselves are the reason that students perform well.) In urban areas HIL elementary and middle schools often operate as magnet or specialized programs. HIL high schools are usually categorized as "alternative" high schools—often a last resort for students who have remained in school long enough for the public system to acknowledge that they need a different approach. Most states have laws that allow alternative high school programs to use different accountability systems than conventional high schools, which is not true in regard to elementary and middle schools. Alternative high school programs disproportionally serve low-income populations, perhaps because families with means who recognize that their child needs alternative supports can afford to remove them from the public system. Unfortunately, by that time the child has often been through many disappointments, perceived failures, conflicts and misunderstandings, at great cost to their confidence in their abilities.

Outside of the formal education system, many homeschooling cooperatives, micro-schools, learning pods and youth-development programs also take an HIL approach, often picking up students who have been failed by the formal education system and/or whose families can afford the time and resources necessary to create hybrid educational programming.[18]

The Next Chapter: From Equity to a Human-Centered/Liberatory Orientation

REALITY

EQUALITY

EQUITY

LIBERATION

The first three frames of the graphic above became popular in the late 1990s. In the three decades since, the graphic has evolved along with our changing definition of *educational equity*. At first it was not enough for state governments to simply provide a uniform per-pupil dollar amount for each student because this neglected the reality that many communities have low tax bases that cannot support supplemental educational spending. Families in high-poverty areas have limited access to basic services like food, housing, healthcare and early education. The education system should level the playing field, we said, by ensuring that each child is given what they need rather than providing the same educational resources to every child. In the late 1990s proponents of new accountability systems were pushing to increase academic proficiency by intensifying standardized assessments. In this version of equity, "seeing over the fence" meant performing well in core, tested subjects.

As we know, this led to an increase in the number of programs that adopted a conventional orientation, endeavoring to make the factory model of school work better through things like longer days, longer years, tighter behavioral management systems and more efficient ways to cover academic content. These schools placed greater focus on reading, writing and math, and they were praised for "closing the achievement gap," as measured by test scores. Over time, however, some cracks began to show. So we bolted solutions onto the conventional model, thus expanding the number of innovative-reform schools. The progress of these schools led us to the third stage in the graphic above, the idea that we can do more than just help kids see over the fence by mitigating the challenges they encountered.

In all of these scenarios equity was understood as producing uniform educational outcomes for all learners in the education system.

This kind of educational equity is ultimately impossible to realize through the Cartesian-Newtonian approach, which is designed to sort people using narrow definitions of *merit* and *intelligence*, because the formal educational accountability process tends to privilege those with certain cognitive strengths over others. Inequality is, in fact, a *desired outcome* in this model—some must always be better than others, and ranking is often how success is acknowledged. Redefining educational equity means expanding our definitions of merit, intelligence and capability—what it means to be smart and capable; and eliminating the biases and values that took hold in Europe after the Scientific Revolution, were exported through colonialism and formed the basis for dehumanizing economic and social systems in America and elsewhere.

This is the moment to embrace liberatory education as it was conceived by HIL thinkers at the turn of the twentieth century, and to set our sights toward an education system designed to recognize the full humanity, diversity and capabilities of children. The liberatory perspective frees us from having to flatten our differences and fit them into preexisting categories in order to rank and judge them as data points on a graph. It allows us to reclaim a holistic and indigenous view of what it means to be a full person—what it means to live in community, connect to the world, understand oneself and contribute to something larger. This is a view that enables our left-hemispheric capabilities to do what they do best: develop technical and conceptual solutions that work *in service* to our humanity, not against it.

By defining equity for so long in terms of academic parity measured by standardized tests, the education system has created an incentive to actually *ignore* developmental needs. It's ironic that this has been especially problematic for the most marginalized students—the ones equity was supposed to help. No one can thrive academically if they're hungry, surrounded by chaos, alienated from their family or their community, or living in fear. In trying for decades to reform a system that minimizes these human needs, we failed the students who most needed our help.

In addition to focusing on demographics and economic strata, our definition of equity must also apply across cognitive profiles. Human-centered/liberatory programs are best suited to respond to what we know about neurodiversity. Like biodiversity—the concept that a diverse ecosystem is best suited for survival—neurodiversity is essential to ensuring that our species can adapt to an uncertain future. Our education system has long labeled and stigmatized children whose brains aren't well suited to conventional learning and testing. Young people with cognitive and emotional strengths that are different from the "norm" are told they have dyslexia or learning differences. They are autistic or have "special needs." Or they receive a diagnosis of vague emotional or affective disorders. Our diagnoses and behavior-management guidelines only reinforce these biases, and end up pathologizing many forms of potential. This is why the socially compliant, logical, verbal learner becomes a star while the gregarious, auditory learner; the dancer; the dreamer; the non-conformer is labeled and demoted. A human-centered/liberatory orientation to education doesn't rely on favoring one set of cognitive skills or tendencies. It doesn't pretend that every child is the same at the various stages of education. And it embraces learning no matter where it happens—at home, at school, at work, at play, at rest.

Many people have legitimate worries about human-centered/ liberatory schools as havens for low expectations. But the left-hemispheric approach to a rigorous education hasn't worked. It hasn't worked in achieving better outcomes. It hasn't worked in helping young people feel smart, capable or confident. It hasn't responded to the unique needs and contexts of a diverse population. Learning happens at the boundary between what we think we can do and what we don't yet know about ourselves—the so-called *zone of proximal development*. For every student to really learn, we need to teach them all to push against real and perceived boundaries and to reject inherited ideas about what they can't do, who they should be and what the world wants from them. A commitment to stop racism, prejudice and unconscious bias should not compel us to forget that all people are different. Instead, this commitment should drive us to see each student as they are, and to design their education according to their particular circumstances and aspirations. No system can be totally human-proofed, and any educational program can be co-opted by unjust powers. The question is whether or not we should continue to invest our time, resources and intentions in a system that has never understood true equity. Can we instead envision a world in which each child learns and grows according to their own resources, their own hopes and their own particular heritage, values and potential?

In any era, education assumes the broader social role of guiding the people who will define future economic and social systems. The professional world of the near future demands two types of wage-earners that the industrial model tends to discourage or neglect: those who know how to work in complex, interdisciplinary ways on multifaceted, ambiguous challenges; and those who engage with the world through the human qualities that can't be replicated by artificial intelligence, such as empathy, compassion, adaptability and creativity.

The decontextualized and mechanistic work that impelled the industrial model will not prepare the students of today for the world they're likely to encounter—a world in which complex, dynamic, system-level problems are the norm and will only be solved through the collaboration of diverse groups of people with divergent ideas. It is a world in which we will be grappling with the intersecting biological and sociopolitical challenges of climate change, the forced migration it will engender, and decisions about whose responsibility it will be to care for those who are displaced. It is a world in which it may be possible for us to "fix" genes that cause diseases and create "designer babies," opening up a Pandora's box of questions at the intersection of biology, technology, ethics and the law. Human-centered/liberatory education immerses young people in lessons that resemble what actual life and work will look like—messy, non-linear, ambiguous and multifaceted. It reflects the reality that young people cannot conceptually prepare to engage with such a world; they need to immerse themselves in it so that they can learn what it means to embody the knowledge, skills and dispositions they will need to thrive.

Emerging technologies and advances in artificial intelligence (AI) mean that machines are now better than humans at many of the things the industrial model is best at training humans to do: organizing, analyzing and applying knowledge; handling and interpreting data; and analyzing and synthesizing. AI loses its edge in domains in which there are unpredictable possibilities, such as organizing community response efforts at the onset of a worldwide pandemic; creating algorithms for self-driving cars that ensure they will make the best maneuver when a small figure on the side of the road unexpectedly darts into a lane of moving traffic; and deciding whether or not to follow orders from a superior in light of ethical considerations. AI is generations away from providing compassionate emotional support to the sick and elderly, empathizing with those who suffer loss or sharing an experience of joy. The world needs our schools to nurture these capacities now more than ever.

We are in the midst of massive changes in our country's social and civic fabric. Debates about education, the environment, healthcare, criminal justice and the economy are rooted in a fundamental tension between left- and right-hemispheric approaches and Cartesian-Newtonian and holistic-indigenous values. There is increasing recognition of the interconnected nature of our reality and of the need to build systems and approaches that reflect that interconnectedness. We are seeing what happens when we don't teach people what it means to be members of civic, political and economic communities—the division and alienation that results. A right-hemispheric perspective allows us to integrate individual differences into the larger whole instead of feeling threatened by them. By centering relationships and community-building, human-centered/liberatory programs become partners to families and community institutions in helping young people develop these skills. Even very young children go out from their schools into the world to learn from workers, elders and neighbors. Whether through expeditions or mentorships, young people are taught to see themselves as contributors to—not just beneficiaries of—a community.

By preparing young people to successfully live in the world they will inherit, human-centered/liberatory schools can begin to restore what centuries of imbalance and inequity have suppressed: our common humanity and our true potential as individuals and as a society.

Applying These Ideas

- HIL programs are designed to allow young people to choose how they access information and how they demonstrate their learning. Many students in these schools gain the profound realization that there's nothing *wrong* with them for the way they process information and communicate; that their preferred style is just as valid and just as much a sign of intelligence or competence as that of others. Are reading and writing your primary modes of learning and sharing information? Are they your preferred modes? *In a world in which speech-to-text and text-to-speech capabilities are rapidly improving, do you think we should we continue to prioritize reading and writing over performance, storytelling and visual modes of communication?*

- In this chapter you learned how HIL programs incorporate aspects of life that in the traditional system are addressed by discrete agencies and departments such as health and human services, child and family services, higher education and labor/employment. *Think about how your local and state governments could change to support HIL programs.*

- This chapter includes a graphic in which three kids stand at a fence trying to watch a ball game. The final frame of this graphic would ideally feature many more than four kids, doing many different things—playing in the game, watching the game, taking down the fence and building something different, painting the fence instead of watching, walking away from the game altogether to take a nap.... Truly liberatory approaches to education embrace the idea that each learner arrives at a *different* outcome and finds different ways to contribute to the world. *Think about why people might be uncomfortable with the idea that every student leaves school with achievements and skills that are different from those of other students?*

PART 3

FUTURE:

Enabling Transformation

CHAPTER 7

A Path Forward

In the 1980s and 1990s people in vast regions of the developing world still had no access to telephones, nor any telephone wires nor the poles to hang them on. And most people in the United States were still using landlines. But a new technology, mobile telephones, was on the rise. International-development professionals faced a choice: Should developing countries invest time and money installing telephone poles and hanging wires, or should they skip over the old technology and start building out the new? They chose the latter, and their decision to leapfrog meant that by the early 2000s even people living in regions without reliable electricity, clean water or reliable transportation could call each other and access the internet.[1]

The knowledge and capacity to make this leap had been developed at institutions like DARPA beginning in the 1980s, well before most civilians were even aware of mobile technology. That foundation enabled the technology to spread rapidly in the general population, transforming the everyday lives of Americans within a little more than 10 years.

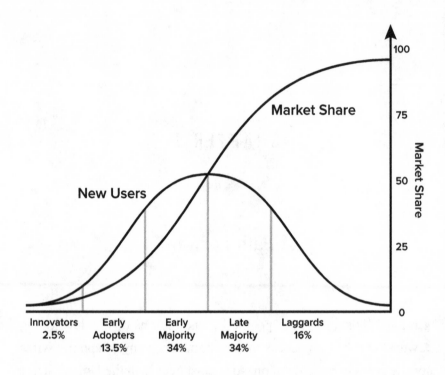

This story illustrates a concept known as the *diffusion of innovations theory*, developed by theorist and sociologist E. M. Rogers, which describes how new ideas and products move from the fringes of society into the mainstream. The theory is illustrated by Rogers's curve above. This process usually begins with a small group of early adopters who, with enough time and the right resources, quietly build the foundation for something world-changing.[2] Initial investment, and infrastructure that can seem incremental, are what ultimately enable fields to leapfrog.

Education is at its own leapfrog moment as we face a choice about whether or not to invest in the "infrastructure" needed to rapidly make human-centered/liberatory education available to all communities. The choice between an HIL approach to education and a Cartesian-

Newtonian approach mirrors a larger tension in America about how we live, what we value, who gets access to opportunity and how we decide to prepare for the future of work. For the first time since the Industrial Revolution, what we identify as being needed in order to sustain healthy communities, economic systems and civic society aligns with the goals and practices of HIL education. Traditional schooling has been failing students and families by every measure for decades, and now a pandemic and a period of broad reckoning have revealed how these failings align with the larger biases and inequities of the culture.

HIL programs already exist all over the country, but at nowhere near the numbers that it will take to leapfrog into a new nationwide vision of teaching and learning. Real change requires dismantling structures that reinforce the status quo; that presume that learning should take place in school only; that mandate that content be dictated strictly by age; and that oblige learners to be judged by standardized annual tests.

The system is reluctant to allow radical change without a clear sense of what will replace the old ways. But 2020 forced us to abandon many of our default practices, and the resulting disruptions revealed how inadequate those practices have been all along. A year of remote schooling has given families and communities opportunities to imagine what learning might look like beyond the walls of conventional schools. Many of the districts and schools that adapted best to the pandemic were those already moving toward human-centered systems and already organized more like HIL programs than conventional programs.[3] For better or worse, many of our most fundamental practices, including all the standardized testing data gathered from students, educators, schools and districts for the 2019–2020 and 2020–2021 school years, have been rendered useless. And these disruptions are not limited to K–12. Higher education will never be the same, and the new era could free students, families and programs from reliance on conventional high school pathways like advanced-placement classes, grade-point averages, the Scholastic Aptitude Test (SAT) and American College Testing (ACT).[4]

We can decide what happens next. Do we leapfrog, or do we settle back into another few decades of the old way and the reforms we know do not work?

This is the moment to build the new systems and structures that will enable and support the work of HIL, a research-and-development engine for transforming the whole American education system. It will not be easy; you have seen how Cartesian-Newtonian values are entrenched in our schools and the culture as a whole, and how resistant this worldview is to fundamental change. Real change will take reinvention at many levels of the system. And, as with any emergent change, the process matters as much as the outcome.

Where We Are as a System and What That Means

Our schools sit within a highly fragmented system, organized into autonomous and insular districts, each one pressured by external demands for standardization, quantification and comparison. This structure originated in America's early days, when communities were geographically distant from one another and most people lived, worked and died in or very close to the locale in which they were born. Communities funded their own schools and took total ownership of their children's education, electing local school boards to manage funds, hiring teachers who would instill the values and lessons deemed most essential to the local community's way of life, and overseeing those teachers. In the decades since, these local units—more than 13,500 autonomous school districts—have fought to maintain control of funding, standards, curriculum, testing, accountability, hiring and transportation.[5] Having local communities invested in the education of their children is a good thing. The problems emerge when a desire for local control pits one community against another or detracts from a community's investment in statewide and national issues related to education. This insularity can limit the flow of ideas, resources and opportunities that an HIL system will need in order to emerge and flourish.

State and federal governments have tried for years to create some uniformity in the public education system, using funding and legislation to influence district decisions. Unfortunately, this meant doubling down on the Cartesian-Newtonian approach: introducing stricter academic standards, reinforcing the division of learning into age-defined curricula, adding standardized tests and building more accountability systems based on student test scores. The federal government provides money to states and districts based on compliance with performance expectations; states pass the money and the mandates to districts; districts impose them on schools; and students and teachers bear the burden.

All this has brought us to the present: Children learn that they're "smart" or "dumb" based on how quickly they master a very narrow set of skills. Schools and districts compete with each other for higher ratings and enrollment, along with the funding enrolled students represent. Parents scramble to have their children labeled "special needs" or "gifted" or "twice exceptional" because this is their best hope for an education that recognizes their child's way of experiencing the world.[6] This is a system in which the majority of young people come to think of school as tedious, uninspiring and even soul-crushing, and in which schools are sometimes closed on the basis of test-score data alone, no matter how important they were to students and families in the community.[7]

The long-term goal of transitioning to HIL is to have a system that promotes and supports what we know about human development and the process of learning and honors diverse ways of knowing, being and contributing to the world. Accomplishing this goal is still a long way off; it might take two decades or more to fully get there. And just as schools cannot really transform except from within, system-level change must begin with the communities and the schools themselves, so the additional challenge is that the transition must begin locally.

Right now America's districts are made up largely of schools within the conventional and whole child/innovative reform orientations, with small pockets here and there of deep HIL practice. Transformation will begin in those small pockets by identifying the HIL educators and leaders already doing the work, helping them replicate and share their ideas and practices, and involving them in the work of building new systems and structures aligned with HIL practice. Over time these practices will come to seem intuitive as HIL becomes the norm. Children will be given credit for learning at home if they speak a second language with a parent, help on the farm or with the family business, cook with their grandparents or field dress a deer on a hunting trip. Districts will allow schools to design curricula that students can complete in any order over the course of three or four years, taking advantage of learning opportunities as they arise, whether at school, at home, in a museum or through an internship. Students will be demonstrating what they know in new ways—through projects they complete, businesses they start, prototypes they design to address community concerns and legislation they help draft or promote. State labor and higher-education departments will support collaborations between high schools, businesses and local colleges to design internships that lead to students earning certifications before graduating from high school. Districts will band together to offer an entire set of high school pathway programs open to students from anywhere in the region, ranging from food production and agricultural science to hospitality, medical technology, elder care, coding and social entrepreneurship. New information-management systems and apps will enable learners from ages 13 to 93 to carry with them a blockchain or electronic resume to which they can add credentials and certificates whenever they acquire a new skill.[8] New accountability systems will rely on coalitions of educators, students, parents and community members who observe such systems in other schools and share their findings with their communities.

Much of this future-facing work is already happening; we are not starting from scratch. We don't know how many HIL programs exist, given that the work often happens in alternative education programs, youth-development programs, learning cooperatives and homeschooling and community-based settings. But we know that HIL-oriented programs probably comprise 5 to 8 percent of the total education landscape, with the majority operating outside public-district and public-charter sectors. These programs serve students and communities in every state, from rural Alaska to rural Florida and every place in between, in urban districts like New York and Los Angeles and in mid-sized urban and suburban communities across the US. Through alternative and magnet schools, HIL programs are already serving a surprising percentage of students who've been left behind by the conventional system, including English language learners, teen parents, adolescents who have gone through the juvenile justice system, children of refugees and children who have experienced trauma. Some students cannot learn in a standardized system no matter how reformed it is.[9] And some can and do perform perfectly well in conventional programs but find themselves uninspired, bored and longing for the more engaging learning experiences available through HIL.[10]

The educators who build and sustain these programs, especially in the public sector, have found ways to work around structural and policy barriers. But this often means compromising their program and limiting the opportunities they can provide to students. Their experiences can help us understand what it will take to establish HIL education as an accessible, mainstream option for all US families.[11]

What It Will Take: An Emergent Theory of Change

In the fall of 2014, Denver Public Schools launched a small project known as the Imaginarium as a setting for trying out new ideas in education. Three dozen schools participated in this "innovation lab." The district had been trying to adopt new programs, but educators needed an infrastructure to support and assess them, and in which to expand the ones that proved successful.

The Imaginarium's tenure was marked by cycles of excitement and profound disappointment. It closed its doors after five years, in May of 2019.[12] An unofficial post-mortem by the staff delivered this final verdict:

Enough! Enough meek compliance with regulations that
fly directly in the face of what we know to be best practice!

Enough turning meaningful ideas into meaningless buzzwords. Personalized learning, whole child education, equity and innovation are real, meaty concepts that have the power to transform education as we know it. But when they're watered down, ingested and regurgitated as pabulum by a system that seeks to make everything bland and inoffensive, then we end up where we are today.[13]

I visited Imaginarium schools as part of the Instructional Orientations project that began in 2015 and is outlined in appendix A. The schools that participated over the course of the project's tenure were a mix of what the project came to call innovative-reform / whole child-oriented and human-centered/liberatory-oriented schools. My interviews with staff and leaders suggested that the project's breakdown was mostly the result of not distinguishing between bolted-on reforms and a genuine human-centered/liberatory orientation. This confusion led the district to limit the autonomy and flexibility that human-centered/liberatory programs were given. They required all Imaginarium educators to receive their ongoing professional development from a graduate school grounded squarely in Cartesian-Newtonian ideas. They used the same outcomes measures for all schools without regard to their underlying design. Schools that were geared toward students who learned best through projects and who struggled with written, timed tests were not offered alternatives to such testing for demonstrating students' learning. The district had no means by which to recognize schools that participated in the project for success in the areas that were, in fact, most central to the project's mission, such as increasing students' agency in their learning process and building a sense of connectedness and belonging.

Everything Imaginarium staff identified as problematic in their final report testified to the challenge of making room for HIL programs in the left-hemispheric atmosphere of the school district, which was ostensibly more progressive in its thinking than most in America. By the time the Imaginarium closed, its most promising HIL programs had either closed or adapted their work to fit district priorities.

Below I lay out a two-phased strategy for spreading the HIL approach throughout the American education market, ultimately providing every family in the country with access to an HIL program for any age learner. The process I envision can be charted on a change-adoption curve like this:

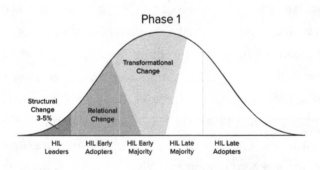

Phase 1 involves the HIL leaders at the far left of the curve codifying their approaches to various aspects of education and developing new models for HIL programs that include outcomes and targets for individual learners, better methods for assessing the full range of outcomes that matter for young people, models for credentialling learning outside of schools, and accountability systems consistent with HIL values.

Phase 2 will focus on disseminating the systems and structures developed in Phase 1. If Phase 1 is like a fallow period, when the soil is being enriched but nothing much changes above ground, Phase 2 is when we see sudden, dramatic growth. The number of communities with HIL programs will suddenly multiply, and will continue to multiply until HIL programs outnumber programs with conventional and innovative-reform orientations, emerging as the most common approach to education in the country. Throughout this phase HIL leaders will engage with families and communities to make the case for HIL, and the successes of HIL programs will be leveraged in districts and states in the push to secure even more support.

In both phases change will happen at three different levels: transformational, relational and structural.[14] Transformational work will change people's minds about the purpose and aims of education. Relational work will change how people engage in the actual work of education in various parts of the system: classrooms, schools, districts, boards of education, state departments of education. Structural work will build the systems and structures needed to sustain HIL education. The transformational and relational changes will take place in communities and among non-HIL practitioners as they begin to shift away from the conventional mindset and open up to the virtues of the HIL approach. In a country that relies so heavily on Cartesian-Newtonian ideas, this is where most of the change will happen during Phase 1. Until the basic values behind factory-model education can be questioned, nothing else can shift. It will be the work of those at the far left of the curve, including HIL practitioners, families and young people who have been through HIL programs—those who have already done the transformational and relational work—to initiate the structural work during this first phase. All three levels of change are essential, and they will often occur in parallel, yet in different orders for different people in different contexts. Taken together, they comprise the complete transition from our current system to a predominantly HIL system.

Although the curves in the graphs above seem to move from left to right, the change process will be emergent, gradual and piecemeal. It can be only this way in a country made up of autonomous districts working toward a transformation that cannot be imposed from the top down. We will see surges of reinvention in some schools, districts and states, and periods of resistance or regression in others as the Cartesian-Newtonian approach fights for survival. The change will be hard to quantify in the short term, encompassing all the doubts, equivocations, experiments and counteractions we expect when a system redefines itself. We'll see a single teacher's revelation in one town and a whole district's revolution a few miles away. But over time, if we keep spreading the word and building intentionally, these gradual and non-linear shifts will converge. We will look up one day and discover a new normal in which the very mention of school will call to mind an experience of interconnectedness, of belonging to a community, of appreciating differences and of individual students evolving *with* their environments rather than being pitted against them—and vice versa.

Phase 1: Creating the Right Conditions for Change and Activating HIL Leaders

Phase 1 should focus on three key areas: engaging people in conversations about what HIL actually is and what it offers, building the relationships needed to make broad changes and providing HIL practitioners all the resources they need to expand and build new HIL-aligned systems.

Transformational and Relational Change

The far left of the curve represents the small subset of HIL leaders, scattered in schools, communities and organizations around the country, who have already internalized the ideas we've been exploring in this book. They have been working holistically, building models that can sustain these new ways of working. They know what it takes to make HIL work with other aspects of America's social, economic and higher-education systems, and will be the leaders of structural change efforts. We'll come back to them in a moment.

Beyond this subset of practitioners, Phase 1 is about engaging with teachers and citizens who are open to change but don't yet know what it will look like or struggle to believe it's possible. Maybe the educators at their school recently added a mindfulness program to the socio-emotional curriculum, even as their teachers still rank students based on their grades. Maybe teachers have worked project-based learning into their classrooms, but they're asking all students to work on the same project at the same time. Perhaps parents have enrolled their children in a Montessori school, but are frustrated by the absence of regular report cards and grades. Educators and parents might not yet have considered a model with a wholly different outlook, but they're drawn to experiences that acknowledge students' full humanity, and already know that relationships are essential to learning.

At this stage the conversations between HIL practitioners, early adopters and the HIL-curious will focus on questioning the purpose of education and demonstrating how an entire school can be governed by new definitions of learning and knowledge. Most people can't understand something they have not experienced or witnessed directly, so this phase involves giving people access to HIL classrooms, teachers and graduates and demonstrating how fruitfully HIL schools interact with their surrounding communities. This brings communities in as partners in education, which ultimately increases demand and support for the work.

In the wake of a devastating flood, leaders in Cedar Rapids, Iowa, modeled this kind of process. Their Billy Madison Project sent a diverse group of adults in the community back to school as a way to show them firsthand what the students experienced. They were astounded and disappointed by what they found. Once these community members understood the problems of the current model, the project leaders, who were long-time HIL practitioners, brought people together to consider alternatives. These community conversations brought forth three themes—passion, projects and community—that ultimately guided the design of Iowa BIG, an HIL high school for students from three adjacent districts. Students at Iowa BIG now learn through a series of team projects proposed and supported by local community partners. The program's success has led to multiple campuses, and the model is being replicated in other parts of the state.[15]

Even as communities engage in these conversations, educators can begin reorienting themselves to their work. On a technical level, many HIL programs design their adult-preparation and professional-learning processes around a residency/praxis model. Just as doctors learn by working under supervision in clinical settings, connecting theory-based learning with actual human life, HIL training programs place aspiring educators in programs full time, where they shadow established HIL teachers in their interactions with students, families and colleagues. Long-term residency models help new educators fully embody HIL relationships, while practices like classroom visits and *learning rounds* (similar to *clinical rounds* for resident physicians) help those who are already working in schools incorporate HIL methods into their classrooms in a practical and coherent manner.

A lab classroom, for example, is a single classroom within a school or district where an experienced HIL practitioner teaches a class to students in their usual manner while being observed by visitors who have some sense of how HIL principles are guiding the work they're watching. At the end of the visit, the host educator and the visitors have an opportunity to debrief, raising questions and concerns in a setting that allows them to make the most of the experience.[16] Thus the lab visit itself becomes a demonstration of HIL—embodied, dialogic and egalitarian.

Regardless of method, the central aim of the work during this phase is to help educators uncover and disrupt the effects that Cartesian-Newtonian values have had on their beliefs and practices. These effects play out in beliefs about young people, in cultural or racial biases and in default approaches to organizing learning that can be difficult to detect in the course of everyday practice. One of the most striking characteristics of HIL programs is the nature of the relationships that undergird the learning community. These heightened, belonging-centered relationships are possible because the adults in these programs have done the deep and often uncomfortable work of surfacing their unconscious beliefs, biases and assumptions and becoming more conscious of how those can unintentionally emerge in the form of limiting language, behavior and practices. Because they have done the work, they have the specific skills and tools they need to change how they show up in relationship to others. This enables them to create the authentic sense of relatedness and belonging that HIL requires, and to model and support young people to do the same for each other.[17]

While it sounds straightforward, it is anything but, because efforts to change people's relationships to the work of education often fall prey to the trap of bolting on change rather than supporting deeper work. Take one specific example of a body of work that seems to be broadly aligned with the HIL orientation but often falls far short: diversity, equity and inclusion (DEI) programs. Far too many of these programs approach the work at the level of "fixing" people or systems, which can include either shaming people with the extent of their ignorance or assuming that the issue to be addressed is a lack of conceptual understanding or a lack of willingness on the part of individuals to make change. They involve short-term professional-development programs that include, for example, training on implicit bias, presentations about levels of oppression or manifestations of white-supremacy culture, and time for self and group reflection. This might be followed by rewriting district or school documents and policies to include more anti-racist language. There might even be a committee assigned to make sure the curriculum becomes more culturally relevant.

While many of these efforts can add value, none of them helps fundamentally change people's relationships with the work of education or with young people. And that is usually because the experience either did not support people in identifying fundamental beliefs and behaviors, or tried to do it in ways that resulted in defensiveness and avoidance.

An HIL approach to DEI work is a healing-oriented, long-term, collective/community-based approach that starts by creating a strong personal connection between participants who see it as their role to witness and support each other along a journey of change. It grounds the work in the idea that the challenge we seek to address sits at the level of worldview—the Western-supremacy culture that has its roots in the assumptions of the Cartesian-Newtonian worldview and has since played out in a cultural stew of social, economic and political systems. These systems impact each of us in real but different ways. Such an approach still provides conceptual frameworks and asks participants to identify the ways in which their daily lives and work reflect this cultural stew of values. However, it also focuses on people's embodied experiences of processing and learning, asking them to notice, name and experience the discomfort that the process of better understanding these dynamics evokes. It encourages the use of breath work and physical movement as ways to let the body alchemize trauma. Practitioners like Resmaa Menakem and Milagros Phillips are among those who speak of "body-centered" or "trauma-centered" activism that aims not to "fix" but rather to elevate awareness and consciousness, to provide concrete tools and strategies and to provide a community in which to continue a journey of personal change and growth.[18] It's about honoring the fact that this is layered, on-going work that is never done because it's about managing the dynamic tension between two different views of the world that are embedded in the structure of our brains and our ways of experiencing the world.

The distinction between bolting on reforms and achieving true transformation through an HIL approach matters; they result in two different outcomes when it comes to how people relate to others and how they relate to the work of education. The latter approach sets the stage for HIL work to unfold and take root, not only in schools but in communities as a whole. As we engage in the relational aspects of change, we must be careful to attend to both what we work on and *how* we undertake the work. This includes *how* we engage communities in these conversations and the work, *how* we engage students in their learning, *how* we design learning experiences and *how* we measure outcomes. Short of attending to the "how," the work we do in service of transformation risks becoming merely performative—a left-hemispheric engagement with the idea and theory of change but without the necessary follow-through that translates into right-hemispheric and embodied ways of doing education differently.

Structural Change

Just as the use of mobile phones could not spread until infrastructure was in place, HIL will not be able to spread rapidly and widely without networks and systems that protect it from the expectations of the status-quo model. This work falls into five general areas which, as a whole, will make a convincing case to parents, employers and policymakers that HIL is a viable alternative to conventional schooling: 1) codifying and disseminating human-centered/liberatory orientation models; 2) organizing learning outcomes into age-band competencies; 3) establishing new ways to track and assess learning; 4) creating new accountability systems; and 5) supporting transitions to post-secondary pathways.

Together these five projects will answer the most common concerns among HIL skeptics: What will children learn?; How can we make sure they've learned it?; How do we know they'll be ready for the transition to work or college?; and How do we ensure programs are serving all students well? HIL programs have been grappling with these questions and crafting workable solutions for decades. Phase 1 will allow HIL advocates to share their answers with each other and with larger communities. It will mean investing in a handful of regional projects that pull together new approaches being created at the school, district and state level in order to craft coherent and internally consistent model ecosystems that show what education can look like with HIL as the dominant approach.

Each one of these five areas of work could be explored in its own book. Below I provide an overview of their importance to HIL in Phase I, and a general outline of the work involved for each area.

Codifying and Disseminating Human-Centered/Liberatory Orientation Models

As we saw with Tom and his team at King's Green School, designing HIL programs without a template often leads to exhaustion and chaos. But even with an instructional model (IM) in place, launching a new program in the current system is challenging. Many schools and districts are likely to benefit from starting with an established, time-tested IM.

An IM provides a core curricular approach, along with methods of tracking and assessing learning, all of which can be very difficult to design from scratch. Beginning with an established IM doesn't mean that there's no room for local communities or schools to adapt; in fact, adapting and improving is generally easier within a reliable, consistent structure. The field of HIL has already generated some sustainable models, and these can be a foundation for the work in Phase 1 even as field leaders continue to build new ones. I single out a few of them below as a starting point. I chose models that have existed long enough to amass extensive curricular materials, assessments and even supporting systems such as adult-preparation and professional-learning programs. Plenty of other models exist, but many are one-off programs in which educators have not yet done the work needed to formally capture and consolidate all the pieces of their work in ways that make them useful for others just starting out.

In early education, the Montessori instructional model has perhaps the most elegant approach to balancing all the needs and inclinations of young children. In Montessori *primary* (ages 3–6) and *lower* and *upper elementary* (1st grade–5th grade) classrooms, children move through an array of sequenced "works," going at their own pace over the course of two- to three-year cycles, which leaves room for the wide variation in how human development unfolds from birth through age eight. Some of the works fall into traditional categories—math, reading and science. Others focus on life activities that speak to children's need to be independent and to feel like significant contributors to their families and environments. Examples of these include cultivating grace and courtesy, pouring and washing, arranging flowers, and cutting and serving. Sensorial works help students develop their auditory, baric and visual senses through discerning minute differences in color and weight—observational skills many adults don't have. A "peace curriculum" is integrated into the learning environment, supporting students as young as three in self-regulating and resolving conflicts independently. Students learn in multiage classrooms, reflecting the reality that children develop skills at different rates and can learn directly and indirectly from one another over time, mimicking the learning and interactions that happen in families and society more generally. Students progress through the carefully designed learning materials in ways that match their individual development and interests, guided by teachers who ensure that students cover all the necessary skills for each learning cycle.[19]

Despite their Euro-centric roots and their association with America's white middle and upper classes, Montessori schools were a cornerstone of desegregation efforts in the US, and the Montessori approach has in recent years been more widely embraced by Black and brown communities than in the past. Montessori programs around the country have been modified to serve racially, linguistically and socioeconomically diverse communities without losing their core strengths.[20]

Other reasonably well-established IMs for the elementary age band include Reggio Emelia, Tools of the Mind, and Expeditionary Learning.[21] The Expeditionary Learning model, developed by Kurt Hahn, works especially well for older elementary-age students since it speaks to the needs of young people in late childhood and early adolescence as they begin to pull away from their families in order to define and discover themselves in relationship to peers. Expeditionary Learning's design emphasizes the structure of multiage "crews" that remain with one teacher for at least two years. Its interdisciplinary academic units include "expeditions" outside the classroom, allowing students to integrate their learning and see its relevance to the world. The model in its original form included room for nature-based adventures, which Hahn believed would connect students of this age to the environment, meeting their need for healthy risk-taking by pushing them beyond self-imagined limits and providing time for solitude and reflection.[22]

Expeditionary Learning changed slightly when funders urged the program to codify expeditions in a format called EL education, which would allow the program to scale more quickly as a model. Some schools now take EL's program and adapt it to an innovative-reform orientation, but the core of the program remains intact and can still provide a strong starting place for new HIL programs to build on.

Strong HIL models are more plentiful at the high school level, in part because so many alternative high school programs adopt this orientation. I have not found a model stronger in its foundational design than Big Picture Learning (BPL). And it is codified in ways that allow it to be adopted across many different communities. Since its inception three decades ago at the Met School in Providence, Rhode Island, BPL has proved to be incredibly successful at serving diverse populations of learners, and has recently released a longitudinal study that demonstrates the impressive outcomes it is able to produce for young people well beyond their time in high school.[23]

After the early-adolescent process of separating from family and trying to conform in order to create peer relationships, older adolescents are ready to identify and embrace what makes them unique in the world. Yet the intense focus on building academic resumes and competing for college admissions leaves very little room for experiences and interactions that help them understand themselves. BPL immerses students in an intense study of themselves—their hobbies, their strengths and weaknesses, and the ways their weaknesses provide insight into their strengths. BPL believes that humans are *situational learners*, and that the best way for students to explore, discover and develop their paths into the world is through well-structured, guided internships. BPL schools flip the secondary model on its head by making internships and other out-of-school experiences the core of its academic program. Instead of organizing around discrete subjects, BPL concentrates on transferrable skills: communication, empirical reasoning, personal qualities, quantitative reasoning and social reasoning. Students work with their families and advisors to identify the specific content and skills they need to master in each of these broad competency areas. A student wanting to pursue a career in the sciences might take traditional courses like calculus and statistics. A student who knows they want to start their own business might focus on financial literacy and accounting. Students keep the same advisor throughout the four-year program, and these advisors help them translate their out-of-school learning into formal skills and content coverage.[24]

Codifying an HIL model takes tremendous time and effort and involves capturing the nuances of a program and moving through high-level theory, student learning progressions, curricular structure, assessment tools and progress trackers. When educators at Iowa BIG started receiving offers from other parts of the state to open up additional campuses, they decided to compile a handbook describing how they work. It took 15 months, and the document is still being updated. Very few new and one-off programs have the time and resources to do this kind of work. Having said that, many of these same programs have emerged out of strong community-based processes with the explicit aim of serving students and communities from non-white, non-dominant backgrounds. In 2004 the Native American Community Academy (NACA) was founded through a community-based process to better serve Native American children; it has since grown into a network of schools committed to taking NACA's core philosophy to other communities around the country. Examples like this demonstrate how important it is to make intentional investment in the codification and dissemination of new HIL models.

Organizing Learning Outcomes into Age-Band Competencies

In place of our current grade-level standards and highly sequenced curriculum, HIL programs need a shared articulation of age-band competencies—a set of knowledge, skills and dispositions that students can be expected to master during each chronological stage of their education, with each stage encompassing multiple years rather than the current nine-month academic year.[25] However, HIL programs will not simply impose these competency frameworks on individual learners; instead, these frameworks will become the backdrop against which to set appropriate but individualized outcomes for each young person.

During Phase 1, HIL programs collectively will need to develop some common procedure by which individual learning plans are developed. Having a commonly articulated process helps mitigate the risk of things such as implicit bias, which can result in building plans that do not adequately reflect students' needs and capabilities. It also provides a concrete point of reference for accountability. Once age-band competencies are established, programs can adapt them to further reflect the values of the community and the goals of the program. A school like NACA serving Native American students, for example, might wish to add the acquisition of a local tribe's language and cultural capabilities as a core competency.[26] A high school HIL program dedicated to serving teen mothers might add outcomes specific to learning about parenting or child development.[27]

These competencies must be paired with measures that can help young people and educators track their progress toward acquisition and mastery.[28] We can say that an eight-year-old student should be able to communicate ideas "appropriately to a range of audience," but what does this mean? Does it mean that they can write a persuasive essay? Organize a fundraising effort? Engage in conversations with strangers? If we expect certain outcomes, we must articulate identifiable tasks and measurable skills. These measures don't need to be comprehensive, and they don't need to be the same for every student, but they must be specific enough that educators, students and families can use them to assess a student's progress over time.

Rather than a sequenced checklist, we can imagine these competencies and outcomes organized more like a bingo board on which students, educators and families can track and check off skills and knowledge as a student masters them. Organizing outcomes in this way enables us to be flexible in thinking about how and when learning happens and "counting" learning that happens outside of formal educational settings. It opens the door for families, out-of-school providers and community organizations to become part of a broader educational ecosystem.

Established HIL networks like Montessori, Expeditionary Learning and Big Picture Learning, as well as the many individual programs that exist, provide a place to begin this work since they already have program-specific growth and learning progressions for the pre-K/ elementary through high school age bands. Other countries have also moved in this direction; New Zealand established comprehensive competency frameworks at a national level.[29] A field-wide articulation of a shared set of expected student outcomes will give the HIL approach greater legitimacy in the eyes of skeptics. It will provide a grounding point for conversations with community leaders and families, and it will help HIL programs develop shared notions of quality practice and effective accountability measures.

New Ways to Track and Assess Learning

For HIL programs, the purpose of assessment is improvement rather than comparison or ranking, and although I discuss assessment separately, it is inextricably linked to how we organize and personalize outcomes and the learning process. How we measure learning reflects broader assumptions about knowledge and measurement. The jagged nature of growth and learning, as well as the personalized outcomes HIL seeks, require us to look beyond Cartesian-Newtonian tools for assessment.[30]

Students can demonstrate knowledge and mastery in many ways, often through some type of performance or some kind of action in the world. This is often referred to as *authentic assessment*. Take swimming: An authentic assessment of my ability to swim is swimming, not writing an essay about swimming. Yet we often find that schools privilege modes of demonstrating knowledge and understanding through verbal expression; a student might not get credit for knowing a math concept on a test unless they can explain in words how they came to the correct answer, even if they are able to perform the computation accurately. Conversely, many students can perform well on a written test about something without really understanding the thing itself; they can master it conceptually without knowing it in any embodied way.

In contrast, HIL programs allow students to engage in real-world projects and receive credit for the work they do and for the results they achieve. Rather than requiring all students to discuss a piece of literature in a written essay, HIL programs allow students to give a presentation or teach a lesson about it to other students. These "performance tasks" require a clear sense of what outcomes we expect from students, expressed using specific performance indicators, sometimes laid out in rubrics that serve two purposes: to set the criteria against which a specific task will be evaluated, and to describe levels of quality for each criterion. A rubric for a restaurant server, for example, might include "knowledge of the menu," "ability to engage with diners" and "service skills," with different levels of performance for each. "Average" performance under "knowledge of the menu" might mean being familiar with popular menu items, being able to make general recommendations and answering questions about ingredients accurately. "Above-average" might include additional skills like being able to recommend wine pairings and answering nuanced questions about how the food is sourced and prepared. Thus the rubric gives us a way to assess the current performance of an individual server while providing them helpful information about how to improve.[31]

Educators, families and researchers have been pushing harder in the last decade to replace standardized test results with data that takes the form of observations, experiences and anecdotes. New Hampshire and Massachusetts have developed alternative assessment systems with a strong focus on performance assessments, as have well-funded initiatives around *deeper learning* and *project-based learning*.[32] The Hawaii Department of Education has launched the Assessment for Learning pilot project, which is focused on creating culturally responsive assessment practices for measuring student progress against the Na Hopena A'o (HA), a set of six interdependent learning outcomes grounded in Hawaiian values, language, culture and history.[33] There has also been considerable recent progress in capturing and tracking student work on non-academic outcomes, an area in which established HIL models and programs, including programs traditionally considered "youth development programs," are far ahead of the curve.[34]

Creating New Accountability Systems

Educators in HIL programs see teaching, learning and growth as emergent, unfolding processes. While outcomes matter, the process itself is just as important, if not more so. Accountability systems are not primarily used to rank and sort but to inform growth and improvement. Our education system generally hasn't been very invested in what is happening to kids as they learn; the question is always: *Did they learn, and if so, how much?*

In the name of ensuring equity and high standards for all students, the conventional approach to accountability has continued in the direction of standardizing outcomes and measuring them in the form of norm-referenced, standardized tests. Such "high-altitude" measurements give us very little insight into the experiences of individual learners or the work of individual schools and educators. Policymakers believed that making results comparable across large numbers of students would lead to higher expectations and better outcomes for traditionally marginalized students. Proponents of this approach argue that too much accountability in the hands of individual principals and teachers leads to widening gaps between different groups of students, whether grouped on the basis of race, class or cognitive ability.

In response, HIL school leaders often point to district and state accountability systems as one of the biggest barriers to their work. These systems equate high scores with "good" schools. But HIL programs often attract students who struggle with standardized, timed, written assessments, and thus no matter how much those students learn from their work at HIL schools, the schools can in the end be flagged for sanction or closure. They are often labeled "alternative" in order to explain why they are being held to a unique and more program-specific set of standards.[35]

We cannot let the shortcomings of the industrial model trap us in this approach to accountability. New approaches aligned with HIL values must be different in three main ways: they must recognize student growth over a multiyear period rather than over nine-month learning cycles; they must honor the value of personalized processes and outcomes for each student; and they must be designed to give support and feedback to schools while providing assurance to stakeholders and communities that all children are being served well.

Collective accountability occurs when organizations balance their internal interests with those of other stakeholders in support of a common goal.[36] In the case of education, the goal is high-quality programs that serve all students well. This collective-accountability approach returns accountability decisions to small communities of educators, students and families, and networks of HIL programs in which educators comprehensively understand the model.

The new accountability process would have room for light oversight by districts and states, but this oversight would be tailored to reflect HIL practice and focused on spot-checking student progress and overall operations rather than ranking students and schools primarily on the basis of standardized testing. A collective-accountability approach would not preclude state-administered standardized tests, but it would shift how the test data are used. Uneven or low performance would not immediately lead to a bad rating, but rather would trigger further examination to better understand the reasons for the performance.

The Student-Centered Accountability Program in Colorado is one such collaborative effort among networked rural districts. Eight years in, their goal is to design and implement an accountability system that is "timely, meaningful, considers the whole child and engage[s] community stakeholders in a continuous cycle of improvement...supported by a community of peers." The program has been welcomed by local communities for its understanding of the schools and educators.[37] Other, more informal networks have had success in the US and internationally. Indeed, systems in UK, the Netherlands, Hong Kong and Finland already integrate such networks into their overall accountability programs.[38]

More than any other part of Phase 1, these new accountability methods will require districts and states to give HIL programs significant freedom from current requirements—perhaps in the form of pilot programs in which schools are allowed to test alternative accountability approaches that are transparent about both the student outcomes being tracked and how the accountability process is being monitored, in exchange for waivers from districts and states.

Supporting Transitions to Post-Secondary Pathways

Admission processes in higher education exert far too much influence on American education. Parents have gone to jail for bribing their kid's way into college. In places such as New York City, they network, connive and finagle to secure spots at the best preschools, assuming this is the first step toward admission at the most elite colleges.[39] High school educators considering new programs find themselves in a bind: how can they assure worried parents that children will be better served by new, more human-centered ways of learning when that means foregoing the traditional measurements that college admissions personnel look at so closely? These worries help keep in place advanced-placement (AP) classes, single-content courses like biology and chemistry, and grade-point-average (GPA) rankings, while discouraging internships, projects and non-traditional learning. This in turn pressures middle schools to prepare kids to be competitive in high school, and so on down the line.

Colleges use SAT and ACT scores, GPAs and AP scores as proxies for evidence that a student has really engaged with school. But we have plenty of evidence that students can elevate their SAT and ACT scores more effectively through targeted test-preparation than by actually studying the material. Most adults acknowledge that scoring well on a test when they were in school was often evidence of how much they could cram into their short-term memories rather than of how much they understood about the subject matter.

Admission processes in higher education can benefit as much as HIL programs from finding new ways to capture qualitative, personalized evidence of students' learning and accomplishments. It's fortunate that such efforts are already under way. The non-profit Colleges that Change Lives was founded in 2006 to advance student-centered college admissions. Administrators of higher education institutions that joined its network helped design college admission processes that ignored standardized test scores in favor of student essays, videos and completed projects.[40] Mastery Transcript Consortium was launched in 2017—a network of private and public high schools around the country whose educators are working to design and promote the use of a digital high school transcript. The Mastery Transcript allows students to upload evidence of learning that is more substantial than scores, such as final projects from internships, letters from supervisors, videos of performances, and travel journals, along with traditional evidence like course grades.[41] Big Picture Education Australia recently released the International Big Picture Learning Credential, a personalized credential that assesses students using six "assessment frames" and developmental progressions: knowing how to learn, empirical reasoning, quantitative reasoning, social reasoning, communication and personal qualities. The tool has been validated by researchers and is already being accepted by higher education institutions around Australia.[42]

In the last five years we have already seen a shift in US colleges' and universities' approaches to admissions, arising mostly from concerns about inherent bias in standardized tests and the reality that many forms of test-preparation are available only to students from wealthy families. Dozens of institutions had already moved to make SATs and ACTs optional prior to the pandemic that began in 2020. The pandemic led dozens more to temporarily waive the tests. And the University of California system announced in May of 2021 that it will drop use of the SAT and ACT entirely from its admission process.[43] Across universities, even GPAs will be weighted differently in admissions for the next several years in light of the challenges of online learning and unequal access to the technologies needed for remote learning.[44]

As universities begin, out of necessity, to devise new admissions processes, Phase 1 should engage them as partners in the effort to capture the kinds of learning and outcomes that emerge from HIL education. Colleges, too, can experiment with pilot programs that include parallel admissions processes for students from HIL schools to see whether the alternative selection criteria lead to more or less desirable student bodies. This would allow educators in the HIL field more time to determine how to capture learning in ways that can be read and appreciated on a college application. A side benefit is that these new ways of capturing and credentialing skills will be more aligned with the types of information needed by employers, enabling students to more easily navigate the dynamic and changing landscape of post-secondary options.

Phase 2: Building Intentional Systems

Phase 2 will multiply the momentum generated in Phase 1, accelerating the growth of HIL as a market share of education overall. The systems and structures designed and/or refined in Phase 1 will be put to work to increase availability and increase the overall quality of HIL programs, which should by this time have a more comfortable foothold in the education system. Phase 2 will continue to connect HIL practitioners with communities, but with a new focus on connecting system leaders with each other across geographies as states begin to translate Phase 1 innovations into actual policies and systems. To be clear, this will be an entirely new period in American education; we have never yet had the opportunity to design and build this level of HIL-aligned infrastructure, nor have we been challenged to do so.

As in Phase 1, the progress in Phase 2 will be non-linear, and different in different places. Communities, regions and states are likely to move from Phase 1 to Phase 2 at different times. However, as the disparate pieces developed in Phase 1 begin to feed each other and policymakers begin to support these changes, the various pockets of momentum will start to converge. The districts and states that are furthest along could enter Phase 2 with the next three to five years.

By that point the field of education will be better equipped to distinguish between bolt-on innovation and HIL-aligned transformation. Districts, states, funders and support organizations will begin targeting money, time and resources toward HIL efforts and striving to keep these efforts separate from bolt-on reforms aimed at improving the conventional system. That said, the two streams of work—transformation and bolting on—will not remain entirely siloed. The lessons and codified resources designed by HIL leaders can be shared with non-HIL programs.

As conventional programs seek to personalize learning, they might, for example, adopt some HIL-developed age-band competencies and begin organizing students into multiage cohorts instead of investing billions more dollars in a rewrite of grade-level academic standards. Instead of another generation of standardized assessments, districts and states might invest in more performance-based assessment.

Relational change in Phase 1 will have transformed the leadership picture in schools, districts, non-profits and government to better reflect the diversity of students and communities. In schools and programs, young people and community members will have more seats at the table, helping to shape policies and practices that further enable HIL work.

At the community level, most families by Phase 2 will have meaningful access to an HIL program in their region, unlike prior years when interest in HIL programs often outstripped capacity. With increased funding and support, educators will now be able to build whole new HIL programs rather than retool conventional or innovative-reform programs or try to build HIL programs within conventional schools. Even when that is not possible, many more educators will be organizing students into multiage classrooms based on HIL age bands and using established, field-wide competency frameworks, performance indicators and rubrics to guide students' learning.

Urban and suburban districts will have at least one HIL option available for students from preschool through high school. The vast majority of rural districts will have incorporated at least some HIL approaches, leveraging technology to connect students with non-local learning opportunities. Furthermore, education may not be as tied to geography by Phase 2, as learning won't be as strictly tied to the school building, and new funding models will have relaxed districts' territorialism. The lines will have blurred between school and community; education and life. Community organizations—museums, non-profits, homes for the elderly, hospitals and other businesses—will be opening their doors for more students to visit, learn, intern and apprentice. Formal and informal systems and structures will facilitate these connections—programs like Big Picture Learning's ImBlaze system[45], and the non-profit organization CommunityShare[46], which helps connect students with community mentors, internships and real-world learning opportunities. Efforts like Remake Learning in Pittsburgh, Pennsylvania, and Reschool Colorado, both committed to increasing the availability of community-based learning experiences for young people, will have inspired similar efforts in communities around the country.[47]

As a result of these relational changes, all students will have much stronger ties to their communities as a whole, and community organizations and businesses will invest more concertedly in local education. By this time there should be more evidence and more consensus among colleges, communities and employers that HIL-program graduates are better prepared than graduates of conventional and innovative-reform schools to navigate the post-secondary world, whether this means enrolling in college or going directly into the workforce.

The Phase 2 structural changes will be in three areas. First, leaders in districts, states, non-profits and advocacy groups will codify and disseminate the collective knowledge of experienced HIL practitioners. Communities shifting toward an HIL approach will have access to new resources: an instructional-model bank; a common set of HIL outcomes to inform accountability frameworks; age-band competencies across the various domains of growth and development, along with performance/mastery indicators; and banks of rubrics—learning progressions and assessment resources aligned to each set of age-band competencies. Second, policymakers will know enough to craft HIL-supportive legislation that can be shared across states, and they will be able to promote state-level support systems that can intervene when communities need outside help. Schools will be authorized to credential and support "anytime-anywhere" learning so that young people can compile life-long records of education incorporating work experience, professional certificates and badges earned through networks of providers. New policies will formalize collective accountability to replace existing state-level accountability systems. State departments of education will facilitate connections between state and national HIL programs, allowing them to continually learn from each other. And third, new educator-preparation programs will emerge in every state, designed around the unique skillsets required in HIL environments. The programs will credential a diverse population of adults to be learning guides and facilitators. Admission to the programs will be based more on a candidate's disposition toward education than on higher-education qualifications.[48]

Over the course of Phase 2, we will see the map of America's education landscape transform. What started in Phase 1 as a map dotted with small pockets of HIL practice—little points of light on the map—will grow as educators and advocates connect and share across district and state boundaries. The lines between learning and life will be blurred as young people learn in museums, businesses and homes, and as they learn to write poems for inaugurations, compose pieces for performance in concert halls and develop lab techniques that can resolve the mysteries of human cognition. The maps of communities will light up, too, as boundaries are crossed, neighborhood divides melt away and institutions and businesses are enriched by the presence of curious, motivated young people learning about the world and sharing their idealism. These new encounters will reignite the connections that underlie any thriving community. As the ideas of HIL spread among schools and among young people, coming generations will learn of the power that comes from interdependence and mutual appreciation. The light spreading over the map is the light of the best in us, set free.

Our Reason

In July of 2018 I sat with thousands of educators from around the country in a cavernous convention hall listening to a young man named Jemar Lee tell the story of his educational journey. His voice cracked slightly as he described how he had spent most of his 16 years hating school, feeling trapped and lacking any sense of purpose. He rebelled and misbehaved as ways to express the hopelessness he couldn't put into words. When he shut down as a young kid and refused to do his work, the punishment was losing out on recess or having his mom come pick him up from school. But as he grew from a young black boy into a young black man in his small Midwestern town, concerned questions evolved into stern reminders that "this is how school is, so just get used to it" and demands that he "push through—other kids do it and so can you."

He tried, but pushing didn't make things better. As his voice continued to be ignored and silenced, he acted out even more, and started losing friends. He got detentions, then suspensions, and eventually disengaged from school completely. Jemar's frustrations ultimately erupted. One afternoon he lost his temper in the school office and was escorted from the school building. He started seeing a counselor, hoping to prove to himself and those in power that there was nothing wrong with him mentally—that the problem was with the education he was receiving.[49]

The convention hall was unusually still while Jemar spoke. I imagine that, like me, many in the crowd were recalling the names, faces and stories of students like him—good kids who ended up on a similar path. We were reliving that crushing feeling that we failed the young people who most needed our help.

Jemar's story ended well. By his sophomore year, Cedar Rapids, Iowa, had completed its Billy Madison Project process and Iowa BIG had opened its doors. Jemar's face brightened as he recalled learning about the school's mission to develop young people who were makers, designers, storytellers, social entrepreneurs and contributors—all within the structure of a program that could see, know and value him as a whole person. His first BIG project emerged directly out of the intersection of his passion—architecture and interior design—and the community's needs: He designed a new learning space for the school, customized for the kind of living and learning that BIG had planned.

"After months of research and putting my knowledge and skills to the test of building something real in the world, I presented my design to the building owner and manager. My plan was not only taken into consideration, it was actually fully implemented." He spent the next three years working in a place he had literally helped build.

BIG saved his life, Jemar said, particularly the relationships he had with educators and other students. The program helped him find his voice, a sense of self and a purpose. He knew—we all knew—how easily he could have wound up in a different type of building, a different type of community.

Jemar is now a young leader in the field of HIL education, travelling the country speaking to leaders in business, education and philanthropy.

He encourages young people to believe that they deserve more from their education. And not just students who obviously struggle as he did; he meets thousands of students who seem to do fine in the current system, but at a huge unacknowledged cost to them and their potential.

"My advocacy for improving the education system for all my peers and the generations behind me has only just started, and I won't stop until every student has the chance to blossom and thrive just like I and many others have in [HIL] environments," he told me. And he tells anyone else who will listen.[50]

This is a unique moment in America. We are now far more aware of what happens when a mechanistic, left-hemispheric view of the world becomes dominant. Old ideas are breaking apart all around us, leaving a vast uncertainty that will either paralyze or catalyze us. We are more aware than ever that our choices about how to balance the values of the left and right hemispheres, individualism and collectivism, progress and sustainability, technology and community, outputs and process, will determine a great deal about the future. They will have impacts on the future of the climate, our economy, our criminal justice system, the weaponization of race in America, and our definitions of human well-being. And education sits at the heart of it all.

Do we continue to raise our children in a system that strips away their humanity and their individuality, and that scolds and stigmatizes the many different ways they might contribute to the world? Or do we build something new? We say we want meaning for our children; we want wellness for them, belonging and genuine fulfillment. We claim to want vital and empowered communities that can care for their own, and a society committed to equality and enriched by differences. We know what it will take to build a system of education and learning that deepens our humanity and that helps young people recognize, care about and be in community with each other. We can see glimpses of that future in the current work of HIL schools and programs.

I am always impressed by the young people I meet who have been shaped by HIL programs—how they make and take their place in the world, whether they are five years old or fifteen. These kids amaze me. But not because they're exceptional. In fact each one is simply a manifestation of the unique brilliance in each of us, if we dare to believe in it and nurture it.

The choice is ours to make.

Applying These Ideas

- Changing the whole education system is a daunting project. It helps to remind ourselves that change can and does begin anywhere. Emergent change takes time, intentional engagement, continued effort, sustained attention and patient capital/resources. *Consider a time in your life or work when it was worth it to "go slow to go fast"; when the best path to success involved slowing down, stepping back and starting again rather than pressing forward.*

- In the most successful communities, everyone is a power broker. Each of us can gather or direct resources, whether that's information, money, time, people or attention. For example, a mother in a recent focus group explained that the volunteer at the front desk of her child's school is an underappreciated resource because he shares information about little-known activities and opportunities in the community. *Think about your sphere of influence when it comes to transforming education. How can you be a power broker—initiate conversations, persuade people, direct resources or mobilize support?*

- Each of us has a vested interest in the education system regardless of whether or not we have school-aged children or work in education. *Visit schools. Listen to young people. Trust your sense of what young people actually need.*

- If you are a student, parent, community member or advocate: *Put together a Billy Madison Project like the one that facilitated Iowa BIG, host a Graduate Profile[51] community conversation to explore what outcomes your community believes are most important for young people to achieve through their education, or go to a school board meeting to push local accountability systems that reflect your values.* (WeAreBornToLearn.org is a good resource for stories from young people and families who are changing their relationships to education.)

- If you are an educator or out-of-school provider working with young people: *Take small steps. Add a Socratic Seminar[52], a Genius Hour[53] or a student-designed project. Offer young people alternative ways to learn and to show what they know. Establish a community circle or restorative practice in your classroom or program. Get to know each young person you work with more deeply by asking them questions and listening to their stories.* (WhatSchoolCouldBe.org is a good resource for details on these approaches and more ideas.)

- If you are a principal: *Do your best to create time and space for your educators to work in transformative ways. Consider advisories as a schoolwide structure.* (Big Picture Learning is a wonderful resource for this.)

- If you are a school board member, state agency head, superintendent or policymaker: *Make room for a pilot program that can lead to transformative work. If you don't have community support, build it. Remove barriers for HIL leaders who are ready to build new systems and structures.*

- If you are a funder: *Invest in long-term wins that might entail short-term risk, and set up metrics for success that value process as well as outcomes. Use your power to invest creatively. Sow the seeds of transformational changes that will move us toward the racial-equality and social-justice goals that have eluded us in education reform so far.*

APPENDIX A

Instructional-Model Elements and Approaches, and Definitions of Instructional Elements

The Instructional Orientations project was aimed at understanding the instructional and systems-level elements that create and support schools that meet the developmental, cognitive and social needs of a wide range of students.[1] It resulted in the development of a framework that provides an understanding of the different ways in which schools organize themselves to meet the developmental and learning needs of students. Providing this understanding is critical to ensuring that parents and students can choose a school that best fits their needs.

Six "instructional-model elements" (IME) emerging out of the IM framework discussed in chapters 5 and 6 were chosen as critical in classifying schools:

- Primary purpose(s)
- How a school addresses the developmental needs of young people
- Approach to discipline and character development
- Beliefs about how learning occurs
- Pedagogical approach
- Ways of assessing student learning

The project found that schools adopt various "approaches" within each of the IMEs. Consider the IME "Ways of assessing student learning." Assessment approaches used by schools include summative (and summative standardized), interim (and interim standardized), student self-assessment, student-developed (including portfolios, exhibitions and passages) and authentic assessment pieces. In some cases it is important to consider subtle distinctions within approaches. For example, all schools address the emotional needs of students in some way. However, educators in some schools adopt policies, procedures and practices around character development, discipline and behavior-management that view emotional development in a more *functionalist* manner than those of other schools, by focusing primarily on emotional management as a way to help students achieve academically. Others adopt what has been described as a *systems perspective* on emotional development, understanding that emotional maturity and development are influenced by age and cognitive maturity as well as by relationships and human dynamics. The policies, procedures and practices adopted in these schools look very different from those at schools with functionalist approaches; they're aimed at helping students recognize, process and manage their emotions in a holistic manner. The nuances are critical to understanding how various schools approach their work and why a school is classified as having a particular educational orientation.

There are guiding beliefs and IME approaches that are correlated and frequently clustered together, in part because many approaches are too contradictory to be adopted by one coherent system. For example, educators who share a theory of learning that is highly linear, sequential and standardized would not adopt a pedagogical approach that embraces the idea that learners don't all master content within the same time frame. These clusters translate into the three educational orientations discussed in chapter 6.

Primary Purpose(s) +Aligned Curriculum	Developmental Needs	Learning Theories	Cognitive Profile Strengths	Pedagogy	Approach to Discipline	Assessment

(1) Academic ("core" focus)
(2) Cognitive (reasoning, remembering)
(3) Physical
(4) Social
(5) Emotional
  • Functionalist
  • Systems
(6) Moral/character education
  • Values articulation
  • Curriculum-embedded
(7) Relationship to community
  • Functional
  • Foundational
(8) Sense of self
(9) Sense of purpose
(10) Social justice
(11) Educational equity
  • Addressing disparities (group)
  • Meet needs of each learner (individual)
	(1) Academic
	(2) Cognitive
	(3) Physical
	(4) Social
	  • Social awareness
	  • Relationship skills
	  • Responsible decision-making
	(5) Emotional
	  • Self-awareness
	  • Self-management
	(6) Relationship to community
	  • Authenticity
	(7) Sense of self
	  • Self-concept (self-understanding, authenticity)
	  • Self-esteem
	(8) Sense of purpose
		Teacher-focused
		(1) Behaviorism
		(2) Cognitivism
		
		Student-centered
		(3) Constructivism
		(4) Connectivism
			(1) Verbal
			(2) Visual/perceptual
			(3) Processing speed
			(4) Working memory
			(5) Attention: executive functioning
			(6) Attention: planning and organization
			(7) Attention: memory
			(8) Socio-emotional factors
				(1) Teacher-directed
				(2) Teacher-guided
				(3) Enquiry-based
				(4) Situational learning
				(5) Design-based learning
				(6) Play-based
					(1) Consequentialist (modified zero tolerance)
					(2) Positive Behavioral Interventions and Supports (PBS)
					(3) Restorative connection
						(1) Summative standardized
						(2) Interim standardized
						(3) Teacher observation
						(4) Student self-assessment
						(5) Student-developed summative projects
						  • Portfolios
						  • Exhibitions
						  • Passages
						(6) Authentic assessment pieces

Definitions of Instructional Elements

A. Purpose; Developmental Needs; Curricular Strands

(1) **Academic**: Primarily defined as reading, writing and mathematics as "core," with science and social studies generally recognized as secondary subjects and often taught through the literacy portion of the day rather than in stand-alone periods. Other subjects are considered "special" (e.g., music, art, and physical education).

(2) **Cognitive:** Pertaining to intellectual efforts such as thinking, reasoning and remembering. Often measured in relationship to reading and mathematics.

(3) **Physical:** Gross and fine motor-development; physical coordination.

(4) **Social:** Social competence refers to a person's ability to get along with others and adapt to new situations. Social skills are the means by which people navigate social and learning contexts, and can be conceptualized as including interpersonal skills and learning-related skills.

    a. *Social awareness*: The ability to take the perspective of and empathize with others from diverse backgrounds and cultures; to understand social and ethical norms for behavior; and to recognize family, school and community resources and supports.

    b. *Relationship skills:* Skills used to establish and maintain healthy and rewarding relationships with diverse individuals and groups. These include communicating clearly, listening actively, cooperating, resisting inappropriate social pressure, negotiating conflict constructively and seeking and offering help when needed.

c. *Responsible decision-making:* Making constructive and respectful choices about one's personal behavior and social interactions based on consideration of ethical standards, safety concerns, social norms, the realistic evaluation of consequences of various actions, and the well-being of self and others.

(5) **Emotional:** Emotional regulation is the ability to control one's emotions and reactions to one's environment. A major part of emotional development in children and adolescents is how they recognize, label and control the expression of their emotions in ways that generally are consistent with cultural expectations.

a. Specific expectations

  i. *Self-awareness:* Accurately recognizing one's emotions and thoughts and their influences on behavior. This includes accurately assessing one's strengths and limitations, and possessing a well-grounded sense of confidence and optimism.

  ii. *Self-management:* Regulating one's emotions, thoughts and behaviors effectively in various situations. This includes managing stress, controlling impulses, motivating oneself and setting and working toward achieving personal and academic goals.

b. *Functionalist perspective:* Emphasizes that emotions serve the function of focusing action to achieve personal goals. Self-management is critical to emotional development because it marks a progressive ability to regulate emotions according to the demands of the physical and social worlds. Often ignores the nuances of developmental capability and the impact of broader social and environmental dynamics.

c. *Discrete states perspective*: Understands emotions as patterns of configurations in the brain, as demonstrated in cognitive neuroscientific studies. Neurochemical processes result in subjective feeling states, with accompanying automatic changes in bodily function and behavior. These give rise to basic emotions. Theorists propose a maturational timetable, beginning in infancy, for emergence of these basic emotions. Emotional development and regulation are dependent on cognition for the most part; cognitive development leads to new abilities to understand and self-regulate basic emotions.

d. *Systems perspective*: Acknowledges the functional utility of emotions and their grounding in discrete feeling states. But it also focuses on how emotions emerge from one's tendency to organize various interacting components such as felt experiences, cognitive appraisals, motivations, functions and control elements. This perspective allows for emotional regulation to be dynamic and open to transformation, since emotions are complex and specific to situations. Emotions also help form the basis of one's self and personality.

(6) **Moral education**
a. *Character education focus/program*: Discrete program that is added to a school's curriculum or values statement.
b. *Infusion approach*: Approach to developing character that includes moral education and student character-development in the central role of education. Includes:

i. Values articulation

ii. Curriculum as a source of moral education and character development

c. *Service learning*: Learning through service, which requires a long-term commitment to an organization or activity. There is an intentional focus on self-reflection and understanding how the process of serving contributed to personal growth and learning. Contrast this approach to those that require students to complete a designated number of volunteer hours.

(7) **Relationship to community:** Starting from birth there is a dialectical process to the development of a person's sense of self in relation to others in the community. Building and sustaining community is critical to supporting this aspect of development.

a. *Functional approach*: Involves establishing a shared set of values or common identity. Students are expected to behave in ways that conform to these shared values and expectations with little regard to the unique needs of individuals.

b. *Foundational approach*: Rests on the assumption that the community and the relationships within it are foundational to a person's personal growth and development. Relationships are seen as intrinsically valuable; their nature, authenticity and quality are considered of primary importance and are understood to shift based on the needs of individual members of a community.

(8) **Sense of self:** Involves answering questions such as Who am I? What am I good at? What are my gifts? Refers to one's perceptions, beliefs, judgments and feelings about who they are as a person.

There are two aspects of the sense of self:

a. *Self-concept*: Assessment of one's own characteristics, strengths and weaknesses. A person's self-concept influences how they behave. Their self-assessment is influenced by how successful their actions have been in the past. Through experience they acquire a sense of efficacy in regard to the degree to which they can do certain things well. Over time a person's specific efficacies for various tasks and activities contribute to their general sense of self.

b. *Self-esteem*: Judgments and feelings about one's own value and worth.

    i. A person's evaluation of themselves depends to some extent on how their performance compares to that of others, especially peers. Adolescents, in particular, tend to judge themselves in comparison to classmates/peers. Those who see themselves achieving at higher levels than others are apt to develop a more positive sense of self than those who consistently find themselves falling short. Research suggests that in order to help students develop a positive sense of self, competition and other situations in which they might compare themselves unfavorably to others should be minimized.

    ii. Children's self-perceptions are affected by how others behave toward them. Adult interest in and engagement with a child is one huge factor in the child's self-perception. Another is membership in one or more groups. In general, children are more likely to have high self-esteem if they are members of successful groups, including their families and ethnic and cultural groups.

(9) **Sense of purpose:** A sense of being involved in something larger than oneself. Transcendental psychology, as a discipline, is relatively new, though the concepts themselves have deep roots in human communities. Transcendental psychologists suggest, as does research into well-being, that it is both a primary human motivation and a human capacity to strive for meaning—to work toward something that transcends self-interests and serves the greater good.

Purpose is a part of one's personal search for meaning, but it also has an external component: the desire to make a difference in the world and to contribute to matters larger than the self. The field of psychology has been slow to recognize the importance of purpose in positive youth development. There are a number of urgent questions concerning how—and whether—young people today are acquiring positive purposes to which they can dedicate themselves.

(10) **Social justice:** The fair and just relationship between an individual and society. This is measured by the explicit and tacit terms that determine the distribution of wealth, social privileges and opportunities for personal activity. Exploring issues of power, privilege and social justice is important for students coming from groups, and/or who identify with groups, that experience social injustice. This includes students from underprivileged, minority and non-dominant identities. However, it is equally important for students coming from groups and/or who identify with groups that benefit from advantage or privilege, since their perspective about the relative "fairness" of social systems relies on their understanding of the origins and structures of these systems.

(11) **Educational equity – two perspectives:**

    a.   Approach to education and schooling in which reforms focus on addressing disparities in educational performance or academic outcomes by increasing funding levels, redesigning school programs, teaching students in different ways and/ or providing comparatively more educational services and academic support to students with greater needs.

    b.   Approach to education and schooling that meets the needs of individual learners. Recognizes that students have different capacities, interests, motivations and aspirations, and makes the individual student (rather than a "group") the unit of analysis and focus. Embraces the goal of ensuring that each student is empowered to leave school with the ability to make the choices they want to make for their future. This looks different for different students.

B. Theories of Learning

(1)   **Teacher-focused:** Theories of learning that are sequential, linear and uniformly paced

    a.   *Behaviorism*: A worldview that assumes a learner is essentially passive, responding to environmental stimuli. The learner starts off as a clean slate and behavior is shaped through positive reinforcement or negative reinforcement. According to behaviorists, learning is a mechanical process of associating stimulus with response, which produces a new behavior. Learning is also defined as a change in the behavior or outcomes that the learner produces.

    b.   *Cognitivism:* The theory that the mind obtains, processes and stores information based on its own cognitive functioning.

This theory was a response to behaviorism. It states that learners are active participants in their learning because the mind functions like a computer processor. Information comes in as inputs, and the mind processes the information and stores it in a way that allows it to be retrieved later. Learning is shaped by helping students strengthen their prior knowledge and attitudes and develop learning strategies. Education is seen as a one-on-one relationship between the learner and the objective material to be learned, so the educational process is often directed toward isolating the learner from all social interactions and distractions.

(2) **Student-centered:** Theories of learning that are developmentally driven, accounting for variations between students regardless of age or grade. Assumes bursts and ebbs in how learning and mastery of concepts and skills occur. Also acknowledges the social context in which learning happens.

　　a. *Constructivism:* The theory that learning results from one's own construction of knowledge. Knowledge is constructed through one's personal experiences and interactions with the outside world. The learner takes in new information and gives meaning to it using their prior attitudes, beliefs and experiences as references. Learners are active participants in the construction of knowledge, while the instructor serves as a facilitator. Constructivists focus on the learner rather than the subject/lesson to be taught, and provide opportunities for learners to learn within a community of learners rather than individually. Learning is a social activity and is intimately associated with our connection to other human beings: teachers, peers, family—even casual acquaintances.

i.   It takes time to learn. For significant learning to occur, people need to revisit ideas, ponder them, try them out, play with them and use them.

ii. Motivation is a key component in learning. Not only is motivation helpful to learning, it is essential for learning.

iii. *Zone of proximal development*: An area of learning that occurs when students are given the hardest tasks they can do, with scaffolding or support, to lead to the greatest learning gains. The teacher must start at the student's level of knowledge and build from there. The zone of proximal development is an area of learning that occurs when a student is assisted by a teacher or peer who has a more developed skill set than theirs. The learner is poised at a moment of growth but cannot complete the task without the assistance of the teacher or peer (students can often complete a task within a group before they are able to complete it on their own). The teacher's job is to move the student's mind forward step by step. Recognition of this zone accepts the fact that teachers cannot teach all children equally; that they must determine which students are ready for which lessons at a particular point.

b.   *Connectivism:* A learning theory in which knowledge exists outside of the learner and the learner makes connections between new and old information to build knowledge. The connections that learners make help them create their own learning network. This connected web helps learners stay up to date with content as it changes. It is important for the learner to be able to identify credible resources. Key ideas include:

i. Learning and knowledge rest in having a diversity of opinions.

ii. Learning is the process of connecting specialized nodes or information sources.

iii. Nurturing and maintaining connections is crucial to facilitating learning.

iv. The ability to identify connections between concepts is important to learning.

v. Decision-making is a learning process, since all information can change and what is viewed as correct one day can be incorrect the next.

C. Cognitive Profile Elements

(1) **Verbal:** The cognitive ability to use and understand language. The ability can be thought of as having a number of components. The most commonly known are:

a. *Language proficiency*: The ability of a person to speak or perform in an acquired language.

b. *Verbal communication*: Communication using language. This can take the form of speech, conversation, handwriting, narratives, manual communication, oral communication, storytelling, vocalization and written communication.

c. *Verbal reasoning*: Understanding and reasoning using concepts framed in words.

d. *Writing skills*: Abilities that enable people to express themselves effectively in writing. These skills are developed through formal education and practice, and include literacy, mastery of written language, vocabulary and verbal ability.

e. *Written communication*: Representation of language in a textual medium through the use of signs or symbols. It is distinguished from illustration, such as cave drawing and painting, and the recording of language using mediums like digital, audio and video.

(2) **Visual/perceptual:** Our visual and spatial skills help us find our orientation in space, perceive objects around us and organize them into a coherent visual scene, or mentally imagine an object that isn't physically present. Mental imagery plays an important part in thought processes, dreams, problem-solving (such as mental calculation), anticipating events, memorizing, understanding a verbal description, reasoning and recognizing objects presented in an unusual way.

(3) **Processing speed:** The pace at which a person takes in visual and auditory information, makes sense of it and begins to respond. It relates to the ability to process information automatically, and therefore speedily, without intentional thought. Key indicators relate to the time taken and speed at which a person performs tasks. A key strategy for people who are slow at processing is to reduce the time pressure associated with a task.

(4) **Working memory/Attention and memory:** Measures of working-memory capacity are strongly related to performance in other complex cognitive tasks such as reading comprehension and problem-solving. People who need to work on their memory skills can have difficulty following directions, immediately recalling information they have just seen or heard, listening to and comprehending lengthy discussions or remembering information long enough to work it through to understanding.

Key strategies are to not overload working memory, to form meaningful associations between new and old knowledge and to develop memory aids.

(5) **Attention—executive functioning:** Executive functions are elaborate functions that control logical reasoning, strategy, planning, problem-solving and hypothetical-deductive reasoning skills. Planning capacities help determine an action plan and define and organize priorities. These are the thinking skills that help individuals plan, set goals, respond to problems and persist on tasks. People who have executive functioning issues have trouble with impulse control, emotional control and flexible thinking.

(6) **Attention—planning and organization:** People who need to work on their attention skills have difficulty sustaining concentration and focusing on an activity while ignoring distractions. They might concentrate on tasks that are exciting or interesting, but have particular difficulty concentrating on activities that are not interesting. These people need support in paying attention, structuring and managing tasks, and organizing work.

(7) **Socio-emotional factors:** As discussed in A(4) and A(5) above, factors to be considered include:
   a. *Social*: Communication and behavioral regulation, arguing, cooperation, temper outbursts, disruptive behavior, socially-appropriate responses to others and impulsiveness
   b. *Emotional*: Sadness, fearfulness, adaptability to change, positive attitude, worry, difficulty rebounding from setbacks, withdrawal.

D. Pedagogical Approaches to Instruction and/or Learning

(1) Teacher-directed

a. Teacher-directed pedagogy, or direct instruction, is explicit instruction that presents information to learners in a way they can easily access, understand and master. All forms of direct teaching share a set of basic principles that include:

    i.   Setting clear objectives for learning

    ii. Systematically organizing instruction to progress from simple to complex ideas and skills

    iii. Ongoing monitoring of student progress

    iv. Frequent questioning and answering

    v. Reteaching content when necessary

    vi. Guided and independent practice

b. Teacher-directed pedagogy operates under the belief that by presenting information to students clearly and explicitly, teachers eliminate the likelihood of misinterpretation. Direct teaching is most suitable for teaching information and skills that are well defined and need to be mastered step by step; for example, mathematical computation, foreign language vocabulary and word recognition and decoding. Research suggests that direct instruction can be beneficial in these situations since it often leads to gains in student achievement and an increase in a student's sense of self-efficacy. Teacher-directed instruction is also often seen as a way to manage students who present difficult behavior in the classroom.

c. Despite these benefits, teacher-directed activities and direct instruction are not always appropriate and/or beneficial. Direct instruction is often inappropriate for children who have learning difficulties, as they often have a limited attention span and are unable to successfully process information presented verbally. This pedagogy also does not incite or develop intrinsic motivation. Direct teaching does not meet social or emotional objectives and does not foster students' creativity and initiative.

(2) **Teacher-guided:** The teacher takes a role in shaping a learning activity for students, modeling and overseeing student execution. This is a form of instruction that falls between teacher-directed and purely enquiry-based pedagogies.

(3) **Enquiry-based:** Enquiry-based instruction starts with the teacher posing questions, problems or scenarios, as opposed to simply presenting established facts or portraying a smooth path to knowledge. The process is often assisted by a facilitator (usually a teacher). Enquirers (students) identify and research issues and questions to develop their knowledge or solutions. Enquiry-based learning includes problem-based learning, and is generally used in small-scale investigations and projects as well as in research projects. Enquiry-based instruction is principally designed to encourage thinking processes and help learners construct meaning.

(4) **Situated/situational learning:** Situated learning was first proposed as a model of instruction among a community of learners. At its simplest, situated learning is learning that takes place in the same context in which it is applied. Theorists argue that learning should not be viewed as simply the transmission

of abstract and decontextualized knowledge from one person to another, but rather as a social process through which knowledge is co-constructed. They suggest that such learning is almost inherently situated in a specific context and embedded in a particular social and physical environment.

(5) **Design-based learning:** A specific type of project-based instruction that engages students in the process of developing, building and evaluating a product they have designed. It encourages a learning context in which students are active participants and construct knowledge instead of passively learning it. Research provides evidence that design-based pedagogy increases students' content knowledge and engagement in working on the design challenge, enables students to transfer knowledge into another task, enables students to learn through collaboration and develops students' positive attitudes toward academic content.

(6) **Play-based:** Play is a complex set of behaviors characterized by fun and spontaneity. It can be sensory, neuromuscular, cognitive or a combination of all three. Play involves repetition of experience, exploration, experimentation and imitation of one's surroundings. Play-based pedagogy stems from research that indicates that what looks like play to adults is actually the way in which young children learn about and make sense of the world. In a play-based program, children choose activities based on their current interests. The play-based classroom is broken up into sections, such as a home, kitchen, science area, water table, reading nook and space with blocks and other toys. Teachers encourage the children to play independently, facilitating social skills along

the way. While this approach is considered relevant primarily in early-childhood and elementary contexts, a growing body of research indicates that it is beneficial in supporting learning for adolescents and adults as well.[2]

E. Approaches to Discipline

(1) **Consequentialist (full or modified zero tolerance):** This approach imposes automatic punishment for infractions of a stated rule with the intention of eliminating undesirable conduct. Zero-tolerance policies forbid even people in positions of authority from exercising discretion or subjectively changing punishments to fit the circumstances. Instead, they are required to impose a predetermined punishment regardless of individual culpability, extenuating circumstances or history. This predetermined punishment need not be severe, but it is always meted out.

(2) **Positive behavioral interventions and support (PBS):** School-wide systems of support that include proactive strategies for defining, teaching and supporting appropriate student behaviors to create positive school environments. Instead of a piecemeal approach using individual behavioral management plans, PBS implements a continuum of support for positive behavior for all students in a school. This includes classrooms and non-classroom settings such as hallways, buses and restrooms. Attention is focused on creating and sustaining primary (school-wide), secondary (classroom) and tertiary (individual) systems of support that make inappropriate behavior less effective, efficient and relevant, and desired behavior more functional.

(3) **Restorative justice / restorative connection:** This approach is based on respect, responsibility, relationship-building and relationship-repairing. It focuses on mediation and agreement rather than punishment. Restorative approaches resolve disciplinary problems in a cooperative and constructive way. If a student misbehaves, they are given the chance to come forward and make things right. The student sits down in a circle with the teacher and the affected parties to work things out together. To facilitate the process, the teacher or mediator asks nonjudgmental, restorative questions like "What happened?" "How did it happen?" and "What can we do to make it right?" Through discussion everyone gains a better understanding as to what happened, why it happened and how the damage can be fixed. Students come up with a plan and fulfill that plan with the intent that their relationship with the affected party will become stronger.

F. Assessments

(1) **Summative:** Summative assessments are used to evaluate student learning, skill-acquisition and academic achievement at the conclusion of a defined instructional period—typically at the end of a project, unit, course, semester, program or school year. Tests, assignments or projects are used to determine whether students have learned what they were expected to learn. Because they are given at the end of the teaching cycle, they are generally evaluative rather than diagnostic (that is, they are better used to determine learning progress and achievement, measure progress toward end goals and make course-placement decisions than they are to help inform improvements to the teaching/learning process).

Summative standardized: Summative standardized assessments are increasingly popular because of the wide variety of assessments available on the market and because of an increased focus on having objective information about student outcomes. Many schools routinely use summative standardized assessments to measure outcomes. The data is then theoretically consistent and can be used to provide uniform professional development and support.

(2) **Interim:** Interim assessments are used to track student learning over the course of a learning unit or project. An interim assessment can be a teacher observation, a short quiz, a review of a writing sample, or a conversation with a student. The critical point is that it is diagnostic and can be used to adjust strategy or pace.

Interim standardized: Interim standardized assessments are becoming more common because of a desire to consistently use data for improvement at a school or grade level. However, the use of interim standardized assessments requires all classroom teachers using the assessment to have taught the same material in a fairly prescribed scope and sequence, which allows far less discretion for teachers to adjust their instruction to meet the needs and interests of students.

(3) **Teacher Observation:** A process by which teachers gather evidence of student learning to inform instructional planning. Specific approaches include anecdotal notes written during lessons that track students' progress toward mastery of learning

targets; anecdotal notebooks; and observation folders for individual students.

(4) **Student self-assessment:** A process by which students monitor and evaluate the quality of their thinking and behavior while learning, and identify strategies that improve their understanding and skills. Student self-assessment depends on teachers providing clear outcomes as well as easily understood and tracked indicators of progress toward those outcomes. Rubrics are the most common tool for facilitating student self-assessment. As students become older they often construct their own rubrics as a way of taking additional ownership of their learning.

(5) **Student-developed summative projects**
   a. *Portfolios*: A student portfolio is a compilation of academic work and other forms of educational evidence assembled for the purpose of (1) evaluating coursework quality, learning progress and academic achievement; (2) determining whether students have met learning standards or other academic requirements for courses, grade-level promotion and graduation; (3) helping students reflect on their academic goals and progress as learners; and (4) creating a lasting archive of academic work products, accomplishments and other documentation. Advocates of student portfolios argue that compiling, reviewing and evaluating student work over time can provide a richer, deeper and more accurate picture of what students have learned and are able to do than more traditional measures that represent a student's achievement at a moment in time.

b. *Exhibitions*: Students present their work through self-selected media in a manner most appropriate to the work and to a relevant community audience.

c. *Passages*: Culminating processes for students in which they present a portfolio of their work over a period of a year or two. Community members (non-teachers) are often involved in the process of reviewing the work and speaking with the student to allow them to explain areas of improvement or particular strengths. Passages often culminate in a formal advancement to a new grade or level.

(6) **Authentic assessment piece**: A student creation that is the natural output of a body of exploration or work that has been undertaken; for example, a performance or a speech to a city council. The final product is determined by the project that was undertaken, not by the need for a certain type of assessment or a specific form of data to be collected that is consistent across a classroom or school. When applying authentic assessment to student learning and achievement, a teacher applies criteria related to construction of knowledge, disciplined inquiry and the value of the achievement beyond the school. Authentic assessment tends to focus on contextualized tasks, enabling students to demonstrate their competency in a real-world setting.

The following image summarizes key defining characteristics of each educational orientation, referencing the definitions above.

ORIENTATION	CONVENTIONAL	WHOLE CHILD/INNOVATIVE REFORM	HUMAN-CENTERED/ LIBERATORY
Purpose	Primarily academic focus aiming towards standardized outcomes	Whole child focus	Individual development
Human development	Limited to little consideration of human development in the design and delivery of curriculum; or school approaches to discipline and culture-building Functionalist approach to social-emotional development, with a focus on strong systems and structures that help direct/manage student behaviors Functional approach to relationship development Self-esteem and self-identity closely tied to values of the school and academic success	Recognition that human development has an impact on school's work; often leads to changes with respect to the social-emotional work of the school, but less on the academic Discrete states perspective on social-emotional development with a stronger focus on helping student manage their emotions More functional approach to relationship development Focus on developing positive self-esteem	Central to school's organization and work; recognition that rates of progress and even student outcomes must be individualized, making standardization difficult Systems perspective to social-emotional development with a primary focus on helping students become self-aware, which in turn leads to self-regulation and management on the part of students Foundational approach to relationship development Students explicitly and intentionally supported in developing a sense of identity as an individual and sense of purpose in relationship to larger community both inside and outside of school
Discipline/ character	Focus on traits aligned to academic success; consequentialist approach Character education/values articulation approach	Character development understood more broadly; often adopt positive behavior intervention and support models Values articulation approach to character building with some elements of curriculum-embedded	Curriculum-embedded exploration of values and character; restorative connections/restorative justice approach Infusion approach to character development; embedded within the curriculum
Theory of learning	Sequential, linear and paced; focus on conceptual learning	Individually constructed; fairly heavy conceptual focus	Developmentally influenced; practical and situational; emphasis on experiential learning
Approach to teaching	Teacher-directed or teacher-guided	Mostly teacher-guided with some room for enquiry-based learning	Primarily enquiry/project-based; situational/internships; career and technical programs emphasized
Assessment of learning	Standardized, norm-referenced summative and interim data	Standardized assessments; some student work	Portfolios; exhibitions; authentic assessments; focus on self-assessment and improved craftsmanship
Cognitive strengths served	Strong verbal, sequential processors; strong working memory; fewer socio-emotional and executive functioning challenges	Strong verbal, sequential processors; reasonable working memory; more capacity to adapt to students with socio-emotional and executive function challenges	High and low verbal processing; high visual-perceptual capabilities; variable processing speed and working memory capability; holistic and sequential processors; can adapt to students with socio-emotional and executive function challenges

APPENDIX B

Examples of Human-Centered/Liberatory Programs in the US

Annie Fisher Montessori (Hartford, CT)
AFM is a Montessori magnet school serving four mixed-age groups: primary (ages 3–6), lower elementary (ages 6–9), upper elementary (ages 9–12), and adolescent (ages 12–14).
https://sites.google.com/hartfordschools.org/anniefishermontessori

Avalon Charter School (St. Paul, MN)
Avalon is a public charter middle school and high school serving students in grades 6 through 12. Avalon places an emphasis on project-based learning.
http://www.avalonschool.org

Blue School (New York, NY)
Blue School is a private school serving approximately 300 "seriously curious" young people from age 2 through grade 8. Teachers balance opportunities to expand students' academic mastery, creative thinking and self and social intelligence with an emphasis on inquiry-based, whole-child education.
https://www.blueschool.org

Boston Day and Evening Academy (Boston, MA)

BDEA is a public charter school serving approximately 400 students in grades 9 through 12. BDEA uses a competency-based model that places students in courses based on their demonstrated skill. https://bdea.com

Boulder Journey School (Denver, CO)

BJS is a year-round private school enrolling over 200 students ages 8 weeks to 6 years. BJS partners with the University of Colorado Denver and the Colorado Department of Education to offer a teacher education program. https://educators.boulderjourneyschool.com

Crosstown High School (Memphis, TN)

First opened for the 2018–2019 school year, Crosstown is currently serving approximately 280 students in the 9th and 10th grades. Crosstown is a public charter school that emphasizes project-based learning and competency-based proficiency standards. https://www.crosstownhigh.org

City-As-School (New York, NY)

City-As-School deploys an external learning model for students who may be at risk of dropping out. City-As-School students are 11th- and 12th-grade transfer students from public, private and parochial schools in New York's five boroughs. https://www.cityas.org

City Garden Montessori (St. Louis, MO)

City Garden is a public charter school serving approximately 275 children

from ages 3 through 14. As a Montessori school, City Garden centers its educational approach on hands-on and individualized learning.
https://www.citygardenschool.org

City Neighbors Charter School (Baltimore, MD)
CNCS is a public charter school serving approximately 230 students in kindergarten through 8th grade. CNCS places an emphasis on project-based learning and arts integration.
https://www.baltimorecityschools.org/schools/326

City Neighbors High School (Baltimore, MD)
CNHS is a public charter school serving approximately 400 students in grades 9 through 12. CNHS's educational philosophy is centered on project-based learning and arts integration.
https://www.cityneighborshighschool.org

Compass Montessori School (Golden, CO)
Compass Montessori is a preschool through 12th grade Colorado public charter school. In keeping with the Montessori model, children progress through a self-paced curriculum at a campus that places an emphasis on indoor and outdoor education and play.
https://www.compassmontessori.org

Compassion Road Academy (Denver, CO)
CRA is a district-managed public innovation school serving at-risk students in 9th through 12th grades. CRA opened in 2013 with the desire to create an educational environment that meets the needs of students who feel left out in a traditional school setting.
https://cra.dpsk12.org

Denison Montessori (Denver, CO)

Denison Montessori is a magnet school that serves nearly 400 children from 3 years old through 6th grade. At Denison children make their way through three programs: primary (age 3–kindergarten), lower elementary (1st–3rd grades) and upper elementary (4th–6th grades). https://denison.dpsk12.org

Denver Academy (Denver, CO)

Denver Academy is a private school serving approximately 750 students in grades 1 through 12. Students are grouped into four divisions: elementary (1st–5th grades), 6th grade, middle school (7th–8th grades) and high school (9th–12th grades). https://www.denveracademy.org

Denver Center for 21st Century Learning (Denver, CO)

DC21 is a district-managed public innovation school designed for students who require a highly supportive, relationship-oriented educational experience. The school serves approximately 165 students in 6th through 12th grade. https://dc21.dpsk12.org

Denver Waldorf School (Denver, CO)

Denver Waldorf School is a private school guided by the educational philosophy of Rudolf Steiner. The school serves children from preschool through 12th grade. https://denverwaldorf.org

Design39Campus (San Diego, CA)

D39C is a public school serving approximately 1,100 students in kindergarten through 8th grade. D39C strives to create a learner-

driven educational environment in which students are given agency of where and how their learning takes place.
https://design39campus.com

Eagle Rock School and Professional Development Center (Estes Park, CO)

Eagle Rock is a private, residential, full-scholarship high school serving approximately 70 students who were not thriving in their previous school, for whom few positive options exist, and who are interested in taking control of their lives and learning.
https://eaglerockschool.org

Embark Education (Denver, CO)

Embark is a private micro-school for grades 6–8 serving 30 students across the three grades. Learning at Embark is embedded into two North Denver businesses, Pinwheel Coffee and Framework Cycles, which ground students' academics in real-world situations.
https://www.embarkeducation.org

Empower Community High School (Aurora, CO)

Empower is a public charter school founded in 2017. As its name implies, Empower was designed to immerse students in an environment that builds and sustains a strong sense of community.
https://empowerhighschool.org

Fannie Lou Hamer Freedom High School (New York, NY)

Fannie Lou Hamer is a public high school that serves approximately 450 students. Located in the Bronx, FLHFHS's academic program emphasizes intellectual development and political and social involvement in society.
https://www.flhfhs.org

Georgia Fugees Academy Charter School (Atlanta, GA)

Fugees Academy is a year-round public charter school that serves students in grades 6 through 12. GFACS was founded to meet the needs of refugee and new American students through English language acquisition, foundational skill study, culturally relevant curriculum and other wraparound supports.
https://www.gfacs.org

Highlands Micro School (Denver, CO)

Highlands Micro School is a non-religious private school in northwest Denver serving approximately 20 students in a mixed-age, learner-centered environment. Students are not assigned homework or grades at Highlands, where a competency-based culture of collaboration, community and curiosity drive the learning for each individual child.
https://highlandsmicroschool.com

High School for Recording Arts (St. Paul, MN)

HSRA is a public charter high school enrolling approximately 200 students that is well known for pioneering the practice of engaging with at-risk students through a hip-hop music program. HSRA has earned the nickname "Hip-Hop High."
http://hsra.org

Innovations High School (Reno, NV)

Innovations High School is Nevada's only Big Picture Learning school, serving approximately 100 students in grades 9 through 12. Innovations encourages students to be self-driven learners in a small, supportive school environment.
https://www.washoeschools.net/innovations

Iowa BIG (Cedar Rapids, IA)

Iowa BIG is a public high school serving students in grades 10 through 12. Iowa BIG places an emphasis on connecting students to their community by splitting learner time between traditional coursework and community-based projects.
https://iowabig.org

Lake Country Day School (Minneapolis, MN)

Lake Country Day is a private school that serves approximately 300 students from pre-kindergarten through 8th grade in the Montessori model.
https://www.lakecountryschool.org

Living School (New Orleans, LA)

Living School is a public charter school serving students in the 9th and 10th grades (as of the 2020–2021 school year). Living School emphasizes project-based learning and a democratic structure designed to include the voices of students, family and staff.
https://www.livingschoolnola.org

The Logan School for Creative Learning (Denver, CO)

The Logan School is a private school that serves nearly 300 students in kindergarten through 8th grade, with the mission of cultivating the curiosity of gifted children.
https://www.theloganschool.org

Lumin East Dallas Community School (Dallas, TX)

LEDCS is a public charter school that serves approximately 600 children ages 3 through 9. LEDCS provides on-site Montessori education for students and a home-visiting parent-education program for pregnant women and for parents with children through age 3. https://lumineducation.org/campus/lumin-east-dallas-community-school

The Met (Providence, RI)

The Met is a network of six small public high schools, three of which are located in Providence, Rhode Island. The Met centers its educational experience on internships, individual learning plans and a college transition program.
https://www.themethighschool.org

Metropolitan Expeditionary Learning School (New York, NY)

MELS is a public school that serves over 840 students in grades 6 through 12, with a stated focus on science, technology and sustainability. The school is located in Queens, New York.
https://metropolitanels.com

MetWest High School (Oakland, CA)

MetWest is a public school that serves approximately 245 students with a focus on internship-based education.
https://www.ousd.org/metwest

Millennium School (San Francisco, CA)

Millennium School is a private school serving approximately 90 students in 6th through 8th grade. As an innovation lab, Millennium School is partnering with universities to develop an integrated educational program based on neuroscience and developmental psychology.
https://www.millenniumschool.org

The Mountain School of Milton Academy (Vershire, VT)

The Mountain School is a private semester program for high school juniors. Each semester 45 students from all over the country come together to live and work on the school's farm in rural Vermont. Courses provide a demanding, integrated learning experience that takes advantage of the school's small size and mountain campus. http://www.mountainschool.org/

Native American Community Academy (Albuquerque, NM)

NACA is a public charter school serving students in elementary, middle and high school (grades K–12). NACA's student body includes children from more than 60 American Indian tribes. https://www.nacaschool.org

The Nautilus School (Chicago, IL)

The Nautilus School is a private school serving children from ages 4 through 9 in mixed-age classes. Their one-room schoolhouse is designed to allow children of various ages and abilities to learn in a shared space. https://www.nautilusschoolchicago.org

Nawayee Center School (Minneapolis, MN)

Nawayee Center School is an alternative public school focusing on American Indian youth in grades 7 through 12. The school provides transformative education grounded in indigenous life-ways and love of learning. http://www.centerschool.org

New Roads School (Los Angeles, CA)

New Roads is a college preparatory K–12 private school serving approximately 500 students in Santa Monica. New Roads houses four programs: Lower School (kindergarten–5th grade), Middle School (6th–8th grade), Upper School (9th–12th grade), and the Spectrum Program. The Spectrum Program is for students in grades 6 through 12 who meet the diagnostic criteria specified in the revised Diagnostic and Statistical Manual of Mental Disorders (DSM–5) for autism spectrum disorder. Spectrum Program students receive accommodations such as extended time on tests, extended time on large projects, peer notes, small-group testing and preferential seating at the front of the room. https://www.newroads.org

Norris Academy (Mukwonago, WI)

Norris is a public school district located in rural Waukesha County. Norris is the smallest school district in the state of Wisconsin, and has developed an innovative learner-centric educational service model. https://norrisacademywi.org

Oak Grove School (Oaja, CA)

Oak Grove School is a private pre-kindergarten through 12th grade school serving approximately 200 children. Oak Grove School is part of the Krishnamurti Foundation, a non-profit organization based on the life and spiritual teaching of Jiddu Krishnamurti. https://oakgroveschool.org

Portfolio School (New York, NY)

Portfolio School is a private school serving students in kindergarten through 6th grade. Portfolio School places an emphasis on immersive,

project-based learning.
https://www.portfolio-school.com

Rock Tree Sky (Oaja, CA)

Rock Tree Sky is a private school serving approximately 105 students ages 5 to 18. Rock Tree Sky provides a learner-centric, "open-walled" educational environment.
https://www.rocktreesky.org

San Diego Met High School (San Diego, CA)

SD Met is a public magnet high school in the San Diego Unified School District, and part of the Big Picture Learning network. SD Met emphasizes Advisory, internships and exposure to college courses starting in grade 10.
https://sdmet.sandiegounified.org

Stanley British Primary School (Denver, CO)

Stanley BPS is a K–8 school guided by an instructional philosophy that can be best described as constructivism. Constructivists believe students must actively "construct" their knowledge and understanding for themselves through firsthand experience.
https://www.stanleybps.org/stanleybps

The Urban Assembly (New York, NY)

The Urban Assembly is a non-profit organization that forms and manages a network of 23 New York City public secondary schools. The Urban Assembly schools are located in Manhattan, Brooklyn and the Bronx.
https://urbanassembly.org

Urban Montessori Charter School (Oakland, CA)

Urban Montessori is a tuition-free transitional kindergarten through 8th grade public charter school serving approximately 430 students. Urban Montessori is based on the teachings of Maria Montessori, in combination with design thinking and arts integration. https://www.urbanmontessori.org

Washington Heights Expeditionary Learning School (New York, NY)

WHEELS serves approximately 950 students from pre-kindergarten through 12th grade in Manhattan. Expeditionary Learning centers on developing students through project-based learning expeditions. https://www.wheelsnyc.net

Workspace Education (Bethel, CT)

Workspace Education is a 501c3 non-profit that emphasizes co-learning to bring students, families and educators together for the shared purpose of learning. Workspace Education serves approximately 65 students ages 5 to 18. https://www.workspaceeducation.org

Sites

Alliance for Public Waldorf Education

The mission of the Alliance for Public Waldorf Education is to support the development of high-quality public Waldorf education.
http://publicwaldorf.org

NACA Inspired Schools Network

NISN is building a movement to create excellent schools that are relevant to the communities they serve. NISN works with Fellows who are committed to Indigenous communities to establish schools that will create strong leaders who are academically prepared, secure in their identities, healthy and will ultimately transform their communities.
http://www.nacainspiredschoolsnetwork.org

National Center for Montessori in the Public Sector

NCMPS works to promote, grows and sustains Montessori education in the public sector.
https://www.public-montessori.org

One Stone (Boise, ID)

One Stone is a student-driven non-profit that promotes student voice and provides high school students with opportunities to drive their learning and practice twenty-first-century skills.
https://onestone.org

Progressive Education Network

PEN's mission is to harness the dynamic power of progressive practice for the next generation of students, schools and democracy. PEN

promotes student-driven learning, elevating the voice of educators and diversity in school and society.
https://progressiveeducationnetwork.org

Reaching At-Promise Students Association

RAPSA's mission is to improve the lives of at-promise students by providing professional development experiences for educators who work with the opportunity youth population.
https://rapsa.org

ENDNOTES

1. Where appropriate these thinkers' works are cited throughout the book, but among those who most strongly influenced my thinking are Karen Armstrong, Jared Diamond, Modris Eksteins, Ibram X. Kendi, Jill Lepore, Madhusree Mukerjee, Leonard Schlain and Barbara Tuchman.
2. I highly recommend the curriculum/courses offered by the Racial Equity Institute for those interested in understanding why and how these forces have come to be particularly entrenched in America's economic, political and legal systems.

Chapter 1

1. *National Center on Education and the Economy,* 1990.
2. *National Commission on Excellence in Education,* 1983.
3. *National Center on Education and the Economy,* 1990.
4. Klein, 2015.
5. Goldstein, 2019, December 3.
6. Kamenetz, 2014; Crisafulli, 2006.
7. McGilchrist, 2009, pp. 16–29.
8. For a helpful overview of his ideas see McGilchrist, 2012.
9. Rowson & McGilchrist, 2013.
10. Ibid.
11. McGilchrist, 2009, pp. 209–237.
12. McGilchrist, 2009, pp. 32–93.
13. McGilchrist, 2009, pp. 428–434.
14. Riser-Kositsky, 2019.
15. Rowson & McGilchrist, 2013
16. Autism Speaks, 2020; Daw, 2001; McGilchrist, 2009, pp. 405–407.
17. Rowson & McGilchrist, 2013.
18. Rowson & McGilchrist, 2013.
19. McGilchrist, 2009, pp. 1–14.
20. Sharma R., 2017.
21. Brenneman, 2016.
22. Riddle & Sinclair, 2019.
23. Riddle & Sinclair, 2019.
24. Twenge, 2019.
25. Pirani, 2018.
26. Child Trends, 2019.
27. Child Trends, 2019.

28. Partnership to End Addiction, 2014.
29. Shlain, 1999, pp. 1-44; McGilchrist, 2009, pp. 32–93.
30. Chapman, 2016; Austin & Pisano, 2017.
31. Meister, 2012.
32. Lund et al., 2019.
33. "Vocational Skills," 2016.
34. Lund et al., 2019.

Chapter 2
1. Becker & Lopatto, 2018.
2. Weiner, 2016.
3. Kirby, 2018.
4. The Audiopedia, 2017.
5. Lepore, 2018, p. 8-9.
6. *Holy Bible*, New International Version, 2011, Gen. 1:28.
7. Lepore, 2018, p. 9.
8. Lepore, 2018, p. 11; Kendi, 2016, pp. 15–21.
9. Crosland, 1971, p. 97.
10. Capra, 1983, pp. 40–41.
11. Russell, 1961, pp. 442–451.
12. Ibid.
13. Capra, 1983, p. 44.
14. Capra, 1991, pp. 166–172.
15. Cranston, 1957, p. 196.
16. Russell, 1961, pp. 740–747.
17. Jackson, 1970, pp. 196–230; Kendi, 2016, pp. 15-20; Lepore, 2018, pp. 10–12.
18. Lepore, 2018, pp. 11–13.
19. Lepore, 2018, pp. 13–15.
20. Mullainathan & Shafir, 2013; Okun, n.d.; Schaef, 1998.
21. Sivin, 2005.
22. Ibid.

Chapter 3
1. Connelly, 2017; Woods, Madeleine. (2018, November 13). Personal interview.
2. Hansen, 2007, pp. 41–50; Miller, 1990, pp. 1–56; Russell, 1961, 742–747; Wardle, 1976, p. 3.
3. Digby & Searby, 1981, pp. 7-10; Wardle, 1976, p. 9–23.
4. Lawton & Gordon, 2002, pp. 116–119; Wardle, 1976, 88–89.
5. Lawton & Gordon, 2002, pp. 101–114.
6. Smuts, 1926, p. 100; Hansen, 2007, pp. 36–40.
7. Ibid.
8. Gleick, 1987, pp. 81–118.

9. Kramer, 1976; Standing, 1998; Hansen, 2007, pp. 57–79.
10. Steiner and Stebbing, 1999; Hansen, 2007, pp. 80–101.
11. Hansen, 2007, pp. 102–123; Luytens, 1975.
12. Hansen, 2007, pp. 129–157.
13. Hansen, 2007, pp. 35–41.
14. Smuts, 1926, pp 13, 95–105
15. Hansen, 2007, 35–41.
16. Ibid.
17. Hansen, 2007, pp 129–147

Chapter 4
1. Laloux, 2014, pp. 2–5.
2. Mandelbrot, 1982.
3. Gleick, pp. 83-98.
4. Brown, 2017.
5. Hansen, 2007, pp. 126–147.
6. Ibid.
7. Hansen, 2007, pp. 147–153.
8. De Craemer, 1983; Hansen, 2007, pp. 147–159; Hogenboom, 2015; Taylor, 1985, p. 97.
9. De Craemer, 1983; Hart, n.d.; Naming Traditions, 2007.
10. De Craemer, 1983; Hansen, 2007, pp. 147–150; Pring, 1984.
11. Hansen, 2007, pp. 165–168.
12. Science of Learning & Development Alliance, n.d.
13. Hansen, 2007, pp. 165–168. This was quite remarkable for the time period; the field of developmental psychology, led by thinkers such as Jean Piaget, wouldn't emerge until the 1920s, and human development as a field of study did not begin until the 1970s.
14. Friedman, 2001.
15. Hansen, 2007, pp. 161–164.
16. Hansen, 2007, pp; 148–163; Transformation Design, 2020.
17. McGilchrist, Iain (2016, October 21). Personal interview.
18. Of course, there are foundational skills that we can predict most students will be expected to master, however, the level of commonality around student outcomes will be most pronounced during the elementary age band, and will gradually decrease as students reach the end of high school. This will be discussed again in chapter 7.
19. Hansen, 2007, pp. 259–260 and pp 165–170.

Chapter 5
1. Kiersz & Gould, 2017
2. Jones, 2020; Sheffield, 2019.
3. Kiersz & Gould, 2017.

4. Costello-Dougherty, 2009; Pappano, 2011; Whitescarver, 2010.
5. Ervin et al., 2010; Freidlaender et al., 2015.
6. The content of this chapter is covered in greater detail in my doctoral dissertation (Hansen, 2007). It can be accessed online through the Oxford University Research Archive with this specific link: https://ora.ox.ac.uk/objects/uuid:6a51f6c8-3821-4fc5-b329-728b02921e47
7. Hansen, 2007, pp 102–123.
8. While I am limiting my examples in this chapter to the models being examined, this robust and authentic engagement of family and community is a hallmark of HIL programs for reasons we will explore more deeply in chapter 6.
9. Lipset, Michael (2021, February 24). Personal interview.

Chapter 6
1. Defense Advanced Research Projects Agency, n.d.; Belfiore, 2010
2. Kaplan & Saccuzzo, 2012; DeVore, Christine (2016, December 16). Personal interview.
3. Hansen, 2017.
4. During the Instructional Orientations project, it was found that this is in contrast to programs in other orientations in which terms like *friend*, *crewmate* or simply *classmate* are more commonly used to refer to students.
5. In response to criticism over the years, Teach for America has tried to strengthen its preparation of corps members; however, the training is still organized around elements of the conventional approach to education, including lesson design and delivery and classroom management. A great deal of their formal training is also completed concurrent to their time as corps members.
6. Strauss, 2019; White, 2015.
7. DeVore, Christine (2016, December 16). Personal interview.
8. Riser-Kositsky, 2019.
9. This claim is based on interviews with conventional orientation school/program leaders (most of whom asked not to be named), as well as a look at longitudinal trends in the performance of college prep / conventional-orientation programs in districts in which portfolio efforts led to concentrated efforts to increase their overall market share between 2005 and 2015. There is no formal research on this question since research funding is often available only for questions that fit into the dominant worldview framework.
10. See Appendix A, which provides descriptions of different pedagogical approaches.
11. Ro, 2019.
12. See Appendix A, which provides descriptions of different disciplinary approaches.
13. I would often describe this to parents using the metaphor of a bowling alley. Imagine children need to roll balls down eight different lanes, each lane representing a different domain like gross motor skills, fine motor skills, literacy, numerical understanding, social skills and emotional skills. They cannot do all of it at the same time. It is perfectly normal for different children to grow within different domains at different

rates and in different orders. The challenge is that educational policies, especially with the more recent focus on grade-level standards and increased accountability for uniform progressions toward "3rd grade literacy," have pathologized "normal" developmental differences. This is also true of expectations around student behavior, including social and emotional skills and self-regulation.

14. See Embark Education in Appendix B.
15. Arnold & Mihut, 2020; New York Performance Standards Consortium, 2012.
16. See Appendix A, which provides descriptions of various pedagogical approaches.
17. Tienken, 2017.
18. See, for example, WorkSpace Education and Reaching At-Promise Students Association in Appendix B.

Chapter 7

1. Juma, 2017.
2. "Diffusion of Innovations," 2021.
3. Battaglia, 2020; Calkins, 2021.
4. Strauss, 2020.
5. "School district," 2020.
6. Belkin et al., 2019; Fox, 2014; Goldstein & Patel, 2019; Jaschik, 2019.
7. Binkovitz, 2016; Ewing, 2018; Jason, 2017.
8. Deloitte, 2020.
9. See Learning Environments page at Education Reimagined, n.d. (not comprehensive); ProPublica, 2017; Montessori Census, n.d.
10. This is based on conversations with dozens of students in programs around the US who have found and enrolled in HIL and/or alternative programs after finding their traditional programs uninspiring. It's interesting that many of them talked about the challenge they faced in adapting to programs in which they were required to take ownership and agency, capabilities they had not been required to develop in their prior programs.
11. A small sampling of programs, which I have visited and/or know reasonably well, can be found in Appendix B.
12. Asmar & Meltzer, 2019.
13. DPS Imaginarium, 2019.
14. Kania et al., 2018 – this model was informed by the FSG systems change model
15. See Iowa BIG in Appendix B
16. Houk, 2010.
17. Hansen, 2007, pp 163-165.
18. Menakem, 2017, pp. 3-133; Phillips, M. A.; https://www.alchemyoftrauma.com
19. American Montessori Society, n.d.; Hansen, 2007, pp. 57–77; Montessori Center School, 2019.
20. Debs, 2016.
21. "Reggio Emilia Approach," 2021; https://toolsofthemind.org/
22. Cousins, 2000; Hanford, 2015

23. Washor et al., 2021
24. Washor & Mojkowski, 2013
25. Achieve, 2015; New Zealand Ministry of Education, 2020; Sturgis, 2018.
26. Native American Community Academy, n.d; Rice, 2020.
27. Rukundo-Karaara et al., 2020; http://www.centerschool.org/ and https://www.newlegacycharter.org/
28. Centre for Teaching Support & Innovation, n.d.
29. New Zealand Ministry of Education, 2020.
30. Safir & Dugan, 2021.
31. Brookhart, 2013.
32. Reaching Higher NH, 2018; http://www.performanceassessment.org/
33. Taira & Sang, 2019.
34. Washor et al., 2021; http://www.performanceassessment.org/research
35. "Alternative School," 2020.
36. Noguera & Noguera, 2018; Schneier, 2012, pp 61–121.
37. Colorado Rural Schools Alliance, 2015.
38. Rothman, 2018; Knecht et al., 2016.
39. Belkin et al., 2019; Fox, 2014; Jaschik, 2019.
40. https://ctcl.org/
41. https://mastery.org
42. White, Viv (2021, January 25). Personal interview. (Big Picture Learning Australia's work on student competencies.)
43. McDonnell, 2021.
44. Jaschik, 2018; University of California, 2020; The College Post, 2020.
45. https://www.bigpicture.org/apps/pages/imblaze
46. https://www.communityshare.us/vision-and-story/
47. https://remakelearning.org/about;http://www.reschoolcolorado.org/out-of-school-learning
48. Interviews with HIL leaders indicate that they often hire based far more on candidates' dispositions toward education and demonstrated ability to work productively with students than on formal training. For this reason HIL programs are far more successful at recruiting and retaining diverse staff and, in many cases, learning guides/educators who come from the communities in which they work. HIL-specific adult-preparation programs are likely to value applicants who are different from those considered by more conventional programs.
49. Aurora Institute, 2018. Note: Jemar is a junior at Morningside University double-majoring in business administration and public policy & social entrepreneurship, with minors in sociology and pre-legal studies. He will graduate in May of 2022. He continues his education advocacy as a fellow with a national non-profit and volunteers for another. He has also been interning with an energy company in the Midwest for four years. Jemar is working with Morningside's administration and faculty to launch the Adventure Program, an effort to embed transformative education practices in the institution.

50. Lee, 2017.

51. A *Graduate Profile* is a way for a community (whether a school or district) to identify and focus on a core set of learning goals for young people, goals that support the development of skills, knowledge and dispositions that a community believes matter in school and beyond. Developing a Graduate Profile should be a community-wide effort that engages as many stakeholders as possible. Not only does this help ensure that the profile reflects a broad set of perspectives, it also sets the stage for engaging a broad set of stakeholders in creating learning experiences for young people. The Global Online Academy has a useful article entitled "Designing a Graduate Profile: Four Essential Steps" that is a helpful reference.

52. A Socratic Seminar is a formal discussion, based on a specific piece of text, in which the leader asks open-ended questions. In the context of the discussion, participants listen closely to the comments of others, thinking critically for themselves, and articulate their own responses. Participants can choose their own topics and gradually learn to take complete ownership of the process.

53. A Genius Hour is a project in the classroom in which students are allowed to explore their individual passions and wonders for a set period of time, from one hour per week to 20 percent of their total class time.

Appendix A

1. Hansen, 2017.

2. Brown, S., 2010.

REFERENCES

Achieve. (2015). *The role of learning progressions in competency-based pathways.* https://www.achieve.org/files/Achieve-LearningProgressionsinCBP.pdf

Adjapong, E. S. & Emdin, C. (2015). Rethinking pedagogy in urban spaces: Implementing hip-hop pedagogy in the urban science classroom. *Journal of Urban Learning Teaching and Research, 2015*(11), 66–77. https://files.eric.ed.gov/fulltext/EJ1071416.pdf

Adorno, T. W. & Horkheimer, M. (1979). *Dialectic of enlightenment.* Verso Editions.

Alcoff, L. & Potter, E. (Eds.). (1992). *Feminist epistemologies.* Routledge.

Alexander, M. (2020). *The new Jim Crow: Mass incarceration in the age of colorblindness.* The New Press.

Allard, J. W. (2005). *The logical foundations of Bradley's metaphysics.* Cambridge University Press.

Alternative school. (2020, December 20). In *Wikipedia.* Retrieved February 10, 2021, from https://en.wikipedia.org/wiki/Alternative_school

American Montessori Society. (n.d.). *5 core components of Montessori education.* Retrieved February 10, 2021, from https://amshq.org/About-Montessori/What-Is-Montessori/Core-Components-of-Montessori

Andersen, K. (2017). How America lost its mind. *The Atlantic.* https://www.theatlantic.com/magazine/archive/2017/09/how-america-lost-its-mind/534231

Andersen, K. (2020, August 7). College-educated professionals are capitalism's useful idiots. *The Atlantic.* https://www.theatlantic.com/ideas/archive/2020/08/i-was-useful-idiot-capitalism/615031

Andersen, K. (2020). *Evil geniuses: The unmaking of America: A recent history.* Random House.

Appelbaum, B. (2020). *The economists' hour: False prophets, free markets, and the fracture of society.* Back Bay Books.

Apple, M. W. (1993). *Official knowledge: Democratic education in a conservative age.* Routledge.

Apple, M. W. (1996). *Cultural politics and education.* Open University Press.

Armstrong, K. (1994). *A history of god: The 4,000-year quest of Judaism, Christianity and Islam.* Ballantine Books.

Arnold, K. & Mihut, G. (2020). Post-secondary outcomes of innovative high schools: The big picture longitudinal study. *Teachers College Record, 122*(8). https://www.esri.ie/publications/post-secondary-outcomes-of-innovative-high-schools-the-big-picture-longitudinal-study

Aronowitz, S. & Giroux, H. A. (1991). *Postmodern education: Politics, culture, and social criticism.* University of Minnesota Press.

Asmar, M. & Meltzer, E. (2019, August 12). *In a postmortem, leaders of Denver's Imaginarium say test scores, bureaucracy are stifling innovation.* Chalkbeat Colorado. https://co.chalkbeat.org/2019/8/12/21108609/in-a-postmortem-leaders-of-denver-s-imaginarium-say-test-scores-bureaucracy-are-stifling-innovation

Aurora Institute [@Aurora_Inst]. (2018, July 23). *Jemar Lee had a lightbulb moment when he transitioned to a student-centered learning environment* [Tweet; video]. Twitter. https://twitter.com/Aurora_Inst/status/1021382421458010114

Austin, R. D. & Pisano, G. P. (2017). Neurodiversity as a competitive advantage. *Harvard Business Review.* https://hbr.org/2017/05/neurodiversity-as-a-competitive-advantage

Autism Speaks. (2020, March 26). *CDC estimate on autism prevalence increases by nearly 10 percent, to 1 in 54 children in the U.S.* [Press release]. Retrieved from https://www.autismspeaks.org/press-release/cdc-estimate-autism-prevalence-increases-nearly-10-percent-1-54-children-us

Ayer, A. J. (1956). *The problem of knowledge.* St. Martin's Press.

Ball, S. (1990). *Politics and policy making in education: explorations in policy sociology.* Routledge.

Barrett, W. (1987). *Death of the soul: From Descartes to the computer.* Oxford University Press.

Battaglia, J. (2020, April 30). *How the Met was ready to pivot thanks to their start-up mindset.* Education Reimagined. https://education-reimagined.org/how-the-met-was-ready-to-pivot-thanks-to-their-start-up-mindset

Bauman, K. J. (2001). Home schooling in the United States: Trends and characteristics. Retrieved September 16, 2007, from https://www.census.gov/content/dam/Census/library/working-papers/2001/demo/POP-twps0053.pdf

Becker, R. & Lopatto, E. (2018, May 15). *Yanny or Laurel? The science behind the audio version of The Dress.* The Verge. https://www.theverge.com/2018/5/15/17358136/yanny-laurel-the-dress-audio-illusion-frequency-sound-perception.

Behr, G. & Rydzewski R. (2021). *When you wonder, you're learning: Mister Rogers' enduring lessons for raising creative, curious, caring kids.* Hachette Go.

Belfiore, M. (2010). *The department of mad scientists: How DARPA is remaking our world, from the internet to artificial limbs.* Harper Perennial.

Belkin, D., Levitz, J. & Korn, M. (2019, May 21). Many more students, especially the affluent, get extra time to take the SAT. *The Wall Street Journal.* https://www.wsj.com/articles/many-more-students-especially-the-affluent-get-extra-time-to-take-the-sat-11558450347

Berliner, D. C. & Biddle, B. J. (1995). *The manufactured crisis: Myths, fraud, and the attack on America's public schools.* Addison-Wesley.

Binkovitz, L. (2016, August 2). *School closures tend to displace black, poor students with few positive outcomes.* Kinder Institute Research. https://kinder.rice.edu/2016/08/02/school-closures-tend-to-displace-black-poor-students-with-few-positive-outcomes

Block, P. (2018). *Community: The structure of belonging.* Berrett-Koehler Publishers.

Bohm, D. & Peat, F. D. (2000). *Science, order, and creativity.* Routledge.

Brenneman, R. (2016, March 22). Gallup student poll finds engagement in school dropping by grade level. *Education Week.* https://www.edweek.org/leadership/gallup-student-poll-finds-engagement-in-school-dropping-by-grade-level/2016/03

Brookhart, S. M. (2013). *How to create and use rubrics for formative assessment and grading.* ACSD. http://www.ascd.org/publications/books/112001/chapters/What-Are-Rubrics-and-Why-Are-They-Important%C2%A2.aspx

Brown, A. M. (2017). *Emergent strategy: Shaping change, changing worlds.* AK Press.

Brown, S. & Vaughan, C. (2010). *Play: How it shapes the brain, opens the imagination, and invigorates the soul.* Avery.

Burke, C. & Grosvenor, I. (2003). *The school I'd like: Children and young people's reflections on an education for the 21st century.* Routledge-Falmer.

Cain, S. (2012). *Quiet: The power of introverts in a world that can't stop talking.* Crown Publishing Group.

Calkins, A. (2021, January 26). *The question everyone in public education should be asking right now.* Next Generation Learning Challenges. https://www.nextgenlearning.org/news/the-question-everyone-in-public-education-should-be-asking-right-now

Capra, F. (1991). *The Tao of physics.* Flamingo.

Capra, F. (1983). *The turning point: Science, society, and the rising culture.* Fontana.

Carnie, F. (2002). *Alternative approaches to education: A guide for parents and teachers.* Routledge.

Carr, D. (2003). *Making sense of education: An introduction to the philosophy and theory of education and teaching.* Routledge Falmer.

Centre for Teaching Support & Innovation. (n.d.). *What are learning outcomes?.* University of Toronto. Retrieved February 10, 2021, from https://teaching.utoronto.ca/teaching-support/course-design/developing-learning-outcomes/what-are-learning-outcomes/

Chapman, G. (2016, August 28). *Autism a Silicon Valley asset with social quirks.* Phys.org. https://phys.org/news/2016-08-autism-silicon-valley-asset-social.html

Child Trends. (2019). *Suicidal teens.* Retrieved February 8, 2021, from https://www.childtrends.org/?indicators=suicidal-teens

Chopra, D. (1989). *Quantum healing: Exploring the frontiers of mind/body medicine.* Bantam.

Chopra, D. (1991). *Unconditional life: Mastering the forces that shape personal reality.* Bantam.

Chopra, D. (1993). *Ageless body, timeless mind: A practical alternative to growing old.* Rider.

Christakis, E. (2017). *The importance of being little: What young children really need from grownups.* Penguin Books.

Clark, E. T., Jr. (1988). The search for a new educational paradigm: The implications of new assumptions about thinking and learning. *Holistic Education Review, 1*(1), 18–30.

Cobb, J. B., Jr. (1988). Ecology, science and religion: Toward a postmodern worldview. In D. R. Griffin (Ed.), *The reenchantment of science: Postmodern proposals.* State University of New York Press.

Colorado Rural Schools Alliance. (2015). *SCAP: Student Centered Accountability Project.* Retrieved February 10, 2021, from http://www.coruralalliance.org/scap.html

Connelly, E. (2017, April 19). Getting medieval on bacteria: Ancient books may point to new antibiotics. *Scientific American.* https://www.scientificamerican.com/article/getting-medieval-on-bacteria-ancient-books-may-point-to-new-antibiotics

Costello-Dougherty, M. (2009, August 31). *Waldorf-inspired public schools are on the rise.* Edutopia. Retrieved February 25, 2021, from https://www.edutopia.org/waldorf-public-school-morse

Cottam, M., Dietz-Uhler, B., Mastors, E. & Preston, T. (2004). *Introduction to political psychology.* Taylor & Francis.

Cousins, E. (Ed.). (2000). *Roots: From outward bound to expeditionary learning.* Kendall Hunt Publishing Company.

Cranston, M. W. (1957). *John Locke: A biography.* Longmans Green.

Crisafulli, T. P. (2006). No educator left unscathed: How no child left behind threatens educators' careers. *Brigham Young University Education and Law Journal, 2006*(2), 613–637. https://digitalcommons.law.byu.edu/elj/vol2006/iss2/7

Crosland, M. P. (1971). *The science of matter: A historical survey, selected readings.* Penguin.

Dahl, R., Allen, N., Wilbrecht, L. *et al.* (2018). Importance of investing in adolescence from a developmental science perspective. *Nature, 554*, 441-450. https://doi.org/10.1038/nature25770.

Damour, L. (2017). *Untangled: Guiding teenage girls through the seven transitions into adulthood.* Ballantine Books.

Darder, A., Baltodano, M., et al. (2003). *The critical pedagogy reader.* Routledge Falmer.

Darling-Hammond, L. (1990). Achieving our goals: superficial or structural reforms? *Phi Delta Kappan* (December). 286–295.

Darling-Hammond, L. (1996). *What matters most: Teaching for America's future.* National Commission on Teaching and America's Future.

Darling-Hammond, L. (2010). *The flat world and education: How America's commitment to equity will determine our future.* Teachers College Press.

Darling, J. (1994). *Child-centred education and its critics.* Paul Chapman.

Davidson, T. (1898). *Rousseau and education according to nature.* Heinemann.

Daw, J. (2001, October). Eating disorders on the rise. *Monitor on Psychology, 32*(9). http://www.apa.org/monitor/oct01/eating

Deaton, A. & Stone, A. A. (2014). Subjective wellbeing, health, and ageing. *The Lancet, 385*(9968), 640–648. https://doi.org/10.1016/S0140-6736(13)61489-0

Debs, M. C. (2016). Racial and economic diversity in U.S. public Montessori schools. *Journal of Montessori Research, 2*(2), 15–34. https://doi.org/10.17161/jomr.v2i2.5848

Debs, M. (2019). *Diverse families, desirable schools: Public Montessori in the era of school choice.* Harvard Education Press.

De Craemer, W. (1983). A cross-cultural perspective on personhood. *The Milbank Memorial Fund Quarterly, 61*(1), 19–34. https://doi.org/10.2307/3349814

Defense Advanced Research Projects Agency. (n.d.). *A selected history of DARPA innovation.* https://www.darpa.mil/Timeline/index

Degruy, J. (2017). *Post traumatic slave syndrome: America's legacy of enduring injury and healing.* Joy Degruy Publications Inc.

Deloitte. (2020). *5 blockchain trends for 2020.* https://www2.deloitte.com/content/dam/Deloitte/ie/Documents/Consulting/Blockchain-Trends-2020-report.pdf

Dewey, J. (1938). *Experience and education.* Collier Books.

Dewey, J. (1944). *Human nature and conduct.* Published for the United States Armed Forces Institute by Henry Holt.

Diamond, J. (1997). *Guns, germs, and steel: The fates of human societies.* W. W. Norton & Company.

Diffusion of innovations. (2021, February 2). In *Wikipedia.* Retrieved February 10, 2021, from https://en.wikipedia.org/wiki/Diffusion_of_innovations

Digby, A. & Searby, P. (1981). *Children, school and society in nineteenth century England.* Macmillan.

Dintersmith, T. (2019). *What school could be: Insights and inspiration from teachers across America.* Edu21C Foundation.

Doidge, N. (2007). *The brain that changes itself: Stories of personal triumph from the frontiers of brain science.* Penguin Books.

DPS Imaginarium. (2019). *Tools from the DPS Imaginarium.* Retrieved February 10, 2021, from https://www.imaginarium.is

Duncan-Andrade, J. M. & Morrell, E. (2008). *The art of critical pedagogy: Possibilities of moving from theory to practice in urban schools.* Peter Lang Publishing.

Education Reimagined. (n.d.). *Explore and discover learner-centered spaces.* https://education-reimagined.org/map

Eiseley, L. C. (1973). *The man who saw through time.* Scribner.

Eksteins, M. (1989). *Rites of spring: The Great War and the birth of the modern age.* Houghton Mifflin.

EL Education. (n.d.). *History.* Retrieved February 10, 2021, from https://eleducation.org/who-we-are/history

Elmore, R. F. (2004). *School reform from the inside out: Policy, practice, and performance.* Harvard Education Press.

Emdin, C. (2017). *For white folks who teach in the hood... and the rest of y'all too: Reality pedagogy and urban education.* Beacon Press.

Ervin, B., Wash, P. D. & Mecca, M. E. (2010). A 3-year study of self-regulation in Montessori and non-Montessori classrooms. *Montessori Life, 2010*(2), 22–31. https://public-montessori.org/wp-content/uploads/2017/03/Ervin-Wash-Mecca-2010.pdf

Ewing, E. (2018, December 6). What led Chicago to shutter dozens of majority-black schools? Racism. *The Guardian.* https://www.theguardian.com/us-news/2018/dec/06/chicago-public-schools-closures-racism-ghosts-in-the-schoolyard-extract

Fielding, M. (1998). The point of politics: Friendship and community in the work of John MacMurray. *Renewal 6*(1), 55–64.

Fielding, M. (1999). Communities of learners. In B. O'Hagan (Ed.), *Modern educational myths* (p. 222). Kogan.

Finser, T. M. (2002). *School as a journey: The eight-year odyssey of a Waldorf teacher and his class.* Anthroposophic Press.

Fischer, C. S., Hout, M., Jankowski, M. S., Lucas, S. R., Swidler, A. & Voss, K. (1996). *Inequality by Design: Cracking the Bell Curve Myth*. Princeton University Press.

Forbes, S. H. (1999). Holistic education: an analysis of its intellectual precedents and nature. [Unpublished doctoral dissertation]. University of Oxford.

Fox, E. J. (2014, June 19). *How New York's 1% get kids into preschool*. CNN. https://money.cnn.com/2014/06/10/luxury/preschool-new-york-city/index.html

Freidlaender, D., Beckham, K., Zheng, X. & Darling-Hammond, L. (2015). *Growing a Waldorf-inspired approach in a public school district*. Stanford Center for Opportunity Policy in Education. https://edpolicy.stanford.edu/sites/default/files/publications/scope-report-waldorf-inspired-school.pdf

Freire, P. (1972). *Pedagogy of the oppressed*. Sheed and Ward.

Freire, P. (1974). *Education for critical consciousness*. Continuum Intl Pub Group.

Freire, P. (1998). *Pedagogy of freedom: Ethics, democracy, and civic courage*. Rowman & Littlefield Publishers.

Friedman, G. (2001). *The sanctity of property in American economic history*. The National Assets Project. https://scholarworks.umass.edu/cgi/viewcontent.cgi?article=1008&context=peri_workingpapers

Froebel, F., Fletcher, S., et al. (1912). *Froebel's chief writings on education*. Edward Arnold.

Fuhrman, S. & Lazerson, M. (2005). *The public schools*. Oxford University Press.

Garber, D. (1978). Science and certainty in Descartes. In M. Hooker (Ed.), *Descartes: critical and interpretive essays*. Johns Hopkins University Press.

Geertz, C. (1973). *The interpretation of cultures*. Basic Books.

Geiger, G. R. (1958). *John Dewey in perspective*. Oxford University Press.

Gerber, A. (1991). Synergy, holistic education and R. Buckminster Fuller: Education for a world in transformation. *Holistic Education Review, 4*(3), 44–50. https://eric.ed.gov/?id=ED367593

Gleick, J. (1987). *Chaos: Making a new science*. Viking Books.

Goldstein, D. (2019, December 3). 'It just isn't working': PISA test scores cast doubt on U.S. education efforts. *The New York Times*. https://www.nytimes.com/2019/12/03/us/us-students-international-test-scores.html

Goldstein, D. & Patel, J. (2019, July 30). Need extra time on tests? It helps to have cash. *The New York Times*. https://www.nytimes.com/2019/07/30/us/extra-time-504-sat-act.html?

Gopnik, A. (2020). *A thousand small sanities: The moral adventure of liberalism*. Basic Books.

Gray, P. (2013). *Free to learn: Why unleashing the instinct to play will make our children happier, more self-reliant and better students for life*. Hachette Books.

Gribbin, J. R. (1995). *In search of Schrèodinger's cat*. Black Swan.

Haidt, J. (2013). *The righteous mind: Why good people are divided by politics and religion*. Vintage Books.

Hammond, Z. L. (2014). *Culturally responsive teaching and the brain: Promoting authentic engagement and rigor among culturally and linguistically diverse students*. Corwin.

Hanford, E. (2015, September 10). *Kurt Hahn and the roots of expeditionary learning*. American Public Media. https://www.apmreports.org/episode/2015/09/10/kurt-hahn-and-the-roots-of-expeditionary-learning

Hansen, U. J. (2007). Holistic education: its philosophical underpinnings and practical application. [Doctoral dissertation, University of Oxford]. University of Oxford Research Archive. https://ora.ox.ac.uk/objects/uuid:6a51f6c8-3821-4fc5-b329-728b02921e47

Hansen, U. J. (2017). Re-imagining high-quality school choice for families: Diverse school orientations and learner-centered schools. https://educatingpotential.com/wp-content/uploads/Instructional-Orientations-Paper-Mar-2017.pdf

Harari, Y. N. (2015). *Homo Deus: A brief history of tomorrow.* Harvill Secker.

Harford, T. (2016). *Messy: How to be creative and resilient in a tidy-minded world.* Little, Brown Book Group.

Hari, J. (2018). *Lost connections: Why you're depressed and how to find hope.* Bloomsbury.

Hart, S. (n.d.). *What is a vision quest?* http://www.sparrowhart.com/what-is-a-vision-quest

Hart, T. (1998). A dialectic of knowing: Integrating the intuitive and the analytic. *ENCOUNTER: Education for Meaning and Social Justice, 11*(3), 5–16.

Healy, J. M. (1991). *Endangered minds: Why our children don't think.* Simon and Schuster.

Heisenberg, W. (1959). *Physics and philosophy: The revolution in modern science.* George Allen & Unwin.

Hofstadter, D. (1979). *Gödel, Escher, Bach: An eternal golden braid.* Basic Books.

Hogenboom, M. (2015, July 6). *The traits that make human beings unique.* BBC. https://www.bbc.com/future/article/20150706-the-small-list-of-things-that-make-humans-unique

Holy Bible. (New International Version). (2011). BibleGateway. https://www.biblegateway.com/versions/New-International-Version-NIV-Bible/#booklist

Hood, B. (2012). *The self illusion: How the social brain creates identity.* Little, Brown Book Group.

Hooker, M. (1978). *Descartes: Critical and interpretive essays.* Johns Hopkins University Press.

Hooks, B. (1994). *Teaching to transgress: Education as the practice of freedom.* Routledge.

Houk, L. M. (2010). Demonstrating teaching in a lab classroom. *Educational Leadership, 67*(9). http://www.ascd.org/publications/educational-leadership/summer10/vol67/num09/Demonstrating-Teaching-in-a-Lab-Classroom.aspx

Howard, A. (2002). The child's descent from the spirit. *Steiner Education, 36*(2), 19–22.

Huxley, A. (1970). *The perennial philosophy.* Harper & Row.

Jackson, J. G. (1970). *Introduction to African civilizations.* Citadel Press.

Jacobs, D. T. (2013). *Teaching truly: A curriculum to indigenize mainstream education.* Peter Lang Inc., International Academic Publishers.

Jaimes, M. A. (Ed.) (1999). *The state of Native America: Genocide, colonization, and resistance.* South End Press.

Jaschik, S. (2018, April 27). *Making the case for test optional.* Inside Higher Ed. https://www.insidehighered.com/news/2018/04/27/large-study-finds-colleges-go-test-optional-become-more-diverse-and-maintain

Jaschik, S. (2019, May 28). *Why are the wealthy more likely to get extra time on the SAT?.* Inside Higher Ed. https://www.insidehighered.com/admissions/article/2019/05/28/new-scrutiny-patterns-which-wealthier-students-are-more-likely-get

Jason, Z. (2017). Bored out of their minds. *Harvard Ed. Magazine*. https://www.gse.harvard.edu/news/ed/17/01/bored-out-their-minds

Jensen, F. & Nutt, A. E. (2014). *The teenage brain: A neuroscientist's survival guide to raising adolescents and young adults*. Harper Paperback.

Jones, B. (2020, September 29). *Increasing share of Americans favor a single government program to provide health care coverage*. Pew Research Center. https://www.pewresearch.org/fact-tank/2020/09/29/increasing-share-of-americans-favor-a-single-government-program-to-provide-health-care-coverage

Jones, B. A., & Nichols, E. J. (2013). *Cultural competence in America's schools: Leadership, engagement and understanding*. Information Age Publishing.

Juma, C. (2017). Leapfrogging progress: The misplaced promise of Africa's mobile revolution. *Breakthrough Journal, (7)*. https://thebreakthrough.org/index.php/journal/issue-7/leapfrogging-progress

Kamenetz, A. (2014, October 11). *It's 2014. All children are supposed to be proficient. What happened?*. NPR. https://www.npr.org/sections/ed/2014/10/11/354931351/it-s-2014-all-children-are-supposed-to-be-proficient-under-federal-law

Kania, J., Kramer, M. & Senge, P. (2018). *The water of systems change*. FSG. https://www.fsg.org/publications/water_of_systems_change

Kaplan, R. M. & Saccuzzo, D. P. (2012). *Psychological testing: Principles, applications, and issues*. Cengage Learning.

Karabel, J. & Halsey, A. H. (Eds.). (1977). *Power and ideology in education*. Oxford University Press.

Kashdan, T. B., Biswas-Diener, R. & King, L. A. (2008). Reconsidering happiness: The costs of distinguishing between hedonics and eudaimonia. *The Journal of Positive Psychology, 3*(4), 219–233. https://doi.org/10.1080/17439760802303044

Kaufman, S. B. (2013). *Ungifted: Intelligence redefined*. Basic Books.

Kendi, I. X. (2016). *Stamped from the beginning: The definitive history of racist ideas in America*. Bold Type Books.

Kendi, I. X. (2016, October 20). *Why the academic achievement gap is a racist idea*. Black Perspectives. https://www.aaihs.org/why-the-academic-achievement-gap-is-a-racist-idea

Kendi, I. X. (2019). *How to be an antiracist*. One World.

Kesson, K. (1991). The unfinished puzzle: Sustaining a dynamic holism. *Holistic Education Review, 4*(4), 44–48.

Kesson, K. (1996). The foundations of holism. *Holistic Education Review, 9*(2), 14–24.

Khan, P. H. & Kellert, S. R. (Eds.). (2002). *Children and nature: Psychological, sociocultural, and evolutionary investigations*. The MIT Press.

Kiersz, A. & Gould, S. (2017, July 3). *12 issues almost all Americans agree on—and one where they couldn't be further apart*. Business Insider. https://www.businessinsider.com/american-attitudes-on-key-issues-2017-6

Kimmerer, R. W. (2015). *Braiding sweetgrass: Indigenous wisdom, scientific knowledge, and the teachings of plants*. Milkweed Editions.

Kindlon, D. & Thompson M. (2000). *Raising Cain: Protecting the emotional life of boys.* Ballantine Books.

Kirby, J. (2018, May 16). *Why you hear "Laurel" or "Yanny" in that viral audio clip, explained.* Vox. https://www.vox.com/2018/5/16/17358774/yanny-laurel-explained

Kirst, M. W. (1984). *Who controls our schools?: American values in conflict.* Freeman.

Kirst, M. W. & Wirt, F. M. (2009). *The political dynamics of American education.* McCutchan Publishing Corporation.

Klein, A. (2015, April 10). No child left behind: An overview. *Education Week.* https://www.edweek.org/policy-politics/no-child-left-behind-an-overview/2015/04

Kliebard, H. M. (1986). *The struggle for the American curriculum, 1893–1958.* Routledge.

Knecht, D., Gannon, N. & Yaffe, C. (2016). Across classrooms: School quality reviews as a progressive educational policy. *Occasional Paper Series, 2016*(35). https://educate.bankstreet.edu/occasional-paper-series/vol2016/iss35/10

Kohn, A. (2000). *The schools our children deserve: Moving beyond traditional classrooms and "tougher standards".* Houghton Mifflin Co.

Kohn, A. (2000). Standardized Testing and Its Victims. *Education Week.* https://www.edweek.org/teaching-learning/opinion-standardized-testing-and-its-victims/2000/09

Kozol, J. (2012). *Savage Inequalities: Children in America's Schools,* Crown.

Kramer, R. (1976). *Maria Montessori.* Basil Blackwell.

Krishnamurti, J. (1981). *Education and the significance of life.* Harper Collins Publisher.

Krishnamurti, J. (1981). *Letters to the schools.* Krishnamurti Foundation India.

Kurzweil, R. (2013). *How to create a mind: The secret of human thought revealed.* Penguin Books.

Lacey, P. A. (1998). *Growing into goodness: Essays on Quaker education.* Pendle Hill Publications.

Ladson-Billings, G. (2009). *The dreamkeepers: Successful teachers of African American children.* Jossey-Bass.

Laing, R. D. (1982). *The voice of experience.* Allen Lane.

Laloux, F. (2014). *Reinventing organizations: A guide to creating organizations inspired by the next stage in human consciousness.* Parker Nelson.

Lancy, D. F., Bock, J. & Gaskins, S. (Eds.). (2011). *The anthropology of learning in childhood.* AltaMira Press.

Langer, E. J. (1997). *The power of mindful learning.* Hachette Books.

Langford, G. (1970). *Philosophy and education: An introduction.* Macmillan.

Lawton, D. & Gordon, P. (2002). *A history of Western educational ideas.* Woburn Press.

Lee, J. (2017, January 5). *Unlocking the door to my future.* Education Reimagined. https://education-reimagined.org/unlocking-door-future

Lemkow, A. F. (1998). Reflections on our common, life-long educational journey. *ENCOUNTER: Education for Meaning and Social Justice, 11*(2), 4–9.

Lepore, J. (2018). *These truths: A history of the United States.* W. W. Norton & Company.

Lerner, D. (1963). *Parts and wholes.* Free Press.

Levin, B. (2008). *How to change 5000 schools: A practical and positive approach for leading change at every level.* Harvard Education Press.

Locke, J. & Cranston, M. W. (1965). *Locke on politics, religion, and education.* Collier Books.

Love, B. L. (2019). *We want to do more than survive: Abolitionist teaching and the pursuit of educational freedom.* Beacon Press.

Lovelock, J. E. (1988). *The ages of Gaia: A biography of our living Earth.* Oxford University Press.

Lukianoff, G. & Haidt, J. (2015, September). The coddling of the American mind. *The Atlantic.* Retrieved January 25, 2021, from https://www.theatlantic.com/magazine/archive/2015/09/the-coddling-of-the-american-mind/399356

Lund, S., Manyika, J., Segel, L. H., Dua, A., Hancock, B., Rutherford, S. & Macon, B. (2019). *The future of work in America: People and places, today and tomorrow.* The McKinsey Global Institute. https://www.mckinsey.com/featured-insights/future-of-work/the-future-of-work-in-america-people-and-places-today-and-tomorrow#

Luytens, M. (1975). *Krishnamurti: The years of awakening.* J. Murray.

Macmurray, J. (1961). *Persons in relation. Delivered at the Gifford Lectures at the University of Glasgow in 1954.* Faber & Faber.

Macmurray, J. & Conford, P. (1996). *The personal world: John Macmurray on self and society.* Floris Books.

Mandelbrot, B. B. (1982). *The fractal geometry of nature.* Times Books.

Markovits, D. (2020). *The meritocracy trap: How America's foundational myth feeds inequality, dismantles the middle class, and devours the elite.* Penguin Books.

McDonnell, G. (2021, May 15). University of California will no longer consider SAT and ACT scores. *The New York Times.*

McGilchrist, I. (2012). *The divided brain and the search for meaning.* Yale University Press.

McGilchrist, I. (2009). *The master and his emissary: The divided brain and the making of the western world.* Yale University Press.

McNeil, L. M. (1999). *Contradictions of control: School structure and school knowledge.* Routledge.

McNeil, L. M. (2000). *Contradictions of school reform: Educational costs of standardized testing.* Routledge.

Mead, W. R. (2008). *God and gold: Britain, America, and the making of the modern world.* Vintage Books.

Mecklin, J. (Ed.). (2021, January 27). *This is your COVID wake-up call: It is 100 seconds to midnight.* Bulletin of the Atomic Scientists. Retrieved February 28, 2021, from https://thebulletin.org/doomsday-clock/current-time

Mehta, J. (2013). *The allure of order: High hopes, dashed expectations, and the troubled quest to remake American schooling.* Oxford University Press.

Mehta, J. & Fine, S. (2019). *In search of deeper learning: The quest to remake the American high school.* Harvard University Press.

Meister, J. (2012, August 14). The future of work: Job hopping is the 'new normal' for millennials. *Forbes.* https://www.forbes.com/sites/jeannemeister/2012/08/14/the-future-of-work-job-hopping-is-the-new-normal-for-millennials/?sh=47f9838913b8

Menakem, R. (2017). *My grandmother's hands: Racialized trauma and the pathway to mending our hearts and bodies.* Central Recovery Press.

Menand, L. (2001). *The metaphysical club*. Flamingo.

Merchant, C. (1980). *The death of nature: Women, ecology, and the scientific revolution.* Harper & Row.

Metzl, J. (2020). *Dying of whiteness: How the politics of racial resentment is killing America's heartland.* Basic Books.

Miller, R. (1990). *What are schools for?: Holistic education in American culture.* Holistic Education Press.

Montessori Census. (n.d.). *School search.* https://www.montessoricensus.org/schools-map

Montessori Center School. (2019, September 2). *Montessori basics: The prepared environment.* Retrieved February 10, 2021, from https://mcssb.org/montessori-basics-the-prepared-environment

Montessori, M. (1989). *Education for a new world.* Clio Press.

Montessori, M. (1989). *To educate the human potential.* Clio.

Montessori, M. M. (1992). *Education for human development: Understanding Montessori.* Clio.

Mukerjee, M. (2011). *Churchill's secret war: The British empire and the ravaging of India during world war.* Basic Books.

Mukerjee, M. (2003). *The land of naked people: encounters with Stone Age Islanders.* Houghton Mifflin.

Mullainathan, S. & Shafir, E. (2013). *Scarcity: Why having too little means so much.* Times Books.

Mumford, L. (1967). *The myth of the machine: Technics and human development.* Harcourt.

Nacson, L. & Chopra, D. (1998). *Deepak Chopra: How to live in a world of infinite possibilities.* Rider.

Naming traditions and ceremonies from around the world. (2007, March 12). Confetti. Retrieved February 25, 2021, from https://www.confetti.co.uk/inspire-and-advice/relationships/naming-traditions-and-ceremonies-from-around-the-world

National Center on Education and the Economy. (1990). *America's choice: High skills or low wages!.* http://www.ncee.org/wp-content/uploads/2013/09/Americas-Choice-High-Skills-or-Low-Wages.pdf

National Commission on Excellence in Education. (1983). *A nation at risk: The imperative for educational reform.* https://www2.ed.gov/pubs/NatAtRisk/index.html

Native American Community Academy. (n.d.). *Curriculum.* Retrieved February 10, 2021, from https://www.nacaschool.org/apps/pages/index.jsp?uREC_ID=1663962&type=d&pREC_ID=1816888

New York Performance Standards Consortium. (2012). *Educating for the 21st century.* https://www.nyclu.org/sites/default/files/releases/testing_consortium_report.pdf

New Zealand Ministry of Education. (2020). *Key competencies.* The New Zealand Curriculum Online. https://nzcurriculum.tki.org.nz/Key-competencies#collapsible2

Nicholson, D. W. (2000). Layers of experience: Forms of representation in a Waldorf school classroom. *Journal of Curriculum Studies, 32*(4), 575–587.

Noddings, N. (1992). *The challenge to care in schools: An alternative approach to education.* Teachers College Press.

Noguera, J. & Noguera, P. (2018). Equity through mutual accountability: Collective capacity building helps educators assess the needs of all students. *Learning Professional, 39*(5), 44-47. https://eric.ed.gov/?id=EJ1194529

Noguera, P. A. (2009). *The trouble with black boys: ...And other reflections on race, equity, and the future of public education.* Jossey-Bass.

Nussbaum, M. C. (2000). *Women and human development: The capabilities approach.* Cambridge University Press.

Oakeshott, M. J. & Fuller, T. (1989). *The voice of liberal learning.* Yale University Press.

Okun, T. (n.d.). *White supremacy culture.* Dismantling Racism. https://www.dismantlingracism.org/uploads/4/3/5/7/43579015/okun_-_white_sup_culture.pdf

Oluo, I. (2018). *So you want to talk about race.* Basic Books.

180 Studio & Eckenhoff Saunders Architects. (2020). *Seed + spark: Using nature as a model to reimagine how we learn and live.* 180 Press.

Oppenheimer, T. (1999). Schooling the imagination. *The Atlantic, 284*(3), 71–83.

Ortiz, P. (2018). *An African American and Latinx history of the United States.* Beacon Press.

Palmer, P. J. (1993). *To know as we are known.* Harper Collins Publisher.

Palmer, P. J. (1998). *The courage to teach: Exploring the inner landscape of a teacher's life.* Jossey-Bass.

Pappano, L. (2011). Waldorf education in public schools: Educators adopt—and adapt—this developmental, arts-rich approach. *Harvard Education Letter, 27*(6). https://www.hepg.org/hel-home/issues/27_6/helarticle/waldorf-education-in-public-schools_515

Partnership to End Addiction. (2014, November). *New research finds 20 percent of college students abuse prescription stimulants.* https://drugfree.org/drug-and-alcohol-news/survey-finds-20-percent-college-students-abuse-prescription-stimulants

Payne, C. M. (2008). *So much reform, so little change: The persistence of failure in urban schools.* Harvard Education Press.

Peters, R. S. (Ed.). (1967). *The concept of education.* Routledge & Kegan Paul.

Phillips, D. C. (1977). *Holistic thought in social science.* Macmillan.

Phillips, M. A. (2016). *8 essentials to a race conversation: A manual to a new dialogue.* CreateSpace Independent Publishing Platform.

Pink, D. H. (2006). *A whole new mind: Why right-brainers will rule the future.* Penguin.

Pirani, F. (2018, July 11). Nearly 1 in 4 teen girls in the US self-harm, massive high school survey finds. *The Atlanta Journal-Constitution.* https://www.ajc.com/news/health-med-fit-science/nearly-teen-girls-the-self-harm-massive-high-school-survey-finds/EQnLJy3REFX53HjbHGnukJ

Pollan, M. (2018). *How to change your mind: What the new science of psychedelics teaches us about consciousness, dying, addiction, depression, and transcendence.* Penguin Press.

Ponton, L. E. (1997). *The romance of risk: Why teenagers do the things they do.* Basic Books.

Pring, R. (1984). *Personal and social education in the curriculum.* Hodder and Stoughton.

ProPublica. (2017). *Alternative schools in U.S. school districts* [Data set]. https://www.propublica.org/datastore/dataset/alternative-schools-in-u-s-school-districts

Purpel, D. E. (1996). Social transformation and holistic education. *Holistic Education Review, 9*(2), 25–34.

Queensland Curriculum & Assessment Authority. (2014). *School-based assessment: The Queensland system*. https://www.qcaa.qld.edu.au/downloads/approach2/school-based_assess_qld_sys.pdf

Radhakrishnan, S. & Moore, C. A. (Eds.). (1967). *A sourcebook in Indian philosophy*. Princeton University Press.

Ravitch, D. (2013). *Reign of error: The hoax of the privatization movement and the danger to America's public schools*. Vintage Books.

Reaching Higher NH. (2018, April 23). *NH's innovative assessment inspires others to explore testing alternatives*. http://reachinghighernh.org/2018/04/23/nh-innovative-assessment-inspires-states

Reggio Emilia approach. (2021, January 23). In *Wikipedia*. Retrieved February 10, 2021, from https://en.wikipedia.org/wiki/Reggio_Emilia_approach

Reid-Henry, S. (2019). *Empire of democracy: The remaking of the West since the Cold War*. Simon & Schuster.

Reinhard, B. (1997, June 25). Public Waldorf school in Calif. under attack. *Education Week*. Retrieved September 16, 2007, from https://www.edweek.org/education/public-waldorf-school-in-calif-under-attack/1997/06

Rice, J. (2020, November 11). *How the wisdom of indigenous lifeways can transform education*. Education Reimagined. Retrieved February 25, 2021, from https://education-reimagined.org/how-the-wisdom-of-indigenous-lifeways-can-transform-education.

Richards, A. S. (2020). *Raising free people: Unschooling as liberation and healing work*. PM Press.

Riddle, T. & Sinclair, S. (2019). Racial disparities in school-based disciplinary actions are associated with county-level rates of racial bias. *Proceedings of the National Academy of Sciences, 116*(17), 8255–8260. https://doi.org/10.1073/pnas.1808307116

Riser-Kositsky, M. (2019, December 17). Special education: Definition, statistics, and trends. *Education Week*. https://www.edweek.org/teaching-learning/special-education-definition-statistics-and-trends/2019/12

Ritzer, G. (1993). *The McDonaldization of society: An investigation into the changing character of contemporary social life*. Pine Forge Press.

Robbins, A. (2007). *The overachievers: The secret lives of driven kids*. Hachette Book.

Robinson, K. (1999). *All our futures: Creativity, culture & education*. Department for Education and Employment, Sudbury, Suffolk, England. https://files.eric.ed.gov/fulltext/ED440037.pdf

Robinson, K. & Aronica, L. (2016). *Creative schools: The grassroots revolution that's transforming education*. Penguin Books.

Ro, C. (2019, October 9). *Dunbar's number: Why we can only maintain 150 relationships*. BBC. https://www.bbc.com/future/article/20191001-dunbars-number-why-we-can-only-maintain-150-relationships

Rodis-Lewis, G. (1978). Limitations of the mechanical model in the Cartesian conception of the organism. In M. Hooker (Ed.), *Descartes: Critical and interpretive essays*. Johns Hopkins University Press.

Rorty, A. (1998). *Philosophers on education: Historical perspectives*. Routledge.

Rose, T. & Ogas, O. (2018). *Dark horse: Achieving success through the pursuit of fulfillment*. HarperOne.

Rose, T. (2016). *The end of average: How we succeed in a world that values sameness*. HarperOne.

Rothman, B. (2018, May 30). *Inspection systems: How top-performing nations hold schools accountable*. National Center on Education and the Economy. Retrieved February 10, 2021, from https://ncee.org/2018/05/how-top-performing-nations-hold-schools-accountable

Rothstein, R. (1998). *The way we were?: The myths and realities of America's student achievement*. Century Foundation Press.

Rothstein, R. (2017). *The color of law: A forgotten history of how our government segregated America*. Liverwright.

Rowson, J. & McGilchrist, I. (2013). *Divided brain, divided world: Why the best part of us struggles to be heard*. RSA. https://www.thersa.org/globalassets/pdfs/blogs/rsa-divided-brain-divided-world.pdf

Rukundo-Karaara, C., Reyes, J. & Bartholomew, S. (2020, May 27). *New Legacy Charter School: A conversation with learner-centered leaders*. Education Reimagined. https://education-reimagined.org/new-legacy-charter-school-a-conversation-with-learner-centered-leaders

Russell, B. (1961). *History of Western philosophy*. Allen & Unwin.

Safir, S. & Dugan, J. (2021). *Street data: A next-generation model for equity, pedagogy, and school transformation*. Corwin.

Saito, M. (2003). Amartya Sen's capability approach to education: A critical exploration. *Journal of Philosophy of Education, 37*(1), 17–33.

Sarason, S. (1990). *The predictable failure of educational reform: Can we change course before it's too late?*. Jossey-Bass.

Sardello, R. (1992). Love as a mode of knowledge. *ReVision, 15*(2), 64–70.

Schaef, A. W. (1998). *Living in process: Basic truths for living the path of the soul*. Ballantine Books.

Schneier, B. (2012). *Liars and outliers: Enabling the trust that society needs to thrive*. Wiley.

School district. (2020, December 28). In *Wikipedia*. Retrieved February 10, 2021, from https://en.wikipedia.org/wiki/School_district

Schwartz, E. (1992). Holistic assessment in the Waldorf school. *Holistic Education Review, 5*(4), 31–37.

Schwartz, J. M. & Begley, S. (2009). *The mind and the brain: Neuroplasticity and the power of mental force*. Harper Collins.

Science of Learning & Development Alliance. (n.d.). *What we've learned*. SoLD Alliance. https://www.soldalliance.org/what-weve-learned

Senge, P. M. (2006). *The fifth discipline: The art & practice of the learning organization*. Doubleday.

Sharma, R. (2017). *The Global youth wellbeing index*. International Youth Foundation. https://www.youthindex.org/full-report

Sharma, S. R. (2011). An east and west divide or convergence?: Similarities between ancient Indian and Greek philosophy on human flourishing. In *Finding meaning, cultures across borders: International dialogue between philosophy and psychology.* (pp. 119–127). Kyoto University. https://core.ac.uk/download/pdf/39271264.pdf

Sheffield, M. (2019, February 7). *Poll: Most Americans want universal healthcare but don't want to abolish private insurance.* The Hill. https://thehill.com/hilltv/what-americas-thinking/428958-poll-voters-want-the-government-to-provide-healthcare-for

Shenk, D. (2011). *The genius in all of us: Why everything you've been told about genes, talent and intelligence is wrong.* Icon Books Ltd.

Shlain, L. (1999). *The alphabet versus the goddess: The conflict between word and image.* Penguin Books.

Silberman, S. (2015). *NeuroTribes: The legacy of autism and the future of neurodiversity.* Avery Publishing.

Simon, B. (1960). *Studies in the history of education, 1780–1870.* Lawrence & Wishart.

Simon, B. (1991). *Education and the social order, 1940–1990.* Lawrence & Wishart.

Sivin, N. (2005). Why the scientific revolution did not take place in China—or didn't it?. University of Pennsylvania. https://www.sas.upenn.edu/~nsivin/from_ccat/scirev.pdf

Smuts, J. C. (1926). *Holism and evolution.* Macmillan and Co.

Sommers, F. (1978). Dualism in Descartes: The logical ground. In M. Hooker (Ed.), *Descartes: Critical and interpretive essays.* Johns Hopkins University Press.

Spear, L. (2009). *The behavioral neuroscience of adolescence.* W. W. Norton & Company.

Spock, M. (1978). *Teaching as a lively art.* The Anthroposophic Press.

Standing, E. M. (1998). *Maria Montessori: Her life and work.* Penguin Books Ltd.

Steiner, R. (1965). *The education of the child in the light of anthroposophy.* Rudolf Steiner Press.

Steiner, R. (1971). *Human values in education: Ten lectures given in Arnheim, Holland, July 17–24, 1924.* Rudolf Steiner Press.

Steiner, R. (1972). *A modern art of education: Fourteen lectures given in Ilkley, Yorkshire, 5th–17th August, 1923.* Rudolf Steiner Press.

Steiner, R. (1980). *Waldorf education for adolescence.* Kolisko Archive Publications.

Steiner, R. (1999). *Towards social renewal: Rethinking the basis of society.* Rudolf Steiner Press.

Steiner R. & Stebbing, R. (1999). *Autobiography: Chapters in the course of my life, 1861–1907.* Anthroposophic Press.

Stern, J. (2001). John MacMurray, spirituality, community and real schools. *International Journal of Children's Spirituality, 6*(1), 25–39.

Stewart, W. A. C. & McCann, W. P. (1967). *The educational innovators: Progressive schools 1881–1967.* Macmillan.

Stixrud, W. & Johnson, N. (2019). *The self-driven child: The science and sense of giving your kids more control over their lives.* Penguin Books.

Stone, D. (2012). *Policy paradox: The art of political decision making.* W.W. Norton & Company.

Stovall, D. O. (2016). *Born out of struggle: Critical race theory, school creation, and the politics of interruption.* SUNY Press.

Strauss, V. (2019, August 29). Some 'no-excuses' charter schools say they are changing. Are they? Can they?. *The Washington Post.* https://www.washingtonpost.com/education/2019/08/29/some-no-excuses-charter-schools-say-they-are-changing-are-they-can-they

Strauss, V. (2020, December 30). Calls are growing for Biden to do what DeVos did: Let states skip annual standardized tests this spring. *The Washington Post.* https://www.washingtonpost.com/education/2020/12/30/calls-are-growing-biden-do-what-devos-did-let-states-skip-annual-standardized-tests-this-spring

Sturgis, C. (2018, February 20). *Progressions? Trajectories? Continuum? Oh my!* Competency Works, Aurora Institute. https://aurora-institute.org/cw_post/progressions-trajectories-continuum-oh-my

Susman, W. (1984). *Culture as history: The transformation of American society in the twentieth century.* Pantheon Books.

Swengel, E. M. (1991). A new wineskin for holistic vintage. *Holistic Education Review, 4*(3), 33–43.

Taira, B. & Sang, K. (2019, April 15). The Hawai'i DOE Office of Hawaiian Education is piloting a proficiency-based assessment model that is culturally responsive and place-based. Next Generation Learning Challenges. https://www.nextgenlearning.org/articles/culturally-responsive-assessment-practices-through-n%C4%81-hopena-a%CA%BBo-h%C4%81

Tart, C. (1986). *Waking up: The obstacles to human potential.* New Science Library/Shambhala.

Taylor, C. (1985). *Philosophical papers volume 1: Human agency and language.* Cambridge University Press.

Taylor, J. B. (2021). *Whole brain living: The anatomy of choice and the four characters that drive our life.* Hay House.

Taylor, S. R. (2018). *The body is not an apology: The power of radical self-love.* Berrett-Koehler Publishers.

The Audiopedia. (2017, February 11). *What is tritone paradox? What does tritone paradox mean? Tritone paradox meaning & explanation* [Video]. YouTube. https://www.youtube.com/watch?v=5oYtQ1VB93U

The College Post. (2020, October 7). *Universities waive ACT, SAT score requirements for admission.* Retrieved February 10, 2021, from https://thecollegepost.com/universities-waive-sat-act

Theisen-Homer, V. (2020). *Learning to connect: Relationships, race, and teacher education.* Rowman & Littlefield.

Tienken, C. (2017, July 5). *Students' test scores tell us more about the community they live in than what they know.* The Conversation. https://theconversation.com/students-test-scores-tell-us-more-about-the-community-they-live-in-than-what-they-know-77934

Tippett, K. (Host). (2020, June 4). Resmaa Menakem – 'Notice the rage; Notice the silence' [Audio podcast episode]. In *On being with Krista Tippett.* The On Being Project. https://onbeing.org/programs/resmaa-menakem-notice-the-rage-notice-the-silence

Transformation Design. (2020). *Explore the transformation design framework.* Retrieved February 26, 2021, from https://www.transformation-design.org/the-framework

Treviranus, J. (1993). The many views of Jane. In P. Lindsay, I. Davidson & J. Light (Eds.), *A Glimpse of Disabilities and Empowerment* (pp. 173–201). Sharing to Learn.

Treviranus, J. (2014). The value of the statistically insignificant. *EDUCAUSE Review.* 46–47. https://er.educause.edu/articles/2014/1/the-value-of-the-statistically-insignificant

Treviranus, J. & Roberts, V, (2006). Inclusive e-learning. In J. Weiss, J. Nolan, J. Hunsinger, et al. (Eds.), *The international handbook of virtual learning environments* (pp. 469–495). Springer.

Tuchman, B. (1978). *A distant mirror: The calamitous fourteenth century.* Alfred A. Knopf.

Tucker, M. S. (2011). *Standing on the shoulders of giants: An American agenda for education reform.* National Center on Education and the Economy.

Twenge, J. (2019, March 14). *The mental health crisis among America's youth is real – and staggering.* The Conversation. https://theconversation.com/the-mental-health-crisis-among-americas-youth-is-real-and-staggering-113239

UK Commission for Employment and Skills. (2014). *The future of work: Jobs and skills in 2030.* https://assets.publishing.service.gov.uk/government/uploads/system/uploads/attachment_data/file/303334/er84-the-future-of-work-evidence-report.pdf

UN Environment Programme. (2021, February 18). *Making peace with nature: A scientific blueprint to tackle the climate, biodiversity and pollution emergencies.* https://www.unep.org/resources/making-peace-nature

University of California (2020, May 21). *University of California Board of Regents unanimously approved changes to standardized testing requirement for undergraduates* [Press release]. Retrieved from https://www.universityofcalifornia.edu/press-room/university-california-board-regents-approves-changes-standardized-testing-requirement

Valenzuela, A. (2017). *Subtractive schooling: U.S.-Mexican youth and the politics of caring.* SUNY Press.

Vander Ark, T. & Liebtag, E. (2020). *Difference making at the heart of learning: Students, schools, and communities alive with possibility.* Corwin.

van der Kolk, B. (2015). *Workbook for the body keeps the score: Brain, mind, and body in the healing of trauma.* Penguin Books.

Villanueva, E. (2018). *Decolonizing wealth: Indigenous wisdom to heal divides and restore balance.* Berrett-Koehler Publishers.

Vocational skills—skilled trades are in demand as boomers retire. (2016, June 7). Adecco. Retrieved February 8, 2021, from https://www.adeccousa.com/employers/resources/skilled-trades-in-demand

Vodicka, D. (2020). *Learner-centered leadership: A blueprint for transformational change in learning communities.* IMPress.

Vollmer, J. (2010). *Schools cannot do it alone: Building public support for America's public schools.* Enlightenment Press.

Wardle, D. (1976). *English popular education: 1780–1975.* Cambridge University Press.

Washor, E., Frishman, A. & Mejia, E. (2021, January 26). *Findings from the Big Picture Learning longitudinal study*. Education Reimagined. https://education-reimagined. org/findings-from-the-big-picture-learning-longitudinal-study/?utm_sq=gn1uxcuqzo

Washor, E. & Mojkowski, C. (2013). *Leaving to learn: How out-of-school learning increases student engagement and reduces dropout rates*. Heinemann.

Waters, M. & McClean, M. (2020). *Indigenous epistemology: Descent into the womb of decolonized research methodologies*. Peter Lang Inc., International Academic Publishers.

Weber, A. (2016). *The biology of wonder: Aliveness, feeling and the metamorphosis of science*. New Society Publishers.

Weiner, S. (2016). These illusions prove that your brain only sees what it wants to see. *Popular Mechanics*. Retrieved February 8, 2021, from https://www.popularmechanics. com/science/a24125/optical-illusions-brain

Wheatley, M. J. (1999). *Leadership and the new science: Discovering order in a chaotic world*. McGraw-Hill.

Wheatley, M. J. (2009). *Turning to one another: Simple conversations to restore hope to the future*. Berrett-Koehler Publishers.

Whitehead, A. N. (1925). *Science and the modern world*. New American Library.

Whitehead, A. N. (1962). *The aims of education and other essays*. Ernest Benn Limited.

White, P., White, J., et al. (1989). *Personal and social education: Philosophical perspectives*. Kogan Page.

White, T. (2015). Demystifying whiteness in a market of 'no excuses' corporate-styled charter schools. In B. Picower & E. Mayorga (Eds.), *What's race got to do with it: How current school reform policy maintains racial and economic inequality* (pp. 121–145). Peter Lang Publishing.

Whitescarver, K. (2010). Montessori in America: the current revival. *Montessori International*. https://www.public-montessori.org/wp-content/uploads/2016/10/Montessori-in-America.pdf

Wiggins, G. P. & McTighe, J. (1998). *Understanding by design*. Association for Supervision and Curriculum Development.

Wilkerson, I. (2020). *Caste: The origins of our discontent*. Random House.

Wilson, C. (1985). *Rudolf Steiner: The man and his vision*. Aquarian Press.

Wilson, F. R. (1998). *The hand: How its use shapes the brain, language, and human culture*. Pantheon Books.

Wilson-Hokowhitu, N. (Ed.). (2019). *The past before us: Moʻokūʻauhau as methodology*. University of Hawaiʻi Press.

Wolf, A. (2002). *Does education matter?: Myths about education and economic growth*. Penguin.

Wolf, E. (2010). *Europe and the people without history*. University of California Press.

Woodard, C. (2012). *American nations: A history of the eleven rival regional cultures of North America*. Penguin Books.

Woods, P. & Jeffrey, B. (1998). Choosing positions: Living the contradictions of OFSTED. *British Journal of Sociology of Education, 19*(4), 547–570.

World Economic Forum. (2016). *The future of jobs. Employment, skills and workforce strategy for the fourth industrial revolution.* http://www3.weforum.org/docs/WEF_Future_of_Jobs.pdf

Wright, R. (1994). *The moral animal: Why we are the way we are: The new science of evolutionary psychology.* Vintage Books.

Zap, J. (1991). Crossing the great stream: Educating the evolving self. *Holistic Education Review, 4*(2), 11–16.

Zervas, P., Kardaras, V., Baldiris, S., Bacca, J., Avila, C., Politis, Y., Treviranus, J. & Sampson, D. G. (2014). *Supporting open access to teaching and learning of people with disabilities.* In *Digital systems for open access to formal and informal learning* (pp. 57–68). Springer International Publishing. https://doi.org/10.1007/978-3-319-02264-2_5

Zinn, H. (1980). *A people's history of the United States.* Harper & Row.

Zukav, G. (1991). *The dancing Wu Li masters: An overview of the new physics.* Rider & Co.

ACKNOWLEDGMENTS

In recent years my sons have levelled the charge that I have a third child, but not in the form of the sister or puppy they both wanted. When I reflect on the energy, attention and resources that have been put into researching and writing this book, I can sympathize with their grievance. I am indebted to more people than can be thanked adequately in a few paragraphs, not least because it is a chain that extends back in time across disciplines, geographies and generations. Nevertheless I wish to express my deepest thanks to a small subset without whom this project might never have been completed.

In 2014 a handful of people saw the potential value of my ideas and the importance of getting them out into the world at a moment when I was struggling to identify my personal and professional trajectory. James Walton Jr. and Cathy Lund: thank you for taking a meeting with me and awarding the grant that made the US-based school research possible. Nora Flood, Bonnie Benjamin-Phariss and Jeff Westphal: I have so appreciated your support of me as thought partners and mentors, and am deeply grateful for your help in securing support for publicity and promotion. Though the timeline for publishing was longer than anticipated, I believe that the ideas will land differently than had my original timeline played out; the whole project has perhaps been a testament to our collective belief in the power of emergence. Craig Lounsbrough, my thanks to you for reminding me about the truth of who I am. You told me to write the book, assuring me that it didn't even have to be good; I just had to write it. I hope I have exceeded that bar. Gillian MacKenzie, I cannot tell you how much it meant for you to sign on as my agent and to take a chance on a new non-fiction author because you believed in the ideas that animated me. I am grateful for your guidance through multiple proposal processes and for your introduction to just the right editor for this project.

Sam Douglas—I had no idea the impact an editor could have on both the process and product of writing. I am eternally grateful for your help over *many* years in holding the vision for this book strongly enough to protect its essence, yet loosely enough to let it evolve; encouraging me to find my voice; and pushing me to refine, organize and communicate these ideas accessibly (and succinctly).

Clarence Burton—I'm so very grateful to City Year for connecting us in 2012! Thank you for your support over many years with research, thought-partnership and the detailed, time consuming work of pulling together ideas, resources and now this manuscript. Thanks to Clara for her patience!

Sandra Luo, Veronica Richmond, Michael Reagan and the broader team at Two Birds/One Stone—it was a gift for this book's graphics to be designed by young professionals like you who have a gift for "untabling the table." It brings to life the book's vision of how the best learning and creation happens! And to Monica Snellings, a huge thank you for your generosity over the years in helping translate complex ideas into beautiful visuals, whether for TED talks, presentations or books.

Christine Kloser, Carrie Jareed, Gwen Hoffnagle, Jean Merrill, Chrissy Das and the team at Capucia—I am so grateful for your commitment to bringing transformational ideas to the world and for your guidance, patience and support in navigating the writing and publishing process. And to Kimberly Benfield, thank you for sharing your amazing gifts as a photographer!

Miguel Gonzalez, Caitlin Long, Ginnie Logan, Kyle Gamba and my other fellow Summer 2020 Iterative Space Residents—it was a gift beyond words to have your energy, encouragement and intentional accountability at a moment when I needed all three to dig into the creative process.

A huge thank you to my early readers for their incisive comments and honest feedback, challenging me to make this book the best it could be: Linda Barker, Sujata Bhatt, Gregg Behr, William Browning, Michelle Culver, Nora Flood, Miguel Gonzalez, Christina Jean, Emily Liebtag, Peter McWalters, Jay Mead, David Nitkin, Anne Olson, Carol Svendsen and Tony Simmons.

Much gratitude goes to additional colleagues, mentors and friends for key experiences and conversations that helped shape the ideas of this book: Darnisa Amante-Jackson, Wisdom Amazhou, Nicole Williams Beechum, Bonnie Benjamin-Phariss, Alin Bennett, Robert Burkhardt, Andy Calkins, Sam Chaltain, David Cook, Deb Cunningham, Mira Debs, Paul "Pablo" Dosh, Anpao Duta Flying Earth, Marcia Fulton, Lynn Gangone, David Grant, Alexis Gwin-Miller, Azella Humetewa, Vernon Jones, Jemar Lee, Caitlin Long, Rebecca Kantor, Amber Kim, Jemar Lee, Thomas Magnell, Colby Mills, Sarojani Mohammed, Lindsy Ogawa, Clarice Olinger, Robert Perry, Trace Pickering, Richard Pring, Christina Quattrochi, Paola Ramirez, Kaleb Rashad, Brian Roberts, Sir Ken Robinson, Fiona Rose, Todd Rose, Andrew Ross, Brittney Sampson, Doug Schuch, Dena Simmons, Nathan Strenge, Regena Thomashauer, Jutta Treviranus, Chelsea Waite, John Watkins, Jeff Westphal, Christin Whitener, Jenee Henry Wood and Elliot Wosher. You have made me a better educator, thinker and person.

To the educators, young people and communities that allowed me to be part of their professional and personal lives over the years—a huge thank you. This includes not only the schools and individuals I mention in this book but the hundreds of others whose voices, experiences and reflections have shaped my thinking, many of whom are now connected within the Education Reimagined Learning Lab, Movement Builder and Spark House communities, which I was honored to help build. I am grateful as well for the opportunity to be part of networks of amazing organizations in the US and globally, committed to working together to transform what learning looks like so that we can unleash the potential of young people: All in This Together, This Is Our Chance Film Festival, Unschooled and the What Made Them So Prepared coalition. If the ideas in this book are to come alive, it will be thanks to the vision, commitment and efforts of these and many other organizations in supporting both the "what" and the "how" of transformative change. This includes the trainers at the Racial Equity Institute who are thoughtfully building the capacity of individuals to organize themselves in service of *groundwater-level* change. A special thanks to Dr. Raúl Quiñones-Rosado, Jamall Kinard and the Reverend Brian Crisp, who are powerful models for what it means to change the narrative.

My thanks go to the Paul and Daisy Soros Fellowship for New Americans, the British Marshall Commission and the Harry S. Truman Foundation for the financial support and (more critically) the communities of amazing thinkers, writers, advocates and change-makers who have helped shape my personal and professional trajectory over the last two and a half decades.

To those not already mentioned who comprise my and my family's extended village: we do not grow as people or raise our children alone. I am so grateful for the gift of friends and "framily" whose presence has been a source of fellowship going back, in some cases, decades:

Katherine Dirks; Jenn and Greg Eure; Sujata and Eric Fretz; Lipika Goyal; Kristina Graff; Diane and Michael Hazel; Nilmini and Eric Hecox; Richard Johnston; Elizabeth Katkin and Richard Waryn; Nick, Sue and Philip Kenrick; Katie Larson; Elise Logemann; Betsy Michel; Nicholas Miller; Leslie Raynor and Wes Scott; Brian Roberts; Anna and Niels Rosenquist; Meena Seshamani; Sapna and Anant Siva; Ian and Elizabeth Skeet; Moira Smith; Lucy and Todd Stribley; Natalie Walker; and Sierra and PJ White.

To the Ladies of the NYMBC (Nilmini Senanayake Hecox, Sujata Fretz, Paola Ramirez, Leah Oliver, Becky Hoffman, Lisa Mortell, Sam Sturhahn and Susan Bross); the Denver Badass and Woke community (Teena Sebastian, Fayoke Longe, Cynthia Pesantez, Alesha Arscott, Jen Sarche and Tolanda Tolbert); and the phenomenal Gilligan's Poddesses (Elisa Ours, Jessica Goldberg, Shanehi Shah, Samantha Elkrief, Sydney Price, Ann Ziata, Lauren Riker, Loveleen Venkitasubramanian, Naomi Nussbaum and Xiaojue Hu): you are gifts I never expected, communities inside of which I get to play all 88 keys and practice both giving and receiving inspiration, gratitude, support and comfort. So much of what I have seen in the schools I love has come alive for me thanks to you.

Too many people do not have the gifts of love, opportunity and an abiding faith in their capacity that my family provides. I am not always good at expressing what I feel but I grow increasingly attentive to the concept of *Ubuntu,* which has deeply shaped my life—I am because we are. Mom, Dad, Amma and Baba—I am deeply grateful to you for the doors that were opened, the journeys that were made possible and the global/cross-cultural perspectives I inhabited because of your choices, sacrifices and presence. I would not be who I am without my brothers and the wonderful women who chose to merge their families with ours—Sameer and Marisa, Aarchan and Rita, Kuntal and Sheetal—my cousin-brothers and -sisters, and extended family—those who have always made me feel that I belonged across cultures, countries, continents, space and time even when I found it hard to find my place. Chris, you have always seen in me what I often could not see in myself, including the potential of this book—thank you for making it possible for me to build and live a life that I love, winding as that path can be at times. Ashwin and Sachin, it is not easy to have a mother committed deeply to ideas, causes and people in the world; I know it can feel that it takes away from time that might otherwise be spent directly with or on you. I am grateful for your continued patience and love. I hope you will one day find the joy of such purpose for yourselves and recognize that I do this work in order to help build a world in which that will continue to be possible. You have always been my inspiration. I am so proud of who you each are, and can't wait to watch who you choose to become.

ABOUT THE AUTHOR

D r. Ulcca Joshi Hansen is a mother, educator, researcher and advocate whose two-and-a-half-decade career has spanned classrooms, non-profit leadership, philanthropy and consulting. She is driven by a vision of education that attends to and supports the development of young people's humanity and creates learning experiences that help them realize their unique potential—the place where who they are and what the world needs intersect.

Ulcca brings a diverse set of experiences working with educators, funders, policymakers, researchers, legislators, business leaders and community advocates in the US and internationally to her work and writing. Her work is aimed at helping transform the foundational values of our educational, cultural and social systems, and building the capacities of educators, families, communities and advocates to work with young people toward new ways of being in the world. She is currently Chief Program Officer for Grantmakers for Education, a membership organization committed to strengthening philanthropy's capacity to improve educational outcomes for all students.

Prior to Grantmakers for Education, Ulcca served as Chief Strategy Officer at Boundless and as Vice President for Partnerships and Research at Education Reimagined. She began her career as an elementary teacher in New Jersey public schools, after which she served as a Program Fellow with the Geraldine R. Dodge Foundation.

Ulcca holds a BA in Philosophy and German from Drew University and a certificate in early childhood and elementary education with a focus on special education. She earned her PhD from Oxford University and a JD from Harvard Law School. She has been recognized nationally for her academic achievements and her commitment to public service through education as a Harry S. Truman Scholar, a British Marshall Scholar and a Paul and Daisy Soros Fellow.

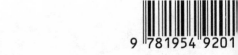